EARLY
BUSTER
KEATON

This book is dedicated to the following folks from BKC and elsewhere who fanned my appreciation of Buster and his work from a small flame into a forest fire: Keith, Bill, Linda, Frank, Amy, Fran, Carol, and Vergil.

EARLY BUSTER KEATON

FROM THE VAUDEVILLE STAGE TO COMIQUE FILMS, 1899–1920

LISA STEIN HAVEN

WHITE OWL

AN IMPRINT OF PEN & SWORD BOOKS LTD.
YORKSHIRE – PHILADELPHIA

First published in Great Britain in 2025 by
PEN AND SWORD WHITE OWL
An imprint of
Pen & Sword Books Ltd
Yorkshire – Philadelphia

ISBN 978 1 52678 076 8

Typeset in Times New Roman 11/13.5 by
SJmagic DESIGN SERVICES, India.
Printed and bound in the UK by CPI Group (UK) Ltd, Croydon, CR0 4YY.

The Publisher's authorised representative in the EU for product safety is
Authorised Rep Compliance Ltd., Ground Floor, 71 Lower Baggot Street,
Dublin D02 P593, Ireland.
www.arccompliance.com

For a complete list of Pen & Sword titles please contact

PEN & SWORD BOOKS LIMITED
George House, Units 12 & 13, Beevor Street, Off Pontefract Road,
Barnsley, South Yorkshire, S71 1HN, England
E-mail: enquiries@pen-and-sword.co.uk
Website: www.pen-and-sword.co.uk

or
PEN AND SWORD BOOKS
1950 Lawrence Rd, Havertown, PA 19083, USA
E-mail: uspen-and-sword@casematepublishers.com
Website: www.penandswordbooks.com

Contents

■■■■■■■■■■■■■■■■■■■■■■■■■■■■■■

Introduction

■■■■■■■■■■■■■■■■■■■■■■■■■■■■■

The relationship between a career on the American vaudeville or English music hall stage and silent film comedy success is always a close one. Charlie Chaplin was hired by Mack Sennett of the Keystone Studios in Glendale, California while he was still performing for Karno's London Comedians on a tour of America. The Marx Brothers simply transformed their vaudeville act to the screen, in films such as *The Cocoanuts* (1929) and *Animal Crackers* (1930) and on and on. Buster Keaton or Joseph Frank Keaton, Jr. was no different, except that he looked down on the 'flickers' because his father Joe, Sr. did. The family had become 'The Three Keatons' just three years after Buster's birth, morphing into 'The Four Keatons' and then 'The Five Keatons' as children were added to the family. 'Buster,' the name given to Joe, Jr., by George Pardee, for his ability to roll down a set of stairs without injury, became his stage name, but would soon translate perfectly into his screen name, one that set him apart as a comedian in a field crowded with greats: Chaplin, Roscoe Arbuckle, John Bunny, Harold Lloyd, and Harry Langdon, among many others.

'The Three (to Five) Keatons' would be a fixture in Buster's life until early 1917, when he met Roscoe Arbuckle at the Talmadge/Comique Studios in New York City and began to toy with the idea of moving his talents to the screen. As a vaudeville performer, Buster was often in stereotypical Irish make-up, complete with Lincoln-style beard and pipe, even when he was a toddler of 3 or 4 years old. Unlike Chaplin and others, he had no formal training in any sort of professional troupe; what he learned he learned from his parents Joe and Myra, who were both in the act, or by developing gags himself. His was a mechanical mind, so whenever he could employ even the most rudimentary of technologies into the act, he would. The 'flickers' finally sold him when Arbuckle spent the time required to demonstrate the intricacies of the technological aspects of the business to Buster in the first few days of his employment.

But he couldn't simply adapt the Keaton Irish caricature, as he and his family had been doing onstage, to the screen. Chaplin had The Little Tramp. Max Linder had his character the dapper yet unconfident gentleman. Roscoe had his charming and endearing fat man. Mabel Normand had her cute yet manipulative wench. Buster would have to create a persona for himself onscreen that stood apart from the others to be successful and recognizable. He would need his tenure with Roscoe and the fourteen films he made at Comique to solidify it. By his first film for Buster Keaton Productions in 1920, *The High Sign*, the Great Stone Face had become Keaton's screen persona and this persona turned out to be one he had honed on the vaudeville stage.

It is important first to acknowledge those who have come before, in regards to Buster Keaton studies, biographies and analyses, for no twenty-first-century writer on Keaton can claim total originality. Since nearly every aspect of Keaton's story and work has been written about in some form, it will be the goal of this book to present a new perspective on Keaton's early life in the entertainment business, beginning with the ancestry, family tradition in vaudeville and moving through the Comique films, Keaton's first foray into the industry. A microscopic approach to this early period has the goal of illuminating in great detail the formative years of Keaton's career, to better understand the brilliance of his 'independence' and the tragedy of his years at MGM, bringing him to a place in entertainment history that celebrates the little gems and sparks of brilliance in his later creative life and career.

This study acknowledges but makes every attempt to move away from the recent work of Dana Stevens and James Curtis, both notable for their particular excellence in telling the Keaton story in different ways. In addition, James Neibaur and Jim Kline's books on the early Arbuckle/Keaton films and Steve Massa's recent work on Roscoe Arbuckle's films (some of which include Keaton) offered both guidance and firm direction about what has already been achieved in the area and, thereby, what still needed to be done and so, attempted here. In addition, work on the Keaton family and its relationship to early American vaudeville, especially as concentrated in the person of Frank L. Cutler, Buster's maternal grandfather, was first considered expertly by both Dr. Vergil Nobel and Linda Neil and serves as the foundation for that part of the story. Cutler, the only performer in the family, and a writer of plays and sketches as well, must have had some influence on his grandson that has not been seriously considered before. This study, then, will differentiate itself from the fine works listed above, and others, by delving deeper into each moment during the specified twenty-four early years of Keaton's life and career, up to and including the transition to his 'independent' productions with Joseph Schenck, beginning with *The High Sign* (1920), *One Week* (1920) and *The Saphead* (1920), his first efforts in the new era. The epilogue will briefly fill out the overall picture of Keaton's remaining career, with an emphasis on moments when a glimpse of the early days can be easily discerned.

Chapter 1

Preamble, or Setting the Groundwork for a Life in Entertainment

■■■■■■■■■■■■■■■■■■■■■■■■■■■■■

Joseph Frank (Buster) Keaton can be said to have lived a life marked by great achievement, deep tragedy and sadness, bad decisions and a maturity graced with love, friendship, and adulation. The great biographers who have taken Keaton on over the years have told this story from many perspectives; they have told it poorly, or well. Keaton himself has offered his own life narrative. None of these, however, has started far enough back in time to flesh out Keaton's unique American-ness, a characteristic that is at the heart of who he becomes as a performer and a filmmaker. Keaton's ancestry includes Quakers, Mormons, and Lutherans. It includes Revolutionary War veterans, Civil War veterans, and veterans who served in every war the country became involved in. It includes both slave holders and abolitionists. It includes esteemed founders of universities, clergymen, Congressmen, and writers. It even boasts one family who survived a voyage on the *Titanic*. With all this honor and esteem in his lineage, then, the entertainment business seems like it would be at the bottom of any list of achievements – that it would bring the reputation of the family down a few pegs. But, in fact, it is Buster Keaton, first as a vaudeville child star and later as a silent film performer and filmmaker who is still the most revered and remembered and whose legacy has had the most staying power.

According to biographers and to family members, the marriage of Joseph Hallie Keaton and Myra Edith Cutler, Buster's parents, was both spur-of-the-moment and ill-considered. Regardless of this unlikely pairing, the result was a conjoining of two families bursting with exceptional stories of the American experience. While the Keatons were known to be Quakers far back into the past, Quakers who never married outside of their faith, facts prove that the woman who was Buster's grandmother, Lydia Shirley Keaton, wife of Joseph Zachariah Keaton, was only two generations removed from the Clore family, who were part of the renowned Germanna settlement of German Lutherans who settled near Culpeper, Virginia in 1717.

The Keaton part of Buster's heritage had a tradition of naming the firstborn male Joseph. As Keaton biographer Marion Meade aptly noted, 'The Keatons, like Plantagenet Kings, believed in economy of Christian names, and for five generations, each firstborn son had been named Joseph.'[1] As she relates, the first Keaton (or Keton) on record in America was farmer Henry Keaton of 1690, although the name itself can be traced back to the eleventh century and a village named Ketton in Leiceistershire in the United Kingdom. Buster's mother Myra's Cutler heritage also extends its roots back to Britain, this time to Oxfordshire and London. The Cutlers themselves are a foundational American family, so much so that they have their own book, the *Cutler Memorial and Genealogical History*, which was compiled in 1889 by Nahum S. Cutler and includes some detailed information about some of Buster's close family members, including his grandfather.

Luke H. Cutler, Buster's great-grandfather, moved to Summer Hill, New York in 1819 where he married Axenia Barber, 'an industrious, energetic woman of happy disposition'[2] who didn't like moving around but ended up doing so quite a bit anyway. Cutler was town clerk and captain of the local militia while in New York. Finally, he landed in Nebraska, living in Rock Bluffs, Plattsmouth and Greenwood, Cass County, which proved to be the location of his passing in July 1887.[3] Along the way, he and his wife had seven children, of which Buster's grandfather Frank was the youngest. Frank Luke, Buster's grandfather, was mentioned in the family book solely by a note that his wife Lizzy had died in 1877 and he was living in Modale, Iowa with two children, Bert and Myra.[4] But, actually, by 1889 and the publication of this memorial volume, Frank had been thinking entertainment for almost 20 years in some way or another, writing plays and sketches at least by 1887, but noted as a traveling minstrel as early as 1871.

Even though there was a considerable rift between the Cutler and Keaton families, supposedly caused by the marriage of Joe and Myra, Buster's parents, little discussion of Frank Cutler has created a great gap in the understanding of who Buster was and how and where he acquired his creativity. It was Grandpa Frank who brought the family into the entertainment business. He not only acted in, managed, and directed his shows and companies of actors, but wrote the scripts for the sketches, scripts that still exist as literary documents, and most of these scripts are comedies.[5] Also, the rift between the families was supposedly caused by the fact that Frank felt that Joe Keaton wasn't good enough for his daughter, but Frank himself had been fairly unsuccessful in choosing a lucrative livelihood over the years, first working on his father's farm, then peddling, then calling himself a traveling minstrel, then clerking in his brother's dry goods store and finally taking to the road in a medicine show put together with tape and a few pieces of sticking plaster. In other words, he was hardly the man to judge.

Luke Cutler moved his wife, son Frank, and his son Martin Barber's two sons (he was a widower) to Berrien, Michigan after his nephew Marcus kindly sold him 10 acres on 2 January 1869.[6] Luke then moved back to Nebraska in early 1875 and his son Frank, with his new wife Lizzy and son Burt, Buster's uncle, born 28 July 1874 in Berrien, moved to Modale, Iowa, where Frank took a post working as a clerk in his brother C. J.'s (Charles's) dry goods store. However, the entertainment bug had bitten him in Michigan, because the 1871 *Michigan Directory & History*[7] lists his occupation as 'traveling minstrel,' and this was only one year after his marriage 27 October 1870. The move to Modale and his growing family suggested that Frank knew he had to support them first. Myra, Buster's mother, was born there on 13 March 1877. Clearly, the period 1875–1887 was the most stable time in the Cutler family's life, because they stayed put. When Brother C. J. sold his store and moved to Rapid City, South Dakota[8] to work a timber claim in 1886 and Lizzy died of consumption a year later, Frank decided to take his kids on the road and become itinerant entertainers – in a medicine show.

Long before that development, however, Frank was building up to it slowly. The first movement towards entering the entertainment business he made is that he started writing scripts for the Ames Theatrical Publishing Company in Clyde, Ohio. Frank's first play appeared in the catalog in 1878 and he had published 15 plays by 1887, or the year that Lizzie died, these also being the years that he was in residence at Modale. He only wrote seven more plays after that, with the last one appearing in 1892. An 1892 *New York Clipper* article listed four more plays/sketches that he had written and was about to put on that aren't even in the Ames catalog, so there could be many more than the 22 he published with Ames.[9] Many were one-act comedy sketches that required only 15 to 20 minutes to perform. There were blackface sketches, ethnic dialogue sketches parodying the Irish, Germans (known as Dutch) or New Englanders.[10] One was a lengthy temperance play, very popular on the medicine show circuit, and two of his later works were lengthy four-act plays that had some popularity and press. At least three of the plays have a cast of characters and locations provided on the title page for their premieres, showing that they had had their first performances in Modale. Frank's wife Lizzy played the lead character Mrs. Blodgett in one of these plays, *Wanted a Husband*, written in 1883. Others performed in the town include *Pomp's Pranks* (1891), *Musical Darkey* (1884), and *Seeing Bosting* (1884).[11] Buster noted in his autobiography that Grandpa Cutler also liked to write verses, which 'concerned everything from politics to the Sullivan-Corbett fight at New Orleans.' Later on when the medicine show was more successful, he would print the poems out and wrap them around whatever current elixir they were trying to sell.[12]

How exactly Frank decided to take to the road and with whom following Lizzy's death on 13 February 1887 is anyone's guess, but he first joined up with the Delorme-Neal Company 22 August 1887, which opened its season at the People's Theatre in Lincoln, Nebraska with a completely reorganized company. Besides Frank Cutler, Harry Langdon, later to gain fame as the baby-faced silent film comedian, was in the cast.[13] Kitty Delorme[14] (soubrette) and Lloyd Neal (comedian) were a married couple that had an act in vaudeville but were looking for employment by 23 March 1889, so Frank was forced to advertise the 'Cutler Comedy Company' by 1890.

Most likely this was the moment he entered the world of the American medicine show, for most of his dates were in Iowa, Nebraska, Kansas, Oklahoma, and Texas. Jeremy Agnew admits that medicine shows 'provided what would at first seem to be a somewhat unusual form of entertainment, but was one that was logical, very popular and widespread in the West.'[15] They were typically a combination of Wild West, circus, minstrel show and vaudeville program in which 'commercial breaks' allowed the fake doctor to advertise his 'patented'[16] elixirs. Admission might be free, or free the first night or there might be special ladies' nights, but all were incentives employed in hopes of persuading the audience to buy products.

By at least 1890, Frank had moved 16-year-old Burt (advertised as 10), by now an accomplished cornetist, and 13-year-old Myra, who would be playing the saxophone soon if not quite then, onstage in starring roles. The *Central City [Nebraska] Courier* noted that

> the most attractive feature of this company is two children,
> a boy and a girl, who have a wonderful faculty of acting the
> part of a child one minute and an adult the next. [. . .] the two

children are doubtless among the best child musicians in the country.[17]

The medicine-show life was a difficult one for adults, never mind for children. As David and Elizabeth Armstrong describe

> Medicine-show performers [. . .] slept in the cramped confines of their vehicles, pitched tents, or stayed in hotels that would accept disreputable show-folk, hostelries with walls 'so thin, you could hear the fellow in the next room making up his mind,' as one veteran of the road wryly recalled.[18]

Combine this with a father distracted by the vagaries of running an entertainment business, deplorable food, and spotty educational opportunities, and the result is an abnormal and challenging childhood. Although Burt would eventually leave the itinerant lifestyle, Myra would go on to foist a similar upbringing on her own three kids, Buster included.

Violinist Fred Batton, with whom Frank was to have a long on-again, off-again relationship, was noted as part of the troupe first in a notice dated 4 April 1890 in Aurora Kansas.[19] By 1892, he had bought into the company with at least a partial partnership, according to the *New York Clipper*: 'Fred Batton, who has been with the Cutler Comedy Company for three years, has lately purchased an interest in the company, and the troupe will now be known as the Cutler-Batton Theatre Co.'[20] One artifact of this partnership was Frank's published play *Peleg and Peter*, which has a cast of characters and the original players listed in the published version, but no premiere venue. Frank's wife of one year at this point, Ida May Trobee, played Isabel Courtney, Fred Batton Captain Hargreaves, Frank Peter Polstein, with Burt as Peleg Potts and Myra as Kate Larky. This was one of F. L. Cutler's most popular Ames plays and was put on widely by amateur theatricals across the Midwest.[21] *Peleg and Peter, or Around the Horn: A Farce Comedy in Four Acts* (1892) was set aboard a steamer, the *Mary Jane*, headed for New York. It combines ethnic humor (Peleg is the Yankee, Peter Dutch and Hannibal black), with mistaken identity, slapstick rough housing between Peleg and Peter, and an unwanted betrothal that is thrown over in the final scene. There's even liberal use of *mal de mer* to comic effect. The token black character, Hannibal (played by Sam Metheney), creates mayhem, but also acts as a sort of chorus. Perhaps the plot is best summed up by Peter's line (in dialect): 'Dhere vos no posey flower mitout stickers!' All in all, the play was a very sophisticated one, that would make any comedy writer proud. One performance in Pleasant Ridge, Nebraska garnered especially high praise: 'Peleg and Peter were sure to bring the house down whenever they came together. Only for the appearance of the captain the audience might have witnessed a pugilistic contest equal to the Corbett-Fitzsimmons mill.'[22]

Still, the Cutler–Batton partnership must have fallen apart by late June 1893, because Frank seems to have joined up with an English couple, Samuel and Violet Bryant and their two children Florence and Billy at about that time. Sam Bryant became Dr. Bryant, whose 'Dr. Bryant's Magic Liniment' was a simple compound made of gasoline and cayenne pepper. He also sold electric belts that were supposed to heal intestinal ailments. Sam Bryant's wife was a noted soubrette from the dance halls of England who could attract a customer or two with her singing, and possibly replace the talents of Fred Batton. While most Keaton biographers call the partnership the 'Cutler-Bryant 10-cent Show,' this name does not appear in the press. In fact, the two families were only together a couple of months. It was Frank's show, and he left the Bryants to their own devices on 19 August. Just over a week before, all seemed to be going well. An 11 August 1893 article in the Edmond Oklahoma *Democrat* lauds the performances of Frank, his son Burt, Violet Bryant and both of her children, suggesting that everyone was performing to great acclaim:

> The tent show on 2nd street has been quite an attraction. Nightly the attendance increases and all seem to appreciate the performance. Young Cutler, the cornetist is out of sight while his father is a professional gentleman on the stage. Mrs. Bryant's singing is heartily received while her two children are loudly applauded. There have been several new acquisitions, and all act their parts well. It is an interesting and refined entertainment and deserving of much better patronage.[23]

Then on 1 September, a notice was published in the Norman Oklahoma *Transcript* signed by Samuel Bryant, stating that he had advertised his show under the name of the Cutler Comedy Company on 24 August, without any right to do so, because Frank Cutler had 'severed his connection' with the Bryants on 19 August.[24] However, that didn't mean the Cutler family was financially stable. Myra remembered that the company arrived in Lincoln for their next performance on different trains with about 25 cents between them.[25]

In the article cited above, the line 'there have been several new acquisitions' most likely referred to Joe Keaton's recent hiring into the company in Edmond, Oklahoma to do odd jobs and play whatever roles were needed. The fact that they were in Edmond at the article's publication, meant, as James Curtis points out, the land run in question was the Cherokee Outlet land run of 16 September 1893, not the Cherokee Strip of 22 April 1889, as was previously believed. Joe Keaton rightly claimed that Frank fired him only to rehire him again and again, because he couldn't find anyone to do the job better. This is borne out by ads in the *Lincoln [Nebraska] Evening Call* that list the acts and cast for the Wonderland Musée where the Cutler Comedy Company landed in December 1893, finding themselves without a tent and needing a venue. They played the Musée throughout December and January 1894, were back the second week of February and then much of April as well. The week of 16 April, Burt and Myra were listed as doing 'specialties,' with Joe Keaton listed next entitled 'the original Fun Maker,'[26] but Frank Cutler and troupe were not listed at all. Supposedly, Frank tried to combat the Joe–Myra attraction by sending Myra to her grandmother Axenia Cutler, 83, and her Aunt Gertrude by marriage (Martin Cutler's widow), who lived in Greenwood, Nebraska,[27] directly after they finished *Waifs of Sacramento* at the Musée the week of 4 December, but there is no indication from the ads that she even departed the company for the Christmas holiday, for following *Waifs*, Myra is cast in the very next Cutler Company play put on at the Musée, entitled *Kathleen Mauvourneen* (as Myrtle Cutler) and then on into January with no discernible break away from the company. In the legendary 1904 article for his hometown paper, the *Terre Haute Morning Star*, Joe suggested that Myra found him at his hotel 'way out west,' she having been in Lincoln, Nebraska since his final ousting from the Cutler Comedy Company, when in fact, he can easily be found alongside her or near her performing at the Wonderland Musée in Lincoln himself, up until the end of April 1894, just a month away from their wedding. Rather than this elaborate story, the truth is probably along the lines of Joe Keaton had finally had enough of old man Cutler and wanted to try his luck elsewhere and Myra went with him. Even before the wedding, Joe is advertised in a 29 May 1894 Mohawk Medicine Show ad in DeWitt, Nebraska,[28] proving that at least he was hired on with the Mohawk Medicine Show troupe (and Myra, too) a few days before they married. DeWitt was just seven and a half miles from Wilber, Nebraska, the county seat, where the couple were married 31 May 1894 between performances.[29] In any event, Frank had lost a saxophonist and a daughter. Vergil Noble has determined that Burt Cutler stayed with the act longer – maybe as long as 1898 or 1899, for he is noted in the 1900 census residing in Columbus, Ohio, where he would live out most of the rest of his life.[30] He became an accomplished composer, band leader and, a little ironically, ended his career playing cornet in a vaudeville and movie house, the Loew's Broad Theater.[31]

Having lost both Burt and Myra from the company by the turn of the century then, Frank was always on the lookout for new acts and performers. It also brought him romantic opportunities, not all of which ended happily. Frank seemed to be collecting wives after Lizzy's death – at least three more of them. In 1891, he married 21-year-old Ida May Trobee in Corydon, Iowa. He was 43 years old. The *People's Reveille* in Hill City, Kansas reported in 1901 that another Mrs. Cutler was in the cast, née Fanny Everett,[32] and nothing is known about this woman's beginning or ending with Frank, for no information can be found out about her. Then, in 1905, he married Nina Metz, aka Sophia Henrietta Metz, who was 26 years old when they married, to Frank's fifty-seven. They had two children, Clinton in 1907 and Marine in 1918. She and Frank were residing together in Stonewall, Texas with Clinton according to the 1910 census and both indicate they were still in show business. But that's not all; there's an enigmatic article in the *Harvard [Nebraska] Courier* 6 April 1907 that seems to create more questions than answers:

> F. C. Cutler, wife and two children, of the Cutler Comedy company, are spending a couple of weeks with Mrs. C's parents, Mr. and Mrs. W. W. Trobee, in this city. Mr. Cutler is enjoying his first "lay off" of any length during the past four years, having played upwards of 1100 nights, since February 1888.[33]

This again is Ida May Trobee, the woman he married in 1891. Frank had married Nina Metz 28 August 1905, so should have been both married to and cohabitating with her at this time. Perhaps more importantly, Nina's son Clinton was to be born on 10 May 1907, about a month from this date. And the two children[34] mentioned? They were probably two sons, born to Frank and Ida May in 1893 and 1896. Was Frank married to multiple women at the same time and parsing out his time with each of them and their children – his children? How would he be able to spend two weeks away from Nina a month away from her confinement without her suspecting? Also, both women were featured in the medicine shows, so how did that work? Nina, it's known at least, married someone else in 1919 and Marine, her son by Frank born in 1918, adopted the new husband's surname, but reverted to Cutler in his adulthood, seeming to suggest that Frank was indeed his father. Both late-life sons served their country in World War II and took wives. Marine gave Frank another grandson, Jerry, in 1943, which he did not live to see, and Buster, therefore, a cousin forty-eight years his junior.

Things were slowing down for the Cutler Comedy Company after both of Lizzie's children left in the late 1890s, so in 1898, Frank could be found with Jordan's Congress of Novelties, touring Iowa and Minnesota. The next year, he was with Spencer Vaudevilles for part of the year. Then in 1901, Fred Batton came back into Frank Cutler's life and they formed a partnership once again on 2 February, which seems to have only lasted until 7 June.[35] Frank and company were on the road in 1902 as the Cutler Comedy Company again – Frank with a wife (probably Fanny Everett), then again in 1906 and years following, in Kansas and environs with new wife Nina Metz, in an act now called the Cutler Theatre Company. In 1909 also, they were performing in Oklahoma and Texas, with the 1910 census reporting them living in Stonewall, possibly only temporarily, with baby Clinton, who would have been 3 at the time (he had been performing in the act since age 2[36]). But, by 1914, an ad appeared in the *Houston [Texas] Post* that read: 'FOR SALE – Large show tent and scenery, dirt cheap. F. L. Cutler, Houston Heights, general delivery, or see tent, corner of Yale and 25th street.'[37] Clearly, the tent show life was over for Frank Cutler and company, although exactly what he did for the next few years is uncertain. An article appeared in the *Austin [Texas] American* in 1924 that suggested F. L. Cutler's life was difficult indeed. The impetus for the article was that Frank had seen his grandson Buster on the screen for the first time, in one of his silent comedies (*Hard Luck*) and it was the first time he'd seen him in any capacity in 20 years. Cutler had come to Rockdale, Texas the previous autumn (1923) in a traveling caravan and set up outside the Sap depot, where he started a jumble store. His sleeping quarters were in the rear of the van, 'surrounded by his beloved books, magazines and "scripts" of which he had a trunkful'[38] – obviously the Ames scripts of all the plays he'd published over the years. He had been touring around the country in the van, painting stage scenery and theatre curtains, wherever he could get the work. Perhaps this had been his occupation since 1914 when he sold the tent and put an end to the Cutler Comedy Company once and for all. The article had one positive effect and that was that it motivated Myra to visit her father after

28 years, which she did in May of that year.[39] No doubt this visit led to an invitation to her ailing pater to move out to California to be closer to her, for he moved to Alhambra, about 20 miles from her little house in Hollywood. He died there on 11 August 1935, having lived to age 85, his death certificate identifying him as a widower of Sarah Elizabeth Cutler and thereby failing to acknowledge any of his other wives or children. And so ended the life of an itinerant showman, Buster's forebear in much more than simple genetics.

The third Joseph Zachariah Keaton, born in 1837 near Terre Haute, Indiana, had the adventure of traveling out to California with his father when he was 18, and staying there about seven years. While he was there, the Civil War broke out, so he signed up with the California Battalion and was discharged at war's end in 1865. Instead of returning to California, he went back to Indiana and married Lydia Shirley in 1886 and had four children, two boys and two girls over the years, eventually moving to Perry, Oklahoma, where his last child, Jesse, was born. Joseph Hallie Keaton, the oldest son, was his father's hope for taking over the family business, milling, but Joe had other ideas. As has been mentioned elsewhere, Joe borrowed $100 and a Winchester rifle from his father and joined the race for property in the Cherokee land run 22 April 1889. In a news article entitled 'Joe Keaton the Boomer,' he tells what is probably one of his usual tall tales about the episode, but one certainly worth the retelling. He and a Canadian named Charley Anderson claimed property adjacent to each other, became close friends and helped to protect each other's interests by visiting every few days. After a couple of months plowing the land and living on it, Joe decided to visit Charley and found some other man plowing his field and wearing his clothes. Joe knew at once that something dire had become of his close friend and after as much as accusing the man and threatening him with the Winchester, with no result, he enlisted the help of Bob Galbreath living in Edmond, who brought along two other men to check out the situation. Back at Anderson's place, the men burned the grass and thereby discovered Anderson's shallow grave, 'with the knees sticking out above the ground. He had been shot through the head.' Joe and his supporters found the interloper eating dinner in Anderson's dugout on the property, marched him out and threatened him with the rifle. He confessed his crime and the men proceeded to string him up on a telegraph pole along the Santa Fe train route, a short distance from

Anderson's property. Two days later, Joe sold the Keaton claim to Robert P. Conner for $900 on 11 March 1890[40] and headed back to Terre Haute, Indiana.[41] Joe returned west to take part in the Cherokee Outlet land run 16 September 1893, which brought him to Edmond, Oklahoma and his destiny with Frank Cutler and his daughter Myra. The land claim went to Papa Keaton, who moved the family to Edmond and eventually ended up in Perry, Oklahoma. Joe and Frank may not have been compatible, but they lived their early lives in similar fashion – flying by the seat of their pants.

When Joe signed up with the Cutler Comedy Company while it was performing in Edmond, he had no talent and nothing to offer, except 'flip-flaps,'[42] but at least a strong impetus to *try*. Frank offered him $3 a week to do odd jobs and play a role here and there as needed. Tent shows like Frank Cutler's necessitated the hiring of a few men to work at least part-time as tent hands. As William Lawrence Slout describes, 'with small shows, actors were required to perform certain duties in putting up and taking down the tent,' a task that did not appeal to 'all dramatic artists.'[43] Joe Keaton may have been fine with the 'odd job' nature of the position, because he needed to see where his talent lay. However, after time passed, and he became more invested in the entertainment end of things, the added duties may have been one source of tension between himself and the boss, Frank Cutler.

After leaving the Bryants on 19 August, and getting their tent repossessed later that fall, Cutler took his troupe to Lincoln, Nebraska for the holiday season and this is where the written record allows some idea of exactly what Joe was doing. The week of 4 December, Cutler's Comedy company was booked at the Wonderland Musée in Lincoln, playing *Waifs of Sacramento, or Old Loder's Will,* while just above on the poster is 'New Acrobatic Specialty – Jos. H. Keating [*sic*],'[44] meaning Joe had been fired by Cutler that week. By the week of 18 December, he had a part in Cutler's *Bob, the Bootblack* (as Tim O'Flaherty) and had teamed up with another player in the company to perform a side gig, *Keaton and Terry – Irish Knockabouts* with Walter Terry.[45] In 1911, a story regarding this partnership hit the papers. Corse Payton, known in his day as 'America's Best Bad Actor,' met Joe just outside the Vaudeville Comedy Club in New York. After ascertaining Payton's identity and then introducing himself, he asked the actor,

'Do you remember a long while ago at Bohannan's Museum in Lincoln, Nebraska hissing a couple of fellows doing a knockabout act, and getting away before they could get to you, though they ran through the stage door after you without taking off their stage whiskers or changing their clothes?' 'I have a faint recollection of something of the sort,' [replied Payton.] 'What of it?' 'Those two fellows were named Keaton and Terry and I'm the Keaton. I've been waiting all these years to have it out with you. Are you ready?' [. . .] I hissed an act that Joe Keaton was in and you're Joe Keaton. Then Joe, you sure must have had a rotten act.'[46]

Into the new year, for the week of 9 January, Joe seems to be both a part of the Cutler troupe and doing a solo as a 'jig and reel dancer.' The Cutlers put on *The Gypsy Queen*, a drama in three acts, with Joe playing the part of 'Cheap John, the auctioneer,' and Myra playing 'Sinzara.'[47] However, later that month, he was fired again, but still working at the Musée according to the ad for the week of 22 January 1894, which promoted 'Joe Keaton, Negro Comedian,' with Cutler Comedy on the same bill performing *Hati, or the Maniac's Wife*.[48] The week of 12 February, Joe had teamed up with someone named Evans, in an act called *Silence and Fun*.[49] The Cutlers weren't even named, but one of their stalwart shows, *Bob, the Bootblack*, was being performed, meaning they were probably in house. A delineated sub-genre of knockabout comedy, the *Silence and Fun* act was originally developed by Fred E. McNish, who performed it in blackface. Essentially, it was a performance of tumbling and acrobatics in a home interior set, either a parlor or a kitchen, set to music.[50] Paul Babiak notes that 'In many of the Silence and Fun acts, the performance was apparently driven by the performer's own sheer delight in executing a series of dangerous stunts. It was an exercise in sheer jouissance.[51, 52] Then for the week of 16 April 1894, Bert (*sic*) and Myra Cutler were advertised at the Musée in 'Specialties,' Joe Keating (*sic*) 'The Original Fun Maker,'[53] and no Frank Cutler anywhere on the bill.

After a short stint with the James Family of Bell Ringers,[54] Joe's next move was to sign on with the Mohawk Indian Medicine Company, Myra in tow, where he was initially advertised as 'Prof. Joe Keaton, a professional acrobat and tumbler.'[55] Together, they were now making $17 a week, with board and transportation. The roster of the company was recorded 6 June 1894, with Dr. Kerrigan, lecturer, Billie Baldwin, song and dance, Katie Davenport, soubrette, Mrs. Myra Keaton, pianist, and Joe Keaton, again labeled a "silence and fun man.' The fact that Joe and Myra's recent affiliations were listed ascertains that they were new to the group.[56]

The Native American medicine companies, so called, were a genre of traveling entertainment all their own. As Brooks McNamara's definitive book on the subject *Step Right Up* describes, the medicine show borrowed every available and popular type of entertainment being innovated in American theatre and culture, such as 'free plays, vaudeville, musical comedy, minstrels, magic, burlesque, dog and pony circuses, Punch and Judy shows, pantomime, menageries, pie-eating contests, and early motion pictures.'[57] Native American medicine show companies also included at least two Native Americans in costume and there were often displays of the tribe members' lifestyle and culture as part of the entertainment. All of this was managed by the pitchman, a fake doctor in most cases, whose main occupation was to arrange all the business details for the show – bookings, accommodation, hiring and firing performers and anything else needed[58] – and to make the pitch for whatever patented concoction was on offer. If it was a Native American medicine show company, the 'medicines' would purport to be from tried-and-true Indian recipes with 'secret' ingredients. Because of the large amount of equipment involved with such shows, it was in the troupe's best interest to stay put for as long as expedient, leading to residences in small towns and cities from two to four weeks, if business was good.[59]

The larger shows eventually morphed into what was akin to Buffalo Bill's Wild West. Certainly, this was not the case for either the Mohawk company or the Umatilla company the Keatons would join up with following Buster's birth. The focus in at least these two companies was entertainment of varied kinds and lots of it. Even the 'doctor's' lectures, seemingly a required aspect of such shows, took a backseat. All Native American named medicine shows, however, were created, owned, and managed by white men. These were not Native American operations.

Joe and Myra had made the move to the Umatilla Indian Medicine Company, No. 90, after their season with Mohawk was concluded in June. This group was based in Detroit, Michigan, and its medicines came from there. In 1896, it had 160 companies on the road selling its products and each company had at least two Native American members.[60] Its roster was reported from residence in Longwood, Missouri for two weeks in June, with Dr. J. W. Kerrigan, lecturer again (meaning he moved companies, too). Other members of the troupe included Mr. and Mrs. Billie Collins in their 'new and original musical act, Mrs. Myra Keaton, soubrette and pianist. Joseph Keaton general all around comedian. Billie Collins is managing the company and everyone lives in camp.'[61] Their tenure with this troupe was short-lived, but they would join up with it again, albeit with a different company, in the new year.

Meanwhile and probably due to continued financial problems and not having his own tent, Frank Cutler had signed his company (himself and Burt, for sure) with the Mohawk Indian Medicine Company in 1895, possibly as early as May or June. The even more surprising aspect of this is that Frank joined forces with two groups this same year that he had already dramatically cut ties with, the Bryants and the Keatons – Joe and Myra. Of course, there were always many companies under the Mohawk Indian Medicine umbrella traveling around at the same time, making it difficult to trace the Cutlers' particular company and its route. The first positively identified venue for Cutler's Mohawk Company is Mapleton, Kansas where they appeared 24 August to 4 September. This is notably the final joint performance of both the Cutlers and the Bryants, who then broke off toward Devon, Kansas, while Frank and company continued on to Weir, Kansas. Sam Bryant would have been the 'Doctor' for the troupe during the joint performances, but following this point, it's Dr. St. George.[62] Another surprise that season was that Joe and Myra joined the Cutler Mohawks, probably because Myra was near the end of her pregnancy and needed the extra moral support. It's not clear when they joined Frank and company, but most likely at the start of the new season, in late June or early July. Their names listed as part of the Umatilla Indian Medicine Company published in the *New York Clipper* 20 July 1895, most likely appeared well after the Keatons had switched allegiances, albeit temporarily.

Leaving Weir on 22 September, the Cutler Mohawk troupe moved on to Bronson, Kansas, where it was in residence until 27, then on to Piqua, were Joseph Frank ('Buster') Keaton was born on 4 October 1895 at the home of Jacob Haen, German-born carpenter and his wife Barbara, assisted by midwife Theresa Ullrich,[63] just across from St. Martin of Tours parish Catholic meeting house,[64] where the Mohawks had to perform after the weather demanded it. A well-known *New York Clipper* piece recounts those first few days in October. Burt's wedding was celebrated 3 October[65] 'and a general good time was had after the show. Mrs. Myra Keaton presented her husband with a fine boy. The mother and baby are getting along nicely. [. . .] At present all is lively with us.'[66] And these may have been the last happy words Frank Cutler wrote about his daughter and grandson. The company was off to Galesburg, Kansas for two weeks 7 October, leaving Myra and baby to catch up when they could. Although their route in the next couple of months can't be ascertained,[67] they were in Ottawa, Kansas 5 to 19 December, just before the holidays and Joe had made it to Edmond, Oklahoma to visit old friends (and probably show off the wife and baby) 6 November.[68] This marked the end of the Cutler–Keaton collaboration, once and for all, for the young Keaton family rejoined their Umatilla colleagues the first of the year.

There has been much discussion about the origin of the 'Buster' nickname – who came up with it, when and under what circumstances. The Keatons themselves developed a story that can now be deemed totally false – that Harry Houdini, during a short period when his group was sharing the same bill with the Keatons, witnessed Buster take a spill down a set of stairs and cried out 'Gee whiz! He's a regular buster!' In fact, the point in time in which the fall down the stairs occurred, near April 1896, when the child was about 6 or 7 months old, makes any of a number of people part of the Umatilla company possibilities for having made the exclamation, and history in the so-doing. Rather than Harry Houdini, who was nowhere near the Keatons at the time, Joe and Myra themselves named George A. Pardey[69] on occasion, the English-born manager of their particular troupe, as the most likely candidate.[70]

1896 then was spent with the Umatilla Indian Medicine & Concert Company, No. 27, which traveled around small Kansas towns and cities. The Umatilla Indian Medicine Co., owned by Dr. M. Campbell and based in Detroit, with the motto 'There May Be Others, but We Lead the Parade,' advertised 'recognized standard and reliable medicines, finely prepared with flash cartoons, present a fine appearance, and create a favorable impression.' Campbell promised 'successful lecturers and good all around specialty performers' as well.[71]

A roster and notes concerning the company, published in January, listed Dr. M. Campbell, proprietor, Dr. George Pardey, manager, Dr. A. L. Bert, assistant manager, Joe Keaton, black face comedian and jig dancer, Myra Keaton, organist and soubrette, Sadie Cheatham, serio-comic singer, and Charles S. Martin, banjoist and comedian. Indians in the troupe were White Cloud and wife, Red Bird, Red Tail, Never Cries, and Red Horse. Red Bird had given her husband a baby boy 21 December 1895. 'Keaton and Farrell's acrobatic songs and dances are quite a feature,' reported *The Clipper*.[72] Keaton and Farrell were again touted in a roster dated 8 February, as part of the same company. The Cherokee Medicine Co., No. 11 noted that Umatilla No.15 (same members as No. 27) had visited them in mid-February (possibly in Montpelier, Iowa the week of 10–15 February).[73] Now entitled Company No. 45, the troupe, still under George Pardey, comprised Charles S. Morton, character comedian, Bill Farrell, Irish comedian, Joe Keaton, black-faced comedian, Myra Keaton, singing soubrette and organist, and five Indians. Both Pardey and Myra shared 13 March as their birthdays and celebrated together in a big company party: 'A fine feast was spread and the scene ended with many wishes and a long and prosperous life to both.'[74] By the end of April, now called No. 27, and touring Iowa, the company was temporarily led by Dr. E. G. Emerson, for Pardey went home for a month's vacation. Farrell and the Keatons were joined by Chief Diebold's family of Indians, which included a chief, squaw, and three papooses.[75]

By 12 September, another roster of the company, now No. 101, appeared in the *New York Clipper*, with

> Dr M. Campbell, proprietor; Dr Geo. A. Lindsay [*sic*] manager and lecturer; his wife, treasurer and head of the culinary department; daughter Mamie, character change, winging step dancing and singing soubrette; Joe Keaton, black face Irish and all 'round comedy acrobatic song and dance and high kicker; Mrs. Joe Keaton, musical soubrette, song and dance and sketch act; Buster Keaton, low comedy; Henry Duso, contortionist and comedian; Charles Armstrong, boss canvas man; Mauzy, the watch, keeps kids at a distance.[76]

The writer noted that the troupe was finishing up a week 'under canvas' and would be moving to the Opera House the week of 20 September. But, perhaps most noteworthy is mention of little Buster, already known by the nickname and only 11 months old, in what is probably his first mention as a performer.

A spate of performances in October and November can be credibly traced, allowing some idea of the type of show the Keatons were performing in. Beginning with two weeks in Scammon, Kansas 5 to 16 October, a review offered that they had 'one of the best troops of the day and their manager Dr. G. W. Pardey [*sic*] cannot be excelled.'[77] The next three-week stop was in Cherokee, Kansas 19 October to 6 November. The Keatons and Pardeys checked into the Hotel Caldwell in Girard, Kansas, 13 miles away, on 30 October. Finally, the troupe landed in Weir, Kansas, where they performed about four weeks, 10 November to 5 December, and received quite a bit of news coverage. One reporter waxed poetic about the 'overflowing house' the troupe had experienced the night of 16 November, while another praised Pardey as 'thoroughly posted in his business and gives a lecture that makes many sales of his medicine.'[78] The program for one night in Weir gives a good idea of the type of entertainment the Keatons were offering:

Tonight:

Curtain raiser – Misteries [*sic*] of a Pawn Shop.

Oleo

Black Art.........................Prof. York, exposing spiritualism and introducing "Dick" the thousand-dollar educated bird.

Myra Keaton in her pleasing songs.

A Farce Comedy entitled A Box of Tacks, or Corbet's Return, introducing the following vaudeville specialties:

William Coy – Musical Expert

Joe Keaton – Rough Irish Specialty

Tommie Chase and Frank Howard – Two Rubes from Rubeville

Arthur Long – Clubs and tumbling

Tommie Chase – The Biddie

Wm. Coy and Joe Brooks – Violin Duet

Frank Howard – Champion Bone Soloist of the World

To conclude with a three-round boxing contest between the Topeka Kid Champion Bantam Weight and Joe Keaton[79]

Three nights later for the same audience, the program changed significantly to include a pantomime called *The Three Lovers*, with Joe Keaton as Pico the Clown, Myra as the White Lily, Tommie Chase as Old Man Nubbins, Chas. Pickett as Chappie Clauda, and Arthur Long as Officer O'Toole, also a 'new' version of 'Burlesque Magic,' Chief Rolling Bear playing a violin solo and Chase and Frank Howard introducing their 'celebrated mind reading.' This night, in addition, the Keatons were featured in a 'comedy sketch introducing singing and dancing, the act to conclude with Joe Keaton's burlesque Skirt Dance.' Finally, the audience could enjoy and participate in a pie-eating contest, with a comedy act entitled 'The Two Imposters' rounding out the evening.[80] The publication of these two programs in the local paper underscores the fact that the troupe went to great lengths to provide new and different entertainment each night of their two- or three-week residence in whatever town. It speaks to their ingenuity, but also their wide-ranging improvisational abilities to do what was necessary to 1) provide good entertainment and 2) sell their products.

Joe Keaton's main desire at this point was to break free from the Indian Medicine show circuits and have an act with Myra and/or one or two others that would be successful on its own. Two of the individuals he would try this out with over the next couple of years he met in the Umatilla companies, W. B. York and Arthur Long. After a brief stint at the end of 1896 into 1897 working as part of George Pardey's P. P. P. P. (Pardey's Protean Pleasure Players[81]), still a sort of medicine show group (without the Native Americans[82]) and a company York and Long were both part of, Joe Keaton and W. B. York broke off and started 'Keaton and York Comedy Pantomime Co.' that included 10 performers and played several dates February through April 1897, in places like La Cygne and Osawatomie, Kansas and Liberal, Missouri. Their first traceable show was 28 and 29 January 1897 in Minden, Kansas, that deemed it 'one of the best shows that ever came to Minden.'[83] The troupe moved on to Liberal, Missouri 1 through 4 February, which was extended two more nights, due to attracting good-sized audiences. The show included most elements of the traveling variety show, with the jugglers and black artist (magician) receiving the most acclaim in this town, whose reviewer noted that 'this company gives one of the best ten-cent shows on the road.'[84] From here they traveled to Pleasanton, Kansas for another week, where Joe Keaton was singled out as 'the strongest member of the company and as a contortionist and funny man generally he is hard to beat.' York was praised as well for his talents in juggling and sleight of hand. Yet, only Monday night, 8 February, was a 'button-burster,' with Tuesday and Wednesday rated not so good.[85] Good reviews were received from Arcada, Kansas, where the troupe performed 15 through 17 February. Then they were on to Paola, Kansas 22 through 24 February, where Joe Keaton was deemed 'a greased eel from start to finish and keeps the house in a roar continually.'[86] The end of that week, they were in Osawatomie, Kansas for three nights with generally good reviews, but when they hit Warrenton, Missouri, it's clear they received some pushback due to the perceived bawdiness or low comedy aspects of the show, for a piece appeared 8 April declaring that a certain Rev. Green and Mr. Stark of the local M. E. (Methodist-Episcopal) Church had objected on moral and financial grounds to their members attending the shows and created a rebuttal of sorts by launching a performance of a quintet composed of church members (cornetists, violinists and a pianist) they chose to dub the 'Green-Stark Comedy Co.'[87]

Perhaps this sort of reaction led to the group's disbanding about this time.[88] In any event, the Keatons spent the summer in Perry, Oklahoma with his family,[89] before taking jobs at the Newmarket Theatre at 4th and Walnut Streets in Kansas City, Missouri for four months, closing out the year, and spending the first month of the new year in the same place.[90] The Newmarket was a rough and tumble place, as evidenced by a 30 March 1897 article in the *Kansas City [Missouri] Journal*, entitled 'Country Boys in Trouble.' One James Stephens got into an argument with the theatre's bouncer, Harry Hatton, in which he drew a razor and tried to slash the man. He was subsequently arrested for carrying a concealed weapon. Then, just two hours later, William Alten and Warner Oliver became angry with their female partners, because they had not reciprocated in buying the four a round of beer. The men drew both a razor and a revolver and were soon carted off to Central Station by the police.[91] During the Keatons' tenure at the venue, May Raymond, a variety actress, drew a revolver and was threatening to shoot a man.[92] It was no place for a young couple like the Keatons to consider for a long period, therefore it can be surmised that they considered their tenure absolutely necessary for financial survival. It was clear they hoped for a move before the end of the year, declaring themselves 'at liberty' in the 13 November 1897 *New York Clipper*,[93] when they would actually find themselves still in Kansas City the end of January 1898.

Buster, now 2-plus years old, began to make his presence felt, both onstage and off. Although his first press mention had come in 1896, 1898 would be the year of his informal stage debut and the last year of his parents' tutelage on the vaudeville stage, for they would take the plunge and move to New York City, in hopes of striking it big there. They would never look back.

Chapter 2

Practically Born on Stage
A Career at Age Three

■■■■■■■■■■■■■■■■■■■■■■■■■■■■

Hovering over the story of the year 1898 in the lives of the Keatons is the spectre of Harry and Bess Houdini. Many have asserted that the Keatons were part of the California Concert Company, formed by Thomas B. Hill (known as Texas Tom) and Dr. Perry Pratt at the end of October 1897,[1] a company which had run aground by February 1898. Harry Houdini and his wife Bess were indeed part of the troupe after it formed, and they did tour around some of the same small towns in Kansas, Nebraska, and Missouri that the Keatons had frequented in the past several years in various troupes. However, there is no evidence that Joe or Myra Keaton were part of this group at any point.[2] In fact, they were listed as part of the roster for the Newmarket Theatre in Kansas City for much of that period. Of course, there is mythology, perpetuated by Joe Keaton himself, that late 1897 to early 1898 was the time when the Houdinis and the Keatons met, being part of the California Concert Company together; this was when Houdini gave Buster his nickname (already disproven) and a mysterious photo appearing in the Rudy Blesh biography supposedly shows the two couples, another man and two Native Americans, which provides proof of all this. In fact, the mystery photo only shows Joe in the middle with Myra on his right. The other couple are clearly *not* Harry and Bess Houdini – not in anyone's imagination.[3] What can be determined and ascertained is that the Houdinis and Keatons appeared on the same bill starting 15 January 1907 at B. F. Keith's Theatre in Boston, Massachusetts, after both parties were well established. Therefore, despite Joe Keaton's best efforts to claim a professional relationship with the Houdinis in 1897/1898, it didn't happen, or at least they weren't on the same bill together. Perhaps they met in some other context.

What did happen in late 1897 through 1898 was significant. The 16 April 1898 the *New York Clipper* presented an 'at liberty' ad for a newish group, Keaton-Long-Keaton, in which the couple joined together with old colleague Arthur (Artie) Long in a continuing attempt to become self-sufficient. The ad noted that the trio would 'furnish singing, talking, dancing sketches. Also, Acrobatic Double Songs and Dances, Double Silence and Fun, Scientific and Burlesque Boxing. Can put on acts, sober and reliant. Stuff for one week.' The 'double' appellation simply meant that two people would be involved in the act, so because this indicates that Joe was bringing back the 'silence and fun' act he tried out four years previous at the Wonderland Musée, he would be performing it this time with a partner.[4] Gigs for this group are not traceable until 11 June, however, when they were promoted for one night in Paola, Kansas as 'high grade entertainment, first class in every respect.'[5] In Liberal, Missouri 16 June, they received enthusiastic applause. A week later, the troupe was in Pittsburg, Kansas, described as a 'fine company of knockabout comedians.'[6] In the ad for their Cherokee, Kansas performance 21 June, besides the fact the group is deemed 'Long & Keyton,' Joe has added 'of the California Concert Company' to his name, in the only mention of a connection to that company (Houdini's) in print.[7] After single night engagements in Galena, Kansas 24 June and Weir, Kansas 25 June, Keaton-Long-Keaton received the most press for their 5 July performance at the Opera house in Hamilton, Missouri, with ads and reviews in several papers. A description of the event that appeared in the *Burlington [Kansas] News* indicated that it was a benefit for the Burlington cornet band to allow them to purchase new music and instruments. The evening's amusements included

> Keating [*sic*], the eccentric comedian, Miss Myra Keating [*sic*] in pleasing songs and dances, Arthur Long in new and novel specialties, John Rollins in songs and cornet solos, Keating and Long in acrobatic songs and dances, besides some of the best home talent in Burlington.[8]

an indication that Keaton-Long-Keaton had incorporated local entertainers, in keeping with the fact the evening was a benefit.

Somewhere during this time,[9] either with Artie Long or later in the summer, Joe later claimed to have brought Buster onstage for the first time (a baby in arms), recalling this event to a reporter in 1923: '"Dad" carried him before the footlights and yodeled a Swiss "go-to-sleep-baby" song.'[10] In just a few months, Little Buster would be listed here and there in the credits.

After posting an ad in the *New York Clipper* 25 June that they were at liberty, the three performers were taken up by the Forest Park Stock company in Pittsburg Kansas in July and, as part of that group, were simply individual performers and no longer part of a partnership or team. Just as a summer stock company today might offer different plays over the course of the season, with members of the troupe playing whatever parts suited them, the Forest Park group operated in a similar manner. The Keatons and Arthur Long were part of at least four different plays that summer, *Old Kentucky* on 15 July, *The Bowery Waif* on 21 July, *The Runaway Wife* on 28 July and *Life on the Ocean Wave* on 29 July. Myra's most compelling review came for *The Runaway Wife*, in which she played two very distinct roles: Aunt Hester, in which she was 'sweet and bewitching' and Lillian Hay, 'ill-featured and sharp-tongued.'[11] Joe's best reviews came for *Old Kentucky*, and *Bowery Waif*. For *Old Kentucky*, the reviewer noted that 'As Neb, he kept the audience in a roar from start to finish. His specialties are of a high order, his dancing being especially fine. When he gets to dancing, it appears as though his legs are boneless.'[12] About a week later for *The Bowery Waif*, Joe played McGoogan, an Irish cop: 'his every appearance was greeted with laughter; when he came through the trap, they yelled.'[13]

In August, the three were set free again and at this point Joe went off to Hollis, Kansas 19 August to join up with Christy's Vaudevilles. The ad he answered appeared in the 13 August *New York Clipper*. It read,

> Wanted a Good Black-Faced Comedian. Salary sure, but you must be a good man and hot comedy in acts. Hams sliced on sight. N. B. if you don't want to work, don't write for it; must change for two weeks. Dr B. Christy, Talmo, Kansas. Republic Co.[14]

In order to take this job, Joe had to leave Myra and Buster behind in Pittsburg for a time. Pittsburg native and amateur actor Guy Fritts[15] related in a 1907 news article that in September, after Joe had arranged for Myra to join him as part of the Christy company, Buster was left behind with Mrs. Ida Fritts, Guy's mother, due to the fact that he was sick and unable to travel: 'My mother took charge of the youngster and kept him until he got well enough to join his parents.'[16] As per the notice published 5 November, Myra had indeed assumed a part in the Christy company, currently playing western Kansas, along with the Seeleys, the Clements, and the Keatons.[17]

Announced in the 19 November edition of the *New York Clipper* was the hiring of Joe and Myra by J. T. R. Clarke's German American Vaudeville Company.[18] The vaudeville part of this troupe was small and ill-advertised, because the main attraction was the doctors. Full-page coverage of the German American doctors filled the pages of the *Wichita [Kansas] Beacon*, where they were in residence for 10 weeks, the *Sterling [Kansas] Bulletin*, Sterling being the location of the premiere of the new season with the Keatons aboard, and the *Lyons [Kansas] Daily News*, 10 miles from Sterling, which also advertised performances of the troupe during the same dates, indicating possibly a splitting of the troupe to take advantage of two locations or performances at different times. The first media blitz in Wichita included a couple of testimonials, including one between patient Sim Travers of 126 North Topeka Avenue and Dr. Clarke (or Clark). Diagnosed originally with an abscess on the brain, which was fatal, Travers gave himself over to the German American doctors and after their treatment and proper diagnosis, he was cured – no charge.[19]

In Sterling, Kansas, the German American doctor group bought an entire page of the local *Bulletin*, page two, filled with such testimonials, all signed by the happy and satisfied patients. The masthead in the center of the page stated 'Are You Sick?' then indicated that the German American doctors would be located in the parlors of the Hotel Morris in Sterling for two weeks, from 9.00 in the morning to 7.30 at night. The doctors were from 'the foremost medical colleges of this country and Europe,' including the City University of New York, University of Pennsylvania, University of Cincinnati School of Medicine, Heidelberg University (Germany), and the Eclectic and Homeopathic Colleges of Philadelphia. Five of these learned doctors had their likenesses adorning the center of the page.[20] In this first huge blitz, the vaudeville troupe affiliated with the doctors received only a brief mention: 'their high-class vaudeville company.'[21]

Yet, the activities and reception of the vaudeville troupe can still be traced. In Lyons, Kansas at the Goodson Opera House, for performances given the same dates as the doctors' residence in Sterling, the reviewer asserted that the show, with only a ten-cent entrance fee, was worth five times that: 'It's chockful of laughter. The costumes worn by Brooks and Floyd cost over $400.'[22] The Brooks was Carney (or Corney) Brooks, troupe manager and advance agent, whose name was nearly the only individual name mentioned in the press for the troupe.[23] He was also *the* black face comedian of the troupe, despite Joe's presence. There were 12 players total at this point. After Sterling and Lyons, they were in Ellinwood, Kansas, then Claflin, Kansas from the day after Christmas until about 6 January 1899.[24] These dates were planned, but the area was hit by a blizzard about 28 November in the area of Lyons, Dighton, and Claflin, all venues for the troupe. The Lyons reporter almost lost an ear due to the cold and three train lines were completely blocked.[25] Of course, being prairie folk, the Kansans made the most of it after everyone acclimated and appeared safe and sound:

> During the blizzard that was raging a week ago last Monday, a man at Claflin bet five dollars that he could run from the hotel to the depot, nearly two blocks away, and back without a stitch of clothing on. The money was put up, the man stripped and ran to the depot and returned against the blinding snowstorm in just two minutes. 'It's an ill wind that blows nobody good.'[26]

In mid-March Clark published a piece in the *New York Clipper*, that asserted his company had been on the road for 104 weeks. Some of the venues they had played included Little River, Garden City, Dighton, Gove City, and Pawnee Rock, Kansas. He had 21 players in the company, including Joe, Mira and Buster Keating (*sic*) and both the Colby and Oliver families, hinting at things to come. They had a nine-piece brass band. He noted that the company had nine more weeks in the opera houses then would go back out under canvas for the warmer months.[27]

In Kinsley, Kansas in late April, Buster had at least one of the two accidents he reports in his autobiography, the severing of his finger. The *Kinsley Graphic* reported that 'the little Keaton boy, who has been appearing on the stage here with the medicine show, had the end of one finger taken off by putting it in the cogs of Mrs. Wolgamot's wringer.'[28] On that same day, Buster recounted that he broke his head open when he attempted to throw a brick at a peach he wanted that hung way up in a tree. The brick flew back and hit him in the head. Mrs. Wolgamot was Altena, from whom the Keatons rented a room. Frank Colby, part of the William Colby family who were performers on the German American Vaudevilles tour, recounted the finger-severing episode in 1942. He remembered that he bore some responsibility for Buster's accident: 'On the porch, a woman was running her washing through a clothes wringer, a machine that neither he nor I had ever seen before. Buster, the more adventurous [one] speculated as to what would happen if one thrust a finger into the quietly meshing gears. "Try it and see," I suggested.'[29]

Being that Frank was three years older than the victim, of course Buster would have taken the dare. Perhaps the most important aspect, though, of this tiny notice in the Kinsley paper was that Buster had been joining his parents onstage, thereby confirming stories his parents told much later.

In mid-May, at a stop in Stafford, Kansas, the troupe (now numbering eight members) encountered some trouble. As the writer related it, 'the "ghost" failed to walk at the proper time when Saturday night came around, which led to an altercation in the dining room of the hotel wherein one of the staff smote a brother with such violence on the jaw that it floored him. The entire troop pulled out for Kansas City'[30] on Monday 8 May, but it may not have been totally due to this altercation. In fact, the city of Stafford had passed an ordinance 1 May, the day of the troupe's arrival, that implemented an occupation tax:

> traveling physicians and surgeons five dollars a day, which we believe to be extortionate. [. . .] Every member of the company spent their money freely in our city. We understand that when these physicians arrived in town and learned of this occupation tax being passed, after all necessary arrangements were made for them to come, they offered to pay the same amount of taxation as resident physicians, which is ten dollars, there being two of these doctors, the sum of their license would have been twenty dollars. They were refused, therefore instead of the city getting twenty dollars, it got nothing.[31]

Their departure was a shame, because the people of Stafford had enjoyed the first week of shows: 'Every member of the company are artists in their line. The fine costumes worn by some of these actors and actresses are extremely handsome and very costly. The privilege of seeing them is well worth the price of admission.'[32]

Still, this turned out to be the last venue for the Keatons as part of J. T. R. Clark's German American Vaudevilles, because once back in Kansas City, they decamped with other troupe members and became part of the new (and short-lived) Oliver and Colby Vaudeville Company,[33] which took a five-night engagement in the Casino at Garfield Park in Topeka Kansas beginning 22 May. Meanwhile, the German American troupe the Keatons had just left went on to Pratt, Kansas and experienced a cyclone first-hand on 2 June. As the reporter noted, the cyclone didn't move level to the ground, but would rise up then dip down and destroy a building but leave the one next to it untouched. For instance, a livery stable in the downtown area was destroyed, but the horse and buggy inside were left unharmed, and the stable next door was completely untouched. More importantly, 'a medicine show was holding forth in the opera house and it was with difficulty that a panic was averted. The building seemed ready to fall to pieces at any time, but fortunately, did not collapse.'[34] Could this have been the cyclone of Keaton mythology, the twister that supposedly blew little Buster out a window? In Joe's version of the story, told in *Photoplay* in 1927, the cyclone occurred on the very day of Buster's birth, 4 October 1895, in Piqua, Kansas and blew away the medicine show's tent and all its properties.[35] By the time Buster himself told the story in his 1960 autobiography, however, the cyclone became part of 27 April in Kinsley, Kansas, for it was the third of the boy Keaton's mishaps of that day:

> This time I was awakened by the noise of a Kansas twister. Getting up, I went to the open window to investigate the swishing noise. I didn't fall out of the window, I was sucked out by the circling winds of the cyclone and whirled away down the road. I had rolled and revolved about a block from the farmhouse when a man saw me, rushed out, scooped me up, and carried me to the safety of the nearest storm cellar.[36]

As divergent as these two tellings are, perhaps first-hand reporting from former colleagues about the event in Pratt simply morphed into the Keatons actually being there (it was the next venue of the German American troupe, after all) and suddenly became the apocryphal life-threatening story. As the only reported cyclone touchdown at the time and in the area, this is highly probable.

Although the *New York Dramatic Mirror* claimed Oliver and Colby had just completed an Australian tour, this is impossible, because both families had been part of the German American Vaudevilles troupe. The Olivers comprised Mr. and Mrs. J. O. Oliver, Flora, Goldie and Guy Oliver. The Colbys were William (Will) and Mrs. Colby, Francis (Frank) and Petite Byrle Colby. The Keatons included Joe, Myra and Master Buster Keaton. Under the management of P. Sisson and T. J. Leathe, the company was supposed to tour the cities of the South and East,[37] but the Keatons' tenure with it would last only four engagements. The first of these, five days at the Casino in Garfield Park, was not well-attended (the 800 attendees were not enough for management), due to the fact, some surmise, that the

Topeka audience was not used to patronizing the new Casino venue inside the park. Here, 'the acrobatic Keatons, Joe and Myra, were enthusiastically received,'[38] A few days later, the troupe was in Junction City, Kansas, performing the same program with the addition of the Colbys in 'their original creation "The German Baker and the Musical Serving Maid."'[39] Then Oliver and Colby moved on to Evansville Indiana, playing five nights in Cook's Park and counting on no rain. Although young Buster was listed as part of the company, his father received the best reviews: 'Mr Keaton presents the most wonderful and novel character pastimes during the action of their sketch that convulses the audience with laughter and applause.'[40] The Colbys were mysteriously absent.

The Keatons' final engagement with Oliver and Colby (the Colbys again absent) took place in Owensboro, Kentucky, 21 to 25 August. In the review of the event, located in Hickman Park under canvas, both Myra and Buster received the most recognition: 'Mr and Mrs Joe Keaton are clever artists, especially Mrs Keaton. She has made many friends here with her charming and catchy songs. Burton [sic] their little son makes a great hit with his dancing and coin trick.'[41] Clearly, Buster was doing more than simply walking on stage and interrupting his parents – at not quite 4 years old.

At the end of August and through much of September, the Keatons, billed with someone named W. O. Stevens in one engagement, but mostly as 'The Keatons' or 'Mr. and Mrs. Keaton,' focused their efforts on venues in Virginia. They were slowly moving east, making their way to their own particular Emerald City: New York. The first engagement in Virginia was at the open-air Ocean View Theatre in Norfolk 28 August to 2 September, interestingly managed by Oscar Sisson, who had been the agent (and a performer) with the Oliver and Colby group. In fact, the Oliver family were booked the week after the Keatons' departure.[42] The Keaton-Stevens-Keaton act, in Norfolk, was deemed 'new, original and laughable.'[43]

In Hampton Virginia at the Buckroe Casino 4 to 9 September, the Keatons were noted here as 'one of the best sketch teams that ever played the casino.'[44] The final Virginia appearance, closing out the season with large and well-pleased audiences, occurred 11 to 16 September at the Auditorium on Broad Street in Richmond, the one-time home of Edgar Allen Poe. The Keatons numbered third on the bill, being described as 'comedy sketch artists par excellence.'[45] Others included Trovollo, the ventriloquist, who had made a particular impression on Buster. As Blesh tells it, Buster began to think that Trovollo's 10 dolls were animate, because after the show, he would talk to them as if they were people. 'How did you sleep last night,' he might ask, and the doll would answer 'Lousy' and provide a few details. Buster's favorite was a red head, freckle-faced doll named Red Top and he decided to steal him one night, but Trovollo was onto him and followed him back to the theatre. As Buster approached the doll, it blurted out, 'Don't touch me, boy, or I'll tell your old man.' Needless to say, Buster was a combination of surprised, scared, and ashamed. Myra found him a bit later in bed crying and shaking.[46] In some way, this may have begun heightening the aura around machines for Buster, adding to what would be a lifelong fascination.

It is thought that the Keatons spent at least a week in September performing at Huber's Dime Museum, 106 E. 14th Street at Union Square in New York City.[47] Dime museums were considered about a half step above medicine shows in the entertainment business. Frank Cullen asserts that they sprung up around the time of the Civil War and were 'vaudeville's early, seedy antecedents.' Showmen such as P. T. Barnum opened the venues, calling them 'museums' to give the places an air of legitimacy and suggest some educational value. In fact, they were filled with side-show freaks and other fraudulent exhibits, placed in high-traffic urban areas in storefronts. On the upper floors of these establishments, the 'entertainers' so-called would perform. Acts usually consisted of magicians, a scantily clad skirt dancer, and a few rag-tag musicians.[48] Andrea Stulman Dennett remarks, however, that 'the process of uniting individual amusements and marketing them as single, 'walk-through' entertainment, suitable for the entire family, was what made the dime museum novel. In a sense it was a so-called environmental entertainment, among whose fixed exhibits mobile spectators could organize their own journey,'[49] thereby legitimizing them somewhat. George H. Huber, the proprietor of both this and Huber's Roadhouse, was a flamboyant fellow of middle age, weighing at least 240 pounds. Huber seemed uniquely adept, though, at booking innovative and unusual acts, especially for his curio department.[50] His typical advertisement for acts requested 'strong features, living curiosities and freaks for Curio Halls, high class variety for theatre.'[51]

Unfortunately, although the freaks in the curio department were well advertised, the vaudeville artists were not. However, one clue as to when the Keatons might have performed at Huber's is a listing for the week beginning 2 October and engaged for two weeks of the five Olivers,[52] indeed the very Olivers of Oliver & Colby, with whom the Keatons had spent the summer months. The headliner in the curio department the first week was Enoch, the Man-Fish, whose stunts were, of course, performed under water, including smoking, playing the trombone, juggling eggs and performing a hoop trick.[53] Joe returned to his 'Silence and Fun' act at Huber's and like the originator of the piece, Fred McNish, tried to add a few exciting elements, namely some shenanigans with a table. McNish implemented two barrels and a chair on the table; Joe just attempted the chair, but would still slip up now and then, especially during the fifth or sixth required show of the day. The feat required a jump of four feet straight up into the air and was not quite perfected, even by the end of the Huber's engagement. Still, despite the lack of press, the risk paid off, for the Keatons had engagements at both Tony Pastor's 14th Street Theatre[54] and Proctor's New York Theatre before they left the city for Massachusetts.[55]

That next stop was Fall River, Massachusetts and the Casto Theatre. The Keatons spent the week of 23 October performing there as part of Star Vaudevilles, and in the third position, described as 'acrobatic comedy sketch artists.'[56] They then traveled south to New York City, playing the week of 13 November first at the Atlantic Garden which extended from 50 Bowery back to Elizabeth Street in Lower Manhattan. Essentially it was a beer hall with an attached outdoor garden, one that by this time, was on the wane.[57] The Keatons were fourth on the bill. Rudi Blesh, probably working from personal interviews with Myra Keaton, offered that the Atlantic Garden only paid its performers after their week was completed, making it a tough time indeed for the family, which claimed only 50 cents to their name by mid-week.[58]

After the week of performances was up and they had been paid at last, that bit of money would have had to last them until the week of 20 November, when they would play the Bon Ton Music Hall, 23rd Street at Sixth Avenue, New York City.[59] They played another dime museum the week following, the Ninth and Arch, which hosted freaks and eccentrics in the curio department and a vaudeville show upstairs. At this particular point in its history, however, the Ninth and Arch was motivated to feature exploitative women's sporting events in the curio hall. This week it was 'The Athletic Amazons' in Female Basketball, who were competing for a purse of $250 in gold.[60]

Although Joe Keaton would later admit that their act, as it existed in December 1899, was nothing but bad, their next engagement at Tony Pastor's 14th Street Theatre in New York changed their professional lives. As Anthony Slide notes, 'Tony Pastor transformed vaudeville from a cheap form of entertainment relegated to the saloons of New York, into an American institution, popular with and suitable for the entire family.'[61]

The 14th Street Theatre, located between Irving Place and Third, near Union Square, was his third venue, and modestly sized with only 1,000 seats. It allowed no alcohol for sale, in the hopes of attracting ladies and families.[62] Due to increasing competition from other houses, Pastor was forced to implement continuous shows[63] in the 1890s, a practice that was in effect when the Keatons came to work there in late 1899, meaning they would be working at least three and maybe four shows a day, every day.

Easily recognizable on the street, Pastor was portly, short and about 67 years old when Joe and Buster met him outside his theatre. Known for being kind-hearted and accommodating to new talent, he agreed to give the Keatons a trial and put them last on the bill for the week of 18 December, the week before Christmas.[64] The Keatons were labeled 'sketch team' in another ad, with no other descriptors, however, they had somehow performed for a week in a legitimate variety theatre and survived the experience. A poem (à la Frank Cutler) Joe wrote and included in an ad that appeared in the *New York Dramatic Mirror* 17 November 1900 both acknowledged the Keatons' one-year anniversary as true vaudeville performers, owned up to their initial deficiencies, and suggested that they had the new act well in hand by the time they played Pastor's.

> It was just one year ago to-day,
> The Man with the Table came East to stay.
> The act didn't go, 'twas bad, for fair,
> And the gong just saved it, Gus Elliott declared.
> We then vamped out, played a joint on the quiet;
> Then twisted our act and at Pastor's tried it.
> Opened the show and broke seventeen chairs,
> We're moved on the bill while they made repairs.
> Before we went on, 'twas a quarter to nine,
> The house it was jammed and the act it went fine.
> Mr. Pastor informed us we had nothing to fear –
> We have played his theatre six times this year.[65]

This poem has been oft misinterpreted. Joe is talking about looking back at the previous year (1899) and recounting its activity, not the year of the poem (1900). One year earlier from the printing of this ad put the Keatons at the Atlantic Garden in the Bowery, so perfecting the new act perhaps from this venue through dates at the Bon Ton Theatre and the Ninth and Arch Dime Museum (the 'joint on the quiet') on to Pastor's 14th Street, which had allowed some perfecting of it, thus 'Mr. Pastor informed us we had nothing to fear –/We have played his theatre six times this year.' Pastor's 14th Street was not the site of a mediocre act, but the site of the beginnings of success and the promise of more and of greater stability.[66]

The Keatons closed out the year 1899 with a week (25 to 30 December) at Proctor's 23rd Street in New York City. F. F. Proctor owned some 50 theatres, his first in New York city proper was the 23rd Street, which he built, instituting continuous vaudeville there.[67] The Keatons appeared listed with 'the others'[68] and, then with no break, the whole show moved over to the Proctor's Pleasure Palace[69] 1 to 7 January 1900 to start out the year.

The year 1900 would bring greater notoriety, traveling further afield from New York City, and an attempt to make Buster a permanent part of the act, despite legal problems involving the Gerry Society, an American child welfare organization. The week starting 14 January, the Keatons visited Albany, the New York state capital, for the first time, playing in the Proctor's Theatre there.[70] Leaving the Proctor houses for their next engagement, the Keatons traveled to Wilmington, Delaware, where they played Dockstadter's Theatre 21 January with Joe receiving high praise in the local paper: 'Joe Keaton is another very superior eccentric dancer and acrobat, a show himself, without accessories.'[71] After Wilmington, the Keatons were on to Boston Massachusetts, where they had two engagements, the first at the Howard Atheneum 28 January. The Howard had been a Boston institution since 1845. Located at 34 Howard Street and Scollay Square, it had hosted the likes of Edwin Booth and Charlotte Cushman, both noted nineteenth-century American dramatic actors. The program on offer during this week was M. M. Theise's popular *Wine, Women and Song*, comprising both a 'travesty,' a burlesque of a more serious work, which included songs and dances, and a 'vaudeville olio,' a program of variety acts. The travesty and olio employed 22 performers, led by the Burke Brothers. An additional vaudeville program employed Mr. and Mrs. Joe Keaton, 'the eccentric comedian and the pert soubrette,' as well as nine other acts.[72] Then, starting 5 February, the Keatons simply walked down the street to Austin and Stone's Dime Museum on Tremont and Scollay Square, 'Boston's oldest and most reliable exhibition resort,' which traditionally featured both freak shows and dancing girls in a low-cost eclectic experience for patrons. The museum was open from 10.00 am to 10.30 pm and cost only 10 cents admission. Mr. and Mrs. Keaton, 'screamingly funny entertainers,'[73] were eighth on a bill containing 21 acts.[74] A gig at another dime museum would seem like a comedown for the Keatons after experiencing Pastor's and the Proctor houses, but it was still early days.

In New Haven, Connecticut, they were booked 12 February at Poli's Wonderland Theatre. Joe and Myra were labeled 'the eccentric tad and the chic soubrette,' with a 'tad' being a street boy or urchin.[75] Sylvester Poli's theatres, after all, were known for being able to accommodate any type of entertainment. By early March, Joe and Myra announced in the *Police Gazette* that they were receiving 'return dates wherever they have played,'[76] however, where they performed during the month is not certain. The next month, however, found them back at Tony Pastor's in New York City from 2 April, for one of those return gigs, with the Mr. and Mrs. Keaton still last on the bill of 14 acts and labeled in one ad 'The Elastic Lady and the Tad.'[77] Back on the road, this time to Philadelphia Pennsylvania, the Keatons performed at the Ninth and Arch Dime Museum beginning 16 April. This particular week, the museum was featuring Female Greased Pole Climbing and Female Rowing Race contests in the Double Curio Hall, with one reporter noting, 'the efforts of the heavyweights to struggle towards the top were something beyond description. And when they would drop back with a thud, everybody roared.'[78] It was here, in Philadelphia, that Buster became part of the act, due to happenstance. Early in the week, Joe sprained his ankle and was unable to continue, so '"Buster" went on and finished the week.' There is no review of this performance, unfortunately, but if they were able to keep the engagement and fulfill the week, it can be surmised that he had done well – at not quite 5 years old. Joe was up and ready to resume the schedule then in Ithaca New York at the Lyceum Theatre, where they were booked for the week of 21 May,[79] then a return engagement at the Howard Atheneum in Boston, but the damage had been done. Could they return to a time without Buster in the act? At the Atheneum 28 May, and labeled 'The Keatons,'[80] they had moved up the bill a bit and were now fifth, instead of last. The next week, starting 4 June, however, they were back down the ladder, performing unattributed as part of the Howard & Emerson Show at the Bijou Theatre in Paterson, New Jersey.[81]

Joe, Myra, and Buster played Henderson's Theatre at Coney Island in New York City beginning 25 June, then moved over to the Atlantic Garden in the Bowery as 'The Keatons' 2 July.[82] From there, they were back again at Tony Pastor's the week beginning 9 July. Again part of a bill of 14 acts, this time, the Keatons, labeled 'The Eccentric Tad and the Soubrette,' had made it to the eleventh spot, instead of dead last before the American Vitagraph, so perhaps Pastor's, the venue at which they had now performed most frequently, was the best judge of their progress in the business (it also didn't allow Buster as part of the act, at least officially).[83]

The Keatons' first experience with Keith's theatres came at the Union Square, managed by the inimitable Edward F. Albee beginning 23 July in the middle of a heat wave. One reviewer noted, however, that 'it was cool and comfortable in this pretty playhouse on Tuesday afternoon when the writer strolled in to look things over. The noiseless electric fans, which are liberally provided, made the use of the palm leaf breeze providers unnecessary.' Mr. and Mrs. Keaton, 'acrobatic comedy sketchists' were third from last on the bill and received no further review.[84]

August was taken up by engagements in northern New York State, the third week at Cayuga Lake Park in Seneca Falls and in Painted Post beginning 25 August.[85] These gigs closed out the summer season for all entertainers and the Keatons could soon be found back in the city (New York) starting up the fall season at Proctor's 23rd Street, a return engagement. The interceding two weeks may have allowed some down time, as their Proctor's performances began on 17 September. Just five days later, the Keatons' first half-page ad[86] in the *Dramatic Mirror* appeared, the tagline 'The Eccentric Tad and the Chic Soubrette' sharing the space with 'The Man with the Table,' which the Keatons described as 'an act suitable for any audience. Full of action. Fifteen minutes of knockabout eccentricities and clever dancing. Concluding with the funniest exhibition of chair and table acrobatic comedy work on the American stage.'[87] Accompanied by a montage of photos from the act, the center image distinctly shows Joe standing by a wooden kitchen table with a chair sitting on top of it. McNish's incarnation of such a 'Silence and Fun' act has been discussed, but others, such as medicine show performer Frank Lexington, known as a professional leaper, also worked in a similar vein:

> Onstage at the beginning of his act was an ordinary kitchen table a little larger than a bridge table. After a very short run from the side of the stage, Lexington would leap over the table without apparent effort. Then, placing a chair on either side of it, he would leap over the three objects. Lexington would continue to leap and to add more chairs until there were three lined up on either side of the table. Next, he placed another chair on top and leaped again, and finally he seated another performer in the chair and vaulted over a total of seven chairs, a table, and the company's blackface comedian.[88]

A writer from *The New York Dramatic Mirror* published a piece specifically on Joe and his new act in January 1901, the first time he had received such acclaim in print. His description of the act is respectfully vague (so as not to give anything away) but does provide some additional information:

> The Man with the Table is a brisk, lively comedy act, different than anything in the same line now before the public. It does not depend upon dialogue, though it is by no means a 'dumb act.' There is just enough gingery repartee to emphasise the merit of Mr Keaton's acrobatic work, which is very amusing. The act embraces eccentric acrobatic dancing, innumerable funny situations, and concludes with an extremely diverting series of tricks, done by Mr Keaton with a table and a chair.[89]

Only a month later, the moniker 'The Eccentric Tad and the Chic Soubrette' was sidelined in favor of 'The Man with the Table' and was never used again.

Proctor's Pleasure Palace was the next stop 24 September, always an expectation following a week at Proctor's 23rd Street. The Keatons were last on the bill,[90] Followed by a return to Tony Pastor's 1 October, for their fifth time performing there in the previous year, this time billed fourth from the bottom. Another of their return engagements occurred at Dockstadter's in Wilmington, Delaware 15 October.[91] The next two weeks were a whirlwind of activity, because the Keatons, as part of Burke's Vaudeville Festival, appeared at a theatre in Easton, Pennsylvania the week of 22 October, then the very next week at the Lyric Theatre in Allentown, Pennsylvania, just 13 miles away. The gig in Easton is significant, because it was there on 23 October that Buster had his official debut with the act, 'his imitations and burlesques were a hit from the start.'[92] Interestingly, the Keatons received some individual notice in the paper there. The description suggested that they were 'two of the best acrobatic comedians, dancers and singers, known to the vaudeville stage, who have recently concluded a long engagement in London,'[93] an obvious untruth (the London part). Then the Burke group traveled back to Wilmington, but just for one day and night, 31 October at the Grand Opera House, and, oddly, only 'Joe Keaton' was listed on the bill. It was again J. K. Burke's Vaudeville Festival that the Keatons took part in.[94] A description and review of the event mentions both Joe and Myra, though, and offers that they were 'two of the best acrobatic comedians, dancers and singers known to the vaudeville stage.'[95] A large ad the Keatons took out in *The New York Dramatic Mirror* 3 November declared them indeed with J. K Burke's Vaudeville and 'The Man with a Table' had now replaced the previous 'Eccentric Tad and Chic Soubrette.'[96]

Off to Ohio in November, the Keatons played the week of 5 November at the London Theatre in Steubenville, best known as the birthplace of singer Dean Martin and for its mining, milling, and glass-making industries. In the *New York Clipper*, the Keatons were called 'Mr. and Mrs. Joe Keaton and Little Buster,' and seem to be at the top of the bill.[97] Touted in the Keatons' 22 September half-page ad was a week following at the Columbia Theatre in Cincinnati, Ohio. Beginning the week of 12 November, the Keatons moved to the first act (or curtain-raiser) on the bill.[98]

From Cincinnati, the young family traveled to St. Louis, gateway to the West, spending the week of 3 December in what would have been a chilly clime. The Columbia Theatre, at Sixth and St. Charles Streets downtown, offered continuous vaudeville, with seats starting at 10 cents and moving up the chain to the lux 50-cent Orchestra chairs.[99] Although billed here as 'Mr. and Mrs. Keaton,' one review noted that the group comprised Mr and Mrs Keaton, 'assisted by "Little Buster" presenting an acrobatic comedy.'[100] Moving back east a bit, the Keatons stopped in Chicago the week beginning 10 December at the Chicago Opera House, again as 'Mr. and Mrs. Keaton,' acrobatic eccentricities and dancing.'[101] They were lucky in that the weather was somewhat mild for December (the wind off of Lake Michigan can be brutal) at only 38°F.

One planned engagement in the American South became two when the Keatons appeared both in Memphis and Nashville, Tennessee on adjoining weeks in December. In Memphis, they appeared at the Hopkins Grand Opera House, 125 to 127 S. Main Street, the week beginning 17 December. The residential stock company, Hopkins New Stock Company, presented 'Sam'l Posen,' an M. B. Curtis comedy. 'Little Buster' made the theatre's ad this time, for Mr. and Mrs. Joe Keaton were 'assisted by' their son in the sketch 'The Man with the Table.'[102] Moving east to Nashville Tennessee for Christmas week, the Keatons shared the bill at the Grand Opera House there, 431 North Cherry Street, with a big production of Marie Doran's *Nell Gwynne* by the residential Boyle Stock Company, prophetically, a play Buster would star in a few years later. Next in importance for the week were 'Mr. and Mrs. Joe Keaton, assisted by Little Buster, in an original comedy creation entitled "The Man with the Sable [*sic*]."'[103]

Little Buster Keaton was part of the act, but not part of it. His parents were still mostly billed as Mr. and Mrs. Keaton, and in the descriptions and reviews of the act, he was usually 'assisted by Little Buster Keaton.'

The year 1900 was about to turn over to 1901 and in this year, Mr. and Mrs. Keaton would become The Three Keatons, with the addition of Buster leading to greater fame *and* greater hardship. Joe had recently employed a stereotypical Irish makeup as his persona for the act: 'His hair is of a fiery red: he is rosy-cheeked, massive, and whiskey-loving. His face is one of simian bestiality, with an expression of diabolical archness written all over it. [. . .] His main characteristics are his swagger, his boisterousness, and his pugnacity. He is always ready with a challenge [and] always anxious to back a quarrel.'[104] Add to these Galway whiskers and a pipe. No explanation for this choice of makeup is given and, because the act is described as knockabout comedy rather than ethnic comedy, it seems odd, especially because the Keatons continued it until the act broke up. Initially, Buster was adorned onstage as a Joe Keaton mini-me, but simple imitation of his father would not be the end of it. As the act evolved, it became a knockabout fest that involved Joe throwing Buster around the stage. This violence, played for fun, would be both misinterpreted and misconstrued (as well as enjoyed), causing problems with the child welfare officials throughout the next few years.

Chapter 3

Life on the Road Becoming 'Buster'

■ ■

The year 1901 dawned with the Keatons in Perry, Oklahoma for six weeks visiting Joe's relatives.[1] Being their first extended 'holiday' at home for many years, the town welcomed them warmly and was ready to celebrate their new-found fame. A piece appeared 11 January, that announced that the Keatons would perform together with several other entertainers the night of 18 January at the opera house: 'Mr Keaton will be remembered as one of the old boomers and made his first appearance in a tent situated on our courthouse square a few days after the strip was open.'[2] The ad for the evening (a good-size) read:

> By Request of Friends and Boomers, Mr. and Mrs Joe Keaton, assisted by Little Buster, the smallest comedian, and several other professional artists will give a high-class Vaudeville festival at the Opera House Friday night, 18 January, on which occasion the Keatons will present their own comedy creation, The Man with the Table, exactly the same as heretofore presented in the large cities. The *New York Journal* says, 'The Keatons have the funniest routine of Table and Chair comedy to be seen in Vaudeville. And the originator of this extremely funny act hails from Perry Oklahoma.'[3]

The Keatons would leave Perry for New York 18 February, but they had been busy booking engagements before they departed. In the months of January and February, they would advertise twice in the *New York Daily Mirror* to try to get their professional ball rolling. The first read,

> Mr and Mrs Joe Keaton. The Man with the Table. Assisted by Little Buster, the smallest comedian, in the busiest comedy

creation in Vaudeville, introducing eccentric, acrobatic, grotesque comedy, dancing and singing, concluding with the funniest routine of Table and Chair comedy before the public today. Vacation address 624 G Street, Perry, Oklahoma, [his father Joseph Z. Keaton's residence].[4]

The next ad, appearing about a month later on 16 February, now had a new headline, 'Joe, Myra and Buster Keaton. The Man with the Table. The Busiest Act in Vaudeville.'[5] Joe and Myra had achieved seven weeks booked into the various Proctor's houses[6] in New York and Buster had become part of the deal. Their first gig of the year was Proctor's Albany New York 25 February, followed the next week by an engagement at the Proctor's New Theatre in Montréal, Canada, 4 March. The Keatons then entered New York City proper for engagements at four other Proctor's theatres, 23rd Street, 125th Street (in Harlem), 5th Street and 58th Street (Proctor's Palace).[7] Proctor's 5th Avenue was played twice. In Albany, already the notices were good for the addition of Buster: 'The Keatons with Buster made a ten-strike.'[8] Just before this engagement, another Keaton ad appeared with the addition, 'Keep Your Eye on the KID.' Weekly ads, as they were called, then appeared for the Keatons in the *New York Dramatic Mirror* two or three times a month. From them, the evolution of the act and the fortunes of the Keatons themselves can be measured. For example, appearing 23 March was a Keaton ad that marked such a difference: 'BUSTER (Keaton), and his assistants were selected as one of the COMEDY FEATURES to appear at the opening of Mr. Proctor's New Theatre, Montreal, Canada. [. . .] More Work for The Man with the Table. Nineteen minutes of refreshing Comedy.'[9] Instead of assisting his parents, Buster was now being assisted by them.

The Keatons' Montréal performance allowed father and son full rein in regards to the physicality of the act. It promised 'Joe Keaton assisted by Mrs Keaton and a little seven-year-old[10] comedian "Buster" will be found to be another funny act.'[11] While most of the Proctor's engagements garnered the Keatons few substantial reviews, the week at Proctor's Palace did result in the substantial

Joe, Myra, and Buster Keaton made the laughing hit of the bill. Buster is a diminutive five-year-old comedian who is unusually funny. He impresses one as a healthy, roguish child with a lively dash in him that is irresistible. Without appearing unnaturally precocious or impertinent, he manages to keep the audiences in roars from the time he is dragged on the stage by his father, sitting on a broom, until his exit, which he makes hanging on to his father's leg. The father does some remarkably clever acrobatic work in a loose-jointed lazy fashion, sorrowfully reprimanding his son for his pranks the while'[12]

This description offers rare detail about the substance of the act at this point.[13] On the same page of the *New York Dramatic Mirror* as this second review, the Keatons were pictured in costume, with the photo accompanied by a descriptive paragraph, which noted, 'The somewhat curtailed figure in the right-hand corner of the picture is one Buster, the Keatons' male heir. Buster, who has inherited the family talent, made his theatrical debut about the middle of this season and was a success at the outset.'[14] The Keatons had visited the prestigious Feinberg's studio,16 W. 14th Street in New York, to shoot the first of many family photographs in costume for publicity purposes, thereby making one more step on the road to success.

Betwixt and between the Proctor's gigs was Easter week at Tony Pastor's 14th Street Theatre 8 April,[15] where they received some positive commentary: 'The Keatons, Myra, Joe and Buster, presented a grotesque comedy act entitled "The Man with The Table," which had clever features galore to recommend it.'[16] Only six weeks later, Buster again took the top spot in his parents' weekly ad: 'BUSTER, the toy comedian, absolutely the funniest imitating and talking comedian of modern times, in a refreshing [eight-person] sketch entitled "The Man with the Table."' They claimed to currently be with the Boom Circuit of Parks, Maurice Boom, manager. The Keatons also offered their current address as 136 East 18th Street, New York City.[17]

This advertising occurred despite the uptick in vigilance on the part of the Gerry Society, more properly known as the New York Society for the Prevention of Cruelty to Children, on the young Keaton, a vigilance that was only a threat to the team within the city limits of New York City. In fact, the Proctor circuit required the Keatons to obtain some sort of permission to allow Buster into the act (and, obviously, to be paid as a performer). The Society began contacting Joe Keaton in December 1900 and in January 1901 founder Elbridge Gerry[18] himself responded to a letter or two from Joe shortly before his retirement. Buster's father hoped to use a loophole to present his young son to New York City audiences for the first time that season, which was that Buster would be doing no singing, dancing, or acrobatics – all skills verboten by the child labor laws.

By May, mayors were getting involved in Buster's ability to perform. One report in *The Brooklyn [New York] Citizen* described a meeting between Mayor Van Wyck, Buster, and Myra, an article that Buster later inserted verbatim into his autobiography. The Keatons were appearing at Tilyou's Steeplechase Theatre at Coney Island and the Brooklyn child welfare authorities were opposed to allowing Buster to play there. Van Wyck sided with the Keatons for the simple fact that he was on the side of the working people who frequented both the park and the theatre (the constituents who had elected him), people he believed deserved to see good entertainment as much as those of higher classes in Manhattan proper, while the child welfare office, Mr. Willis, suggested those audiences were an evil influence:

> 'As far as your suggestions about Coney Island go,' said the Mayor, 'I can say for myself that I never saw a disorderly crowd there. [. . .] These great crowds of people are just as much entitled to their amusements as anyone else. [. . .] I do not think it will do any harm to give this child a license.'[19]

After another week at Proctor's 5th Avenue 5 May, the Keatons began their summer performances at Street Railroad Park in Putnam, Connecticut 10 June.[20] However, by the middle of June, Joe and Maurice Boom had a parting of the ways that involved money. Initially, Boom secured eight weeks on a summer park circuit for the act at what seemed to be a high wage. However, just a couple of weeks into the season, Joe strongly suggested to Boom that he could get $20 a week more with another agency and purported to end his contract unless another $20 a week began to appear. Boom gave him a full release, but Joe then had second thoughts and asked to be taken back:

> Boom might have done so had he not received that morning a letter, written two days before, the manager of one of the parks handled by him, enclosing a communication from Keaton in which the latter announced that he was willing to work for the manager at an increase of fifteen dollars, and stating that he had severed business relations with Boom.[21]

Joe was either just bad at negotiating business or had become overly confident about his act, given some of the fine press they had received in the preceding months. In any event, he couldn't refrain from posting an inside joke about this incident in his 13 July ad in the *New York Dramatic Mirror*: 'Now we are all right, we had our *Boom*.'[22]

Back on the Keith circuit in Atlanta, Georgia starting 24 May at the Lyceum Theatre, they then played the Atlantic Garden[23] in New York. At the Lyceum, all were comedy acts and part of *Anderson's Polite Vaudeville*,[24] with ventriloquist Trovollo leading the pack. Buster was named as the head of the Keaton act, 'which is made up of fancy and comedy dancing. He is said to be great as a child dancer.'[25] After the first night's performances, however, the reviewer decided Joe was the real star:

> Little Buster is said to be the feature of the Keaton act, a grotesque acrobatic act, but he is not ace high beside Joe Keaton. He does marvelously funny things in, around and under a table, besides dancing and playing a game of baseball all by himself. The act started well and went better as it neared the end. Myra Keaton is a pretty little woman that does some artistic dancing and is all around clever.[26]

The Keatons were featuring the newish song 'Tobie, I Kind 'O Likes You' in their act[27] at this time and receiving praise for it:

> I always said I'd never wed, ma heart I'd never lose,
> I thought I'd ramble through a life alone.
> Still, I'm afraid a little maid will make me change ma views,
> but you can gamble she's all my own.
> Now to tell the truth, I love her! An' I'm tryin' to discover
> exactly what a pool I've got with ma own baby dear.
> And I really thought t'would daze her,
> but it didn't even faze her
> when on ma breast her head I pressed an whispered in her ear:
> Tobie, I kind o' likes you; can't I steal a kiss?
> Maybe you'll let me squeeze you, baby!
> I loves to tease you! Tell me, just how it strikes you when
>   I whisper this:
> My Tobie, I kind o' likes you![28]

Because of the act's physicality and the need for the rhythm of music to structure it, the Keaton act continued to depend on it playing an integral role.

49

The Keatons' next Keith Circuit date was at Keith's, Union Square, which they had played before. Scheduled there beginning 8 July, it was during this engagement that Buster received his first notice in the *New York Dramatic Mirror* as an individual performer. The piece, entitled 'A Diminutive Comedian,' appeared 13 July.[29] It places his birth in 1893, two years early, in order to continue the fiction that he was past 7 years old. Unlike later accounts, it gave the origin of his nickname to someone in the particular company of players with whom his parents were traveling, not yet Harry Houdini. The 'biographer' noted that 'the tiny comedian is perfectly at ease in his work, natural, finished, and artistic, and his specialties have proved a fetching addition to the favorite act of the Keatons that is known all over the land by its title, The Man with the Table.'[30]

They traveled to Philadelphia and played Keith's Theatre the week of 15 July. Like the other Keith's houses, this one promised that it was cooler than the outdoor venues, even illustrating their ads with graphics of thermometers clearly showing that inside the theatre was a cool 70°F.[31] From here they left the Keith Circuit and returned to the parks, performing in Electric Park Baltimore Maryland 22 July,[32] then on to Toledo Ohio 18 August at the Hanner's Farm Theatre. Once a private club, located at the northern end of Collingwood near Cherry and Berdan, the Hanner Brothers built a theatre on the site in February 1900. Business the week of the Keatons' engagement was reportedly 'good.'[33] Then, they had a two-week engagement (supposedly held over due to Buster's popularity[34]) in Chicago at Ferris Wheel Park.[35] Called 'Ferris Wheel Park' due to the fact that it contained the first-ever Ferris Wheel, it was designed originally for the World's Columbian Exposition in 1893 in Chicago, but had been moved to Lincoln Park. Then the week of 8 September was spent visiting the family in Perry, Oklahoma before they were to begin a run of engagements that would take them to 3 February 1902 without a break.[36]

After his unfortunate experience with Maurice Boom, it seems like madness for Joe to have signed with the Orpheum Circuit's Martin Beck for the rest of the season, but sign with him he did. Beck held the top job at the largest circuit of theatres located in the western United States, the Orpheum. He was known to be taciturn and sometimes abusive; he once noted, 'I will have no liars about me and want nothing but the truth.'[37] Achieving the Orpheum engagements was indeed a coup for Joe Keaton; the question was whether or not he could work within Beck's rigid parameters for an extended period. Joe had accomplished this contract before the end of the summer season, for the list of performances appeared in the Three Keatons ad for 31 August in the *New York Dramatic Mirror*. Joe had begun referring to the act as the Three Keatons in the 13 July ad for the same paper. The act would keep this name now until a new child, Harry, would join it sometime in 1905.

The Orpheum Circuit venues included (in chronological order) Kansas City Missouri, Omaha Nebraska, San Francisco and Los Angeles California,[38] taking the Keaton family west for the first time since they had played with the Oliver and Colby troupe at the end of the previous century. By the week of 6 October, the Keatons were in San Francisco, completely new territory for them. They were booked at the Orpheum there for two consecutive weeks, then held over for a third.[39] One reviewer focused solely on the Keaton act:

> The Orpheum was packed to the doors last night, and there was not a vacant seat at the matinee performance. Joe, Myra and Buster Keaton appear in one of the old-time turns. Buster Keaton is a four-year-old comedian who possesses unusual precocity and made a big hit with the audience.[40]

Their final Orpheum circuit engagement then was one week in Los Angeles, California beginning the week of 28 October. One reviewer, late in the first week, was determined to provide negative reviews to everyone on the bill, the Keatons included: 'Joe, Myra and Buster Keaton do a turn that is intended to show how much Joe can slam himself about without breaking his neck and how precocious is the little Keaton, who is made up with whiskers like his daddy. The juvenile Keaton has within him the makings of a comedian. The feminine Keaton doesn't do much in particular.'[41] Perhaps the highlight of the week came when the performers presented Buster with a 'handsome gold-headed cane, which was handed over the footlights.'[42]

The Keatons were set up for a week at the Empire in Denver, Colorado 10 November and the Hopkins at Chicago Illinois 22 December (Christmas week), and soon were able to fill other open dates, with a week at Park Theatre in Youngstown, Ohio, the Duquesne Theatre[43] in Pittsburgh, and the Bastable in Syracuse. In Youngstown, the Keatons were the curtain-raisers: 'The bill closes with a hurrah, and it begins with one. The first number is Joe, Myra and Buster Keaton and they're in the first row at that. Little Buster is a good one and you are put in good humor at once by this trio.'[44] Buster once commented later in life that being the curtain-raising act was only a negative thing if the act failed, because if it was a huge success, all the other acts had to work harder to live up to it. Being scheduled last on the bill was another thing, however, for much of the audience failed to stay to see it. At Hopkins Opera House Christmas week the Keatons experienced some excitement their last night on stage when the old Park Theatre next door caught fire in the basement and threatened the Hopkins as well. The old Park was being used to exhibit penny slot machines, electric pianos, and other automatic musical instruments, all of which were destroyed, at a cost of $60,000. The manager of the Hopkins kept his head and successfully evacuated some 2,000 guests, without causing a panic.[45] The Keatons' bravery that night – they kept on with their act while the audience filed out – was reported as far away as Davenport, Iowa.[46]

With that good deed to their credit, the Keatons were rewarded with a week in Richmond, Virginia and warmish weather to begin the new year, playing the Bijou Theatre there starting 6 January. The new year 1902 would prove to be another of paying dues, becoming known, running from the Gerry Society officials and, therefore, staying far afield from New York City for much of the year. What happened to their affiliation with the Orpheum Circuit is unclear, because by all indications, they had been especially successful in San Francisco, but did well at the other three venues as well. Still, they would not darken an Orpheum theatre door this year. Yet Buster was fast becoming the most popular part of the act and in some locations, his name was featured over those of his parents. The word 'midget' did come into play this year in descriptions of the young comedian, but even though Joe promoted this idea to increase his age (and did so also by having him wear a complete adult male costume when on the street, with derby hat and suit), Buster himself rejected the pejorative term, mainly because he wasn't a dwarf or little person, but simply height-challenged (he would top out at 5 foot 4 inches), a fact that was made worse by the stark difference in height between him and his father, who stood at nearly 6 feet: '"You are very short," his father says to him. "Yes, and if I were not, you would be when pay day comes," he answers, which is doubtless true.'[47] This exchange brought the issue directly into their act on occasion and so it became both accepted and expected.

With the evolution of the act and Buster's part in it over the course of this year and next (before the next Keaton child was born), many iconic elements of his later film persona came into being. Although one reviewer thought Little Buster should smile more, in fact it was decided that smiling lessened laughs received, so Buster adopted a solemn, even pathetic expression early on. The oft-recounted story went something like this:

'If something tickled me and I started to grin,' Buster says, 'the old man would hiss, "Face! Face!" that meant freeze the puss. The longer I held it, why, if we got a laugh the blank pan or the puzzled puss would double it. He kept after me, never let up, and in a few years it was automatic. Then when I'd step on stage or in front of a camera, I couldn't smile. Still can't.'[48]

And so, the deadpan expression of his well-known film persona was born. The other aspect of his increasing skill that Buster would carry into films was his physicality.

A luggage handle had been sown into the back of his jacket, that allowed Joe to grab it and throw him around the stage and even out into the audience on occasion. Generally, Buster had been taught how to fall without getting hurt from the very early days. A poem entitled *The Keatons*, written by A. G. Burgoyne, the All-Sorts Man, provides some fine evidence of Buster's costume as well as his role in the act:

> The son, a most precocious lad,
> Presents a faithful duplicate
> In face and make-up of his dad.
> Alike they are in shape and gait,
> A dress suit, too, the youngster sports
> That on a scale a world too vast,
> And old misfortunes thus he courts,
> Which come upon him thick and fast.
>
> They catch Young Hopeful by the slack
> Of his unmentionabler stout
> And toss him forward, toss him back,
> And up and down and in and out,
> Across the footlights he is hurled,
> And overhead he seems to fly;
> Yet while from place to place he's whirled,
> He seems all danger to defy.
>
> A table in the centre stands,
> And serves for many a funny play
> Which agile feet and agile hands
> With unexampled skill essay.

'Tis one great game of knockabout,
Kept up by mater, dad and son,
Till one concludes, beyond a doubt,
They're made of rubber, ev'ry one.[49]

This year of 1902 would be the year, as well, in which the tried-and-true 'Man with the Table' act would be retired in favor of a general knockabout act in which Buster played the unruly son, Joe and Myra his long-suffering parents. As the new year dawned in Richmond, Virginia, however, they were still hanging onto it. Again, the Keatons opened the show 'with some very good work. Master "Busbee" [*sic*] is a very good "kid" comedian.'[50] Another reviewer concentrated his piece on Buster, noting he 'has made a good impression. He is at the top of the class of youngsters seen at the Bijou, and there have been some of the best at the popular Broad-Street house.'[51]

The Keatons traveled to Wilmington, Delaware for the week of 20 January, which would be spent at Dockstader's Theatre. This was the venue at which Buster supposedly first received pay for his work ($10) in the many apocryphal stories that exist about it. Dockstader's is one of many such theatres on the Keaton's schedule in 1900 that came to be labeled 'the debut venue.' Performers (and others) are not above creating stories about their origins that become embellished more and more over the years, as in the Houdini naming event. In any event the Keatons were back in a familiar venue and spent a successful week.[52]

They snuck back into New York City for a week at Tony Pastor's beginning 27 January, risking the wrath of the child protection officers.[53] Then it was on to Washington, D. C.'s Chase Theatre, making this the Keatons' first trip to the American capital city,[54] then Poli's Wonderland Theatre in New Haven, Connecticut, home of Princeton University, one of the most prestigious ivy league schools in the country.[55] Next was Jacques Opera House in Waterbury, Connecticut,[56] and the Lyceum Theatre in New London, in between the plays put on by the Harcourt Comedy Company, with which the Keatons were now traveling. Charles K. Harris was the manager and leading man of the stock company and was presenting Ouida's *Under Two Flags*.[57]

About a month later, the Keatons traveled to Syracuse, New York to play again at the Bastable Theatre beginning the week of 17 March,[58] then Rochester's Cook Opera House,[59] followed by the Temple Theatre in Detroit, where the Keatons opened 'the evening list of sketches with some breezy comedy skits, which do well for an appetizer.' Perhaps the most eye-opening of acts on the bill this time was called Tom Eck's Motorcycle Whirl: 'In addition to the usual tricks on the dizzy inclined track, Stone and Judge have some exciting motorcycle races, while Lottie Brandon does some fast riding paced by one of the motorcycles and Frank Armstrong adds a few bicycle specialties.'[60] From Detroit, the Keatons traveled to the Columbia in St. Louis Missouri,[61] Chicago Opera House,[62] then the Grand in Nashville, Tennessee.[63]

It was high time for a break. The Keatons went home to Perry, Oklahoma for two weeks following Nashville, invited back by Policeman Sam Brafford and his wife. They punctuated their time there with a Perry Commercial Club Band Benefit 19 May. Ads for the event began 15 May and featured a photo of Buster in his Irish makeup with his recent positive review from Proctor's Palace (25 May 1901) as the text underneath it. A description of the coming event that contained a brief 'history' of Joe's career, stated that the act had been contracted for a year's work in Australia at $150 a week. If this information had any truth to it at all, it's clear that the offer fell through, because the Keatons made no such trip.[64] Held at the Grand Opera House in town, nearly every seat was filled that Monday night. The first part of the show featured the band in question, made up of 14 musicians and its director Frank Smith. Joe's brother Jesse (later known as Bert) was a member and played solo cornet. The vaudeville portion of the show began with the Keatons, and Buster was the most noticed:

> 'Buster' Keaton kept the audience in convulsions of laughter
> from the time he came upon the stage until the curtain fell on
> the last scene. He is not more than seven or eight years of age,
> and has a world-wide reputation as a comedian, which he most
> amply deserves. Mr and Mrs Keaton are very fine actors also
> and the three make a trio hard to beat.[65]

The band received $107 after all expenses had been taken care of.

While in Oklahoma, the Keatons began the summer park season 1 June at a familiar venue nearby, Forest Park in Pittsburg, Kansas. Here in the home country, reviewers lauded the Keatons and their increasing success.[66] The Sunday afternoon premiere 'was attended by immense crowds.'[67] Next was Lake Contrary Park at the Casino Theatre in St. Joseph, Nebraska, beginning the week of June 8. The Keatons received a nice introduction in the *St. Joseph News-Press*, one that focused on Buster's reputation: 'Buster Keaton, the juvenile member of the trio, has been pronounced by critics and public alike to be the coming comedian of the American stage. There is probably no other juvenile performer now appearing before the public that stands as well in the opinion of managers as he.'[68] A hop, skip, and a jump away was their next venue, the Lakeside Theatre in Galena, Kansas, where they opened for a week 16 June.[69] From Galena, they would play the end of the month at Lakeside Park Theatre in Muskegon, Michigan, a venue that would become a much-needed refuge in years to come.

The Keatons found themselves sashaying between Chicago and St. Louis the month of July, performing first at the Ferris Wheel Park in Chicago,[70] then at West End Heights in St. Louis, located at the southwest corner of Forest Park and the World's Fair grounds.[71] The Keatons' act was described as 'a conglomeration of singing, dancing, eccentric acrobatic work and a large number of absurdities. They went right well, the little half-size Keaton making more fun than the others.'[72] Another reviewer noted the act 'was the laughing hit of the bill,'[73] a phrase that had almost become a common refrain in the Keatons' publicity. While in St. Louis, they also played Koerner's Garden, located at the corner of King's Highway and Arsenal. In existence since 1880, it catered especially to German-speaking audiences and hosted a stream of popular vaudeville acts in what is thought to be the first open-air venue in the city. The Keatons were described in a German newspaper as an act *welche in einer hübschen Stizze auftreten,*'[74] (who appear in a pretty sketch). Back in Chicago beginning 27 July, they were booked at Sans Souci Park, located at 60th and Cottage Grove and noted as 'Chicago's Only Summer Resort.' Eagle Eye and his troupe of Sioux and Winnebago Indians were on hand as well in this park boasting the 'largest electric fountain in America.'[75]

August found the Keatons in Grand Rapids Michigan at the Ramona Theatre,[76] then the Empire in Columbus Ohio. The show opening night got started an hour late, moving the close of the show to nearly 12.30 am. The Keatons' act was renamed 'The Man under the Table' by the reviewer and they 'are seen to good advantage in the production.'[77] From the week in Columbus, the act traveled up to Toledo, Ohio to play the week of 17 August at the Farm,[78] then went south again to Idlewilde Park's Casino Theatre in Newark, Ohio. The vaudeville program started at 2.30 pm, with other activities, such as horse racing, a watermelon-eating contest, a car race and the Circle Whirl.[79] The Keatons received good notices, with one reviewer noting 'The feature of the week is The Keatons, Joe and Myra, with little six-year-old "Buster" in their humorous act, which is well worked from start to finish and elicits applause from the most fastidious of audiences.'[80]

At the end of the summer season, the Keatons headed east and landed in Elmira, New York the week of 8 September, playing in Rorick's Glen Park, a venue managed by Henry Farnsworth Dixie, the owner/manager of their forthcoming venue in Scranton, Pennsylvania.[81] The Keatons

> made good without half trying. The act is a combination of dialogue, music and acrobatic stunts, giving sufficient range for the talents of the three performers. Buster, a boy not yet in his teens, is a wonder for his age and succeeded in keeping the audience every moment of the time he was before the footlights. Miss Myra's saxophone solo was well received, as was Joe Keaton's grotesque acrobatic performance.[82]

They then ended the season in Scranton, Pennsylvania at the Dixie Theatre before returning to their ultimate goal: New York City.[83] Directly after this engagement, the Keatons were off to the familiar and comfortable Tony Pastor's 14th Street Theatre the week of 22 September to begin the fall season, hoping to go unnoticed by the Gerries. This time, for a week's engagement, they were successful, even with Little Buster advertised in the paper as part of the act. It is with this engagement that 'The Man with the Table' was semi-retired, for the new title for the time being was 'Fun and Nonsense,'[84] still a version of the old 'Silence and Fun' genre of knockabout act. Now the focus would be on dysfunctional family dynamics, with Buster as the recalcitrant child who must be corrected by Joe in some graphically physical way, with Mother Myra providing some singing or saxophone playing. Nearby in Newark, New Jersey, they played Proctor's, then Proctor's 23rd Street the week of 6 October, the Keatons received a nice review of the new act ('Nonsense and Fun'): 'Joe, Myra and Buster Keaton had some new and very excellent material in their act, with the best of older tricks retained, and they scored well.'[85] On another page of the same issue of the *Clipper* as this review, the Keatons' ad started a tradition of featuring poems by various and sundry poets, again à la Frank Cutler. This first one is most likely Joe's: 'Buster was born in America,/ The Sun Flower State of the West,/ A big Taylor trunk was the kid's only bunk,/With a sugar tit stuck in his face.'[86]

The week of 13 October, they had moved over to Jersey City, New Jersey to the Bon Ton Theatre, their first time at this venue. Interestingly, the Keatons' act was labeled 'The Man with the Table' here again,[87] probably because they hadn't played this venue before, so had no worry of repeating themselves. Nearby in Brooklyn, the Keatons began a week at the Grand Opera House,[88] then at the Portland Theatre in Portland, Maine,[89] where 'The Three Keatons come in their very funny act, which keeps the audience in constant laughter. Young Buster Keaton is certainly a most wonderful young comedian, and he is ably assisted by his father, who is a very good comedy acrobat.'[90] Perhaps this review was motivated by a piece in the 18 October issue of *Billboard* that ran in the 'Vaudeville' column: 'Buster Keaton, of the Three Keatons, is today regarded as one of the brightest of the juvenile comedians upon the vaudeville stage.'[91] This sentiment was fast becoming universal. November was finished out at the City (or City Hall) Opera House in Dover, New Hampshire, then the Nashua Theatre in Nashua, New Hampshire.[92]

Back in New York City beginning a run with the Keith's circuit 15 December at Keith's, Union Square, the Keatons took the opportunity to splurge on a nearly half-page ad in the *New York Daily Mirror* 20 December and a smaller but similar ad in *The New York Clipper* the same day. The ad included their schedule through to March, which was open, then continued into April and also described the act and focused on Buster's role in it:

> WHAT WE DO
> Our act is entirely NEW, ORIGINAL, and UNIQUE in every feature. It is immensely different from the ordinary run of acts. We copy nobody's ideas, but, as 'imitation is sincerest flattery,' you will find we are being highly flattered by others. The acrobatic work in our act is extremely FUNNY. Everyone says so! It is so funny that we don't have to talk to make an audience laugh but when we do talk —!!
>
> THE FEATURE
> The feature of our act is little 'BUSTER' the cutest little bundle of jollity that ever wriggled into the hearts of an audience. 'Ginger'[93] is Buster's watchword, and he owns a ginger plantation, right in Gingerville, which gives him a fresh supply twice a day. His fond parents think he's great, but don't take their word for it. See him, or ask the managers who shell out the cold, hard dollars that are so hard to get nowadays.[94]

Being the Christmas issue, the *Mirror* also featured a paragraph description/ review of the Keatons, which described the act as 'new, original and diverting.' Beginning with Joe, it described him as 'an expert comedy acrobat, who scorns to copy the old-fashioned tricks that have done duty for a generation. He uses a table but makes it a very interesting adjunct to his act.' Myra 'is a clever instrumentalist and dancer and is noted for her good taste in dress.' Buster, described as a precocious boy, was the feature of the act and 'bids fair to become a great eccentric comedian some day. The house is in a constant uproar while he is on the stage, as he has a knack of giving the audience frequent surprises.'[95] The *New York Clipper* ad differs a bit, most notably in the text that attests that 'Buster is not a midget performer but a revelation in eccentric juvenile talent properly directed to produce the lasting comedy effects. A miniature comedian who presents irresistible comedy with gigantic effects, making the ladies hold their sides, and the men, too.'[96] This is Joe's attempt to deflect the 'midget' moniker that some theatre managers and reviewers were using carelessly and too often.

The final full week of the year, then, was spent at Keith's, Boston beginning 22 December. Here, Winscherman's Monkeys 'for the children' were enhanced by 'The Funny Keaton Midget,' with no sign of his parents on the bill.[97] Obviously this theatre did not read Joe's plea to venues to stop using that moniker. Sometime this fall/winter season, Buster had started handing out candy to children after the matinées, instead of autographs, which turned out to be very popular. The act received a hearty review 23 December: 'The Keatons in their grotesque acrobatic act brought down the house as usual. Their business is unique and much of its success is due to the wee bit of a man who is thrown around like a bundle of rags and always lands right side up.'[98] The last few days of 1902 into 1903 were spent at Keith's, Providence, Rhode Island, beginning 28 December. The audience battled inclement weather to see the acts on the bill this week in what was described as a 'cozy house.' The Keatons, 'grotesque acrobatic comedians bring down the house, little "Buster" proving an especial winner of applause. The act is one prolonged laugh and takes well.'[99] Despite the weather, then, the act ended the year on a very high note.

Sunday night 4 January only, the Keatons played Manager Ted Marks's New York Theatre, Broadway at 45th Street.[100] Back on the Keith circuit the very next day, the Keatons played at the Keith's New Chestnut Street Theatre in Philadelphia, Pennsylvania. At Tony Pastor's the following week the act was so well known, that the Keatons were almost family. Joe had decided to sneak into the city again, having succeeded in doing so at the New York Theatre a week earlier, and test the Gerry waters. This time they weren't so lucky. A child protection officer pulled Buster from the bill early in the week and the act missed him sorely. An inspection of the ads for Tony Pastor's provides no hint of this,[101] but one reporter who interviewed the Keatons while they were playing the Portland Theatre in Maine the second week of February 1904, managed to get the whole story:

> 'When we were at Pastor's in New York once, some members of the Gerry society for the prevention of cruelty to children saw our act and ordered the "kid" taken off. Now the manager wouldn't let us play without Buster, but he saw there was no way out of it, so my wife and I hatched up a sketch without him.'[102]

Buster was upset by this development and came up with a plan to get even that involved putting himself in the way of the cold January weather selling papers on the street and then sleeping out at night. He envisioned being rescued by a policeman, who would take him before the judge, to whom he would reveal his name and that he had been ripped away from his family, where he was earning a respectable wage. The judge would then understand and send him back to the theatre with permission to play. Of course, Joe wouldn't allow this. However, when it happened again, the society officer filed a complaint stating that the boy had to be black and blue with bruises and that the local mayor would agree. In fact, the mayor looked Buster over from head to toe and found nothing, thereby providing him a special license. Joe ended the tale with 'I only wish the Gerry society had tried to do something more. Ella Wheeler Wilcox, who is a great friend of Buster's, just wanted to take up the matter, and then there would have been something said.'[103] Although the audience's view of the act rarely made the papers, at least one example, probably from 1905, suggested that not everyone enjoyed the 'abuse' unreservedly:

> The Keatons amused the spectators with a 'rough-house' acrobatic sketch, but there were many persons among the onlookers who felt sorry for the boy 'Buster.' Perhaps the rough-handling he experienced did him no harm, but the spectators were kept on the edge all the time the youngster was on the stage. There was some repugnance felt, too, when a mere tot was urged upon the stage to add to the intended merriment.[104]

In any event, the Keatons were off to Washington, D. C. for an engagement at Chase's Theatre again, beginning 19 January. As one writer noted, 'in the role of an Irish comedian, [Buster] poses, jokes, sings, imitates prominent performers, with the gusto of a veteran, and the added interest of an infant phenomenon.'[105] The next two engagements included Shea's Theatre in Buffalo, New York and Shea's Theatre in Toronto.[106]

The Keatons traveled next to Chase's Empire Theatre in Cleveland Ohio,[107] to Cook's Opera House in Rochester, New York,[108] and then spent a week in Detroit, again at the Temple Theatre. At the end of the month, the Keatons were featured in the *New York Clipper's* 50th anniversary issue with a paragraph description accompanied by a group photo in costume. While most of the description was similar to what had already been written, it's important to note that Joe is still called 'The Man with the Table' and it's emphasized that Buster 'is a child comedian and not a midget,'[109] clearly another effort to relieve the youngster of that pejorative moniker. At the Park Theatre in Youngstown, Ohio the first week of March, the Keatons were well received, with the reviewer noting that the 'tiny comedian' Little Buster 'pleased and made a big hit. The imitations of Little Buster were clever.'[110] As Buster became older, his facility with mimicking other acts on the bill or just well-known characters and celebrities started to become legend. Several undated reviews specifically from Proctor's various theatres included in the scrapbook Myra kept of their act's career, alluded to this mimicking ability and its popularity with audiences. One noted that 'His burlesque of melodrama was clever.'[111] Another mentioned '"Buster" Keaton of the Three Keatons, eccentric comedians, with his clever imitations of Dan Daly, Press Eldridge, Jimmie Russell and other stage celebrities is one of the star features.'[112] Eldridge was a blackface performer and comic singer, who titled himself 'The Commander-in-Chief of the Army of Fun.' In 1905, Buster was described in one review as parodying sharpshooter Colonel Gaston Bordeverry at Proctor's 23rd Street Theatre, an imitation that touched Bordeverry so much that he loaned Buster one of his small rifles for the week.[113] Bordeverry, a Frenchman considered the world's greatest marksman, 'dislodges lumps of sugar from human heads, plays a piano by bullet and concludes his performance by disrobing a young lady by a rifle ball.'[114] Any one of those features would have been easy fodder for parody and Little Buster took advantage of them.

After Youngstown, it was a week beginning 8 March at the Avenue Theatre in Pittsburgh, Pennsylvania. Buster was described as 'probably the funniest child comedian on the stage,'[115] and the entire act was rewarded with a photo in *The Pittsburgh Dispatch* 8 March. Then the Keatons re-entered the Proctor's circuit, first in Newark, New Jersey 16 March[116] and then moved into New York City proper at Proctor's 23rd Street Theatre the week of 23 March, where they were still advertised as performing 'The

Man with the Table,'[117] but the *Clipper* noted that 'bright little Buster [was] cleverer than ever.'[118] The *Mirror* went further: 'Joe, Myra and Buster Keaton scored heavily. Buster is getting more clever every day and does seven or eight minutes all by himself now. He is a smart "kid" and his work shows that he is far more intelligent than the average prodigy.'[119] The week of 30 March, the Keatons had moved over to Proctor's 125th Street Theatre in Harlem, where the week was punctuated by a performer's no-show on that Wednesday (1 April)[120] and subsequent removal from the bill. Several other acts from the week before followed them to Harlem and Buster 'brought down the house,' but the Keaton family must have gone to their performances that week feeling as if they were on borrowed time.

The week of 6 April, they traveled up to Lynn, Massachusetts to the Lynn Theatre, where they received tremendous reviews, which were noted as of the first performance of the week:

> In the evening they made the biggest kind of hit, and 'Buster' Keaton, 'the little feller,' received an ovation and a curtain call that would have flattered a professional many years his senior, [. . .] a wee mite of a chap, not much bigger than a pint of cider who has inherited much of the original cleverness of his daddy. [. . .] The act [includes] dancing and saxophone solos by Mrs Keaton, who is as clever as she is personally attractive, tumbling, amusing side talk and humorous impersonations by the boy and his father. The act throughout is undeniably funny.[121]

By Friday of that week, the Keatons had been eliciting laughter from the audience almost at the moment they came onstage, with 'the big Keaton [throwing] Buster around'[122] being deemed one of the funniest things ever seen in the theatre there. The week of 13 April, the Harcourt Comedy Company (with the Keatons in tow) made it up to Lewiston, Maine to perform at the Music Hall, where the star act on the bill was the Three Keatons.[123] Here in Lewiston, they were the only vaudeville 'specialty' on the bill. The rest of the entertainment came from the Harcourt cast and whatever play they performed each night. Other venues the Keatons played as part of the Harcourt Company included the Opera House in Bangor, Maine,[124] Calais, Maine,[125] and the Portland Theatre in Portland, Maine. They seemed to have left the Harcourt Comedy Company at this point to take this engagement.

The Keatons, one reviewer noted, 'still contain for their star number little Buster Keaton whose pa takes a delight in making a veritable football of him to the amusement of the audience and seemingly nonetheless to him and their act went with laughter and applause.'[126] They entered the Keith circuit again at Keith's, Union Square Theatre 18 May. They had taken up residence at the Ehrich House on 38th Street, a professional boarding house that they considered their home address and would be their New York City residence until at least 1917, when the act finally broke up.

Playing the Keith's, Union Square would prove to be their next challenge with the Gerries. Although Joe tried and failed to get permission beforehand, he did modify the act such that Buster's role in it caused no offense. And so ended the Keatons' confrontations with child protective services until the next Keaton child performer came along. Buster continued his great success, especially at the kids' matinées.[127] Their first big mention in *The New York Times* 21 May occurred in response to their appearance at Union Square. It provides a nice blow-by-blow account of the Keatons' act, or at least part of it, beginning with their makeup and costuming:

> Keaton pere comes on the stage in the full glory of red galways,[128] a comic makeup, consisting of face white-plastered to the cheek bones, where a rosy flush forms a sharp angle, coming to a point just beneath the eyes. He wears loose, baggy trousers, no coat, and white spats. Baby Buster is made up and dressed exactly like the father, but diminutive face and figure increase the ludicrous effect in his case.

The two then engaged in 'grotesque acrobatics,' the boy imitating his father in this. The banter that accompanied and followed, however, is what the reviewer found most compelling. It involved Buster describing the Keatons' antics in cheating the ticket takers on whatever train they were taking by pretending to be younger than they were (in Myra's case) and not human (in Buster's case – a dog, in fact). Pa responded with 'You're a blockhead.' Buster then countered with 'Well, I'm a chip off the old block.' And on it went, until the two ended up down by the footlights and Buster sang 'What Right Has a Man to Buy a Collar Button When He Has a Wart on the Back of His Neck.' More banter ensued, then Buster began his celebrity imitations, and thereafter father and son chased each other off the stage.[129]

At Keith's Theatre in Boston, Massachusetts 25 May, they appeared with Press Eldridge, who was making his first engagement since his London tour,[130] thus giving Buster the chance to add the impersonation of this celebrity to his repertoire. The Keatons then opened the month of June at Keith's, Chestnut Street Theatre in Philadelphia, Pennsylvania.[131] One reviewer noted,

> The Keatons, particularly little 'Buster,' the exceedingly small third member of the family, win applause and laughter in large volumes with their acrobatic nonsense. Mr. Keaton's stage falls are remarkably executed, while 'Buster' also does some tall tumbling worthy of remark, and his imitations of 'Dan' Daly and other footlight celebrities are exceedingly clever.[132]

This closed the Keatons' performances on the Keith Circuit this season. Joe announced in his *Clipper* ad that he had signed with Eddie Shayne to work the Western Parks over the summer, beginning in Toledo at the Farm 14 June, allowing them a couple of weeks off in between. Joe was also advertising the fact that the act was now managed by Joe Paige Smith and that they had few dates open in the fall already.[133] After the Farm, the Keatons played the McBeth Park Theatre in Toledo where they topped the bill.[134] They next played Sam Reeves Park in Arcadia, Ohio, which was on the Toledo, Fostoria, and Findlay electric line. It was a 12-acre sugar grove adorned with tennis courts, a baseball park, a pavilion, booths and a grandstand.[135] The Keatons were top of the bill for a two-week engagement, a mistake made by the manager, Joe asserted.[136] Buster kept 'the audience in an uproar from the time the curtain [went] up until he [disappeared] behind the scene.'[137]

Moving west, the act arrived in Chicago at Sans Souci Park the week of 12 July.[138] Before arriving in Mannion Park, St. Louis, Missouri, for an engagement beginning 19 July, Joe printed in *The Clipper*, 'Arrived safely in the West, after a long absence East, and will continue North until we go South.' Buster's photo in costume appeared in the paper along with reviews of the acts. The Keatons headed the bill and Buster was given acclaim as 'one of the most gifted children on the vaudeville stage.'[139] The *Mississippi Blätter*, one of St. Louis's German American newspapers, featured a photo of the whole Keaton family, and *Westliche Post*, a review of the bill at Mannion's, which referred to Buster, probably for the first time in print as a '*Wunderkind*,'[140] certainly an apt descriptor at this point. In St. Joseph,

Nebraska for the week of 2 August at Lake Contrary Park,[141] the Keatons played alongside Little Elsie Janis,[142] a child star who had also experienced the wrath of the Gerries in New York. In August, they played Ingersoll Park in Des Moines, Iowa, Delmar Gardens in Oklahoma City, then the Standard Theatre in Guthrie, Oklahoma, where Manager Richard Reaves seemed quite pleased that he had booked the Keatons, who, in Guthrie, were practically on home territory, so they did something unusual and put on DeWolf Hopper's Humplutu sketch.[143] Finally, the Keatons closed out the summer season at Forest Park in Kansas City, Missouri, the week beginning 6 September, staying pretty much near 'home,' which they planned to visit after the week was up. Colonel John D. Hopkins, manager of the vaudeville programs at the park, provided a quote for Joe's *Clipper* ad of 1 August: 'Like old Kentucky whiskey, Buster improves with age.'[144] Hopkins had arranged the bill to especially appeal to children, so it included Professor Howard's trained ponies, monkeys and dogs, Mr. and Mrs. Jack Burch, experts in legerdemain, and La Gette, the arial gymnast.[145]

All their engagements completed, the Keatons went home to Perry, Oklahoma beginning the week of 14 September and stayed until Friday 9 October, when they would head back east to begin the fall vaudeville season. It would be their last break together as a family of three, for 1904 would see them welcoming another child.

Chapter 4

A Year of Solo Stardom and a Fourth Keaton

■ ■

A fter completing the summer season in the Western parks, the Keatons visited Perry four weeks in the early fall of 1903. They arrived in town 18 September[1] and enjoyed about a week of relaxation before their names began to appear in the paper. As had become a tradition, they had volunteered to appear at the local Commercial Club Band benefit, this one to be held 28 September. Performers Will Armstrong and Mazie Holly, in town visiting Joe and Myra, had been commandeered into offering their services as well.[2] They had just played alongside Armstrong & Holly in their sketch 'The Expressman' 17 August in Oklahoma City. A review of the Perry show appeared 2 October and focused on Buster: 'The most wonderful progeny that ever appeared before the footlights is Little Buster. Being only seven years of age, and displaying the talent of one of mature years, he was the center of the attraction and proved himself a buster[3] right.'[4] Another reviewer made the word 'buster' the center of his piece: 'Little Buster is a buster of all precedents in the line of juvenile comedy turns. And he nearly busted everyone with laughter. Oh, Buster, truly thou art a buster! Thou did'st bust every side of every person at the Opera last night.'[5] The hometown crowd proved once again to be in support of their native son and his family.

The Keatons left Perry 9 October[6] for St. Louis, playing Crawford Theatre there, located at 14th and Locust Streets.[7] Buster, 'a precocious youth who is very comical'[8] hogged the publicity for the Keatons that week. Joe wrote about the engagement in the *Clipper* that Buster 'came near spoiling a clever melodrama on account of his rich humour. He held the stage so long, and the audience laughed so continuously that interest in the plot was lost.'[9] The week of 19 October, the Keatons traveled to Louisville Kentucky to play at the Hopkins Theatre along with the Hopkins Trans-Oceanic Star Specialty Company. Buster was 'the best Lilliputian in the world,'[10] thereby attaining another label of sorts. Not only that, but he achieved a column to himself in the paper, entitled 'A Juvenile Comedian.' The article at first focused on the fact that good stage comedian that he was, he was still a young boy, playing among the settings and stands behind the scenes when he was not on stage and enjoying the toy train he recently purchased. As a young boy, too, he was characterized as preferring his grandfather's ranch, where he 'rides horses and carries water to the threshers'[11] to the stage life. In fact, Papa Joe had included some description of Buster on the ranch in their *Mirror* ad: 'Buster is winning leather medals breaking broncos (whatever that is) on the ranch at home.'[12] That Oklahoma ranch was where Buster would rather be.

Shortly thereafter, Buster had a brush with death involving a steam roller. Showing a propensity for machines that would be displayed later in his films, Buster stopped on his way back to the theatre from purchasing the toy train on 4th Street in Louisville to inspect a steam roller sitting on the street. Buster crawled under the barriers around the roller without being seen and stood in front of the roller just as it was started. A shout from an onlooker woke the boy up, and 'the rough and tumble work of "Buster" on the stage was probably responsible for his salvation,'[13] for he jumped out of the way and behind a car before the driver knew what had happened. Thus ended one of many such close calls with machinery Buster would have in life.

The Keatons then played in Indianapolis, Indiana beginning the week of 26 October at the Grand. The Keatons were first on the bill and somehow escaped the wrath of the reviewer who harshly critiqued almost every act on the bill, even bringing in aspects of the performers' personal lives to do so. Buster's photo in costume, a full length one both front and back, appeared 25 October in the *Indianapolis Star*. The next day another report appeared again centered on the fact that Buster was just a young boy that enjoyed play. This one discussed the fact that he was incredibly popular at the Imperial Hotel where the Keatons were staying and that the neighborhood children would lie in wait for him after the matinée, in hopes that he would join them. One afternoon, Myra allowed him to do so, which he did in his fancy city suit, but regardless, still became 'just one of the boys' before long. On the Statehouse lawn, Buster and the boys practiced their gymnastics, with Buster bursting the buttons of his suit in the exertion. The festivities were concluded when two velocipedes were discovered and Buster and another boy were goaded into racing them around the square: 'The race was an exciting event and the boys howled with delight when "Buster" seemed to be coming in an easy winner,' but in the homestretch Buster ran into a dog and went headlong into the pavement – with no injuries. He hopped up and ended by giving the boys a bit of his monologue.[14]

From Indianapolis, the Keatons played the Columbia Theatre in Cincinnati, Ohio, then Chase's Empire Theatre in Cleveland, Ohio and later the Park Theatre in Youngstown. One reviewer noted that Buster was 'a diminutive comedian who is the hit of every bill he is in. In fact, he is usually featured wherever he plays. His imitations are rendered with almost absolute perfection.'[15] They followed this engagement with one at the Avenue Theatre in Pittsburgh, Pennsylvania, where Buster was deemed 'the greatest boy comedian the stage has ever known, whose imitation and singing always elicit great applause and laughter.'[16] At the end of November, the Keatons moved on to the Temple Theatre in Detroit, Michigan,[17] then to the Jeffers Theatre in Saginaw, Michigan. One reviewer offered that 'Buster is a diminutive chap, but with aged actions and wise enough to be a grandfather. He and Joe are certainly the limit in laugh-making, and their antics are diverting in the extreme, while at the same time there is a great deal of cleverness in the stunts they do, and they are given able assistance by the lady member of the trio.'[18] The last two weeks of 1903 were spent at Shea's Garden in Buffalo, New York and Shea's in Toronto.[19]

The year 1904 would see Buster reach great heights as a respected performer, so there were more articles about his life and his start in the entertainment industry, most provided by Joe. The result was that a litany of false and embellished stories began to be disseminated about Buster, and these stories slowly took hold as actual fact over the years, making it difficult to discern the truths among the fictions. The other major event of the year was the birth of Harry Keaton in August. Myra would be out of commission for several months, affecting their schedule, and then the new child would have to be welcomed into the act, probably earlier than was expeditious. Despite these coming life-changing elements of the year, it started out in a predictable way, with the Keatons working the Keith's theatres. The first was Keith's, Boston, beginning 4 January, where they scored big: 'The real comedy in the show will be provided by Buster Keaton, the midget comedian, who appears with his parents, Joe and Myra Keaton. This little chap is easily the funniest bunch of humanity in the business, and unmistakably clever in other lines, too, as he gives imitations of several well-known stage favorites that are really clever and lifelike.'[20]

Joe had announced late in 1903, that Buster was now performing 12 solo minutes of such impersonations, songs, and other funny stuff during the turn. A photo and one of those 'bios' that would become common this year accompanied a review on the next page. This time, Buster's life story, provided by Joe, already included the mythology about the cyclone, the fall down the stairs (resulting in his nickname) and the severing of his finger all occurring on one day, a triumvirate of events that made it all the way into Buster's autobiography published in the early 1960s. Another seminal story was about Buster being toted around in a trunk, sleeping first in the hat compartment therein and later in the entirety of the trunk itself, from which he would crawl out and wander onto the stage, thereby effecting his debut. The final vignette printed in this piece was about Buster's 'actual' stage debut at Dockstader's Theatre in Wilmington, Delaware, if, in fact, that was the location,[21] how Mr. Dockstader first thought the boy had failed onstage, and later changed his mind, placing him back in the act for the children's matinée, which resulted in a great success. Joe related: 'Nothing I could do would amuse or entertain anybody. The audience couldn't see me at all, and Buster was one scream from start to finish.'[22] And with this interview, Joe had created another apocryphal Buster Keaton creation story.

The week of 11 January, the Keatons had moved on to Keith's, Providence, Rhode Island.[23] Buster again received rave reviews, with one critic admitting, 'It is impossible to describe the convulsingly funny antics of the little fellow, but everything he said or did brought about a vociferous round of applause or laughter.'[24] Nine days later, this newspaper published a paraphrased version of Joe's life history of Buster, with the addition of his method in becoming proficient in imitating others: 'At first Buster watched everything that was said or done, but did not attempt to act any himself. Then, as he grew more accustomed to the strangeness of it, he began to imitate the other people on the stage.'[25] Next at Keith's Union Square Theatre,[26] Buster was receiving good reviews, especially for his mimicry:[27]

It is seldom that such hearty laughter is heard in a theatre as that which greeted the efforts of 'Buster,' who is an exceptionally clever lad. Every word and action set the house in a roar, and his imitations of Dan Daly, James Russell, and Sager Midgely brought him so much applause that it is a wonder his little head is not turned completely around. 'Buster' does not give the impression of having been taught: his work is so spontaneous and so accurate that it shows him to be above the average performer of his age in intelligence and indicates that he understands the value of pause and emphasis as well or better than many a performer of mature years.

Joe, too, was praised: 'He is as limber as a piece of whalebone and as spry as a kitten.'[28]

Hardly recovered from all the adulation, the Keatons traveled to Keith's New Theatre in Philadelphia beginning 25 January,[29] then the Empire in Hoboken, New Jersey, Keith's Bijou Theatre in Philadelphia the week of 8 February, and Portland Family Theatre in Maine, a place in which they always received great reviews and were heartily welcomed [30] Buster was noted as having 'a true sense of humour and creates screams of laughter.'[31]

The week of 22 February, the Keatons found themselves in Salem, Massachusetts at Mechanic Hall, a first-time venue.[32] Buster was noted to be 'unusually bright and naturally clever. One would think, to see the way he is thrown about, that it would hurt the youngster, but as he knows how to land, and his father knows how to throw him, there is not even a jar to the tiny lad.'[33] Back then in Boston at Howard's Atheneum, the Keatons' growing popularity could be measured by the fact that they had been booked in Boston three times already in 1904 and it was only the end of February. The entire month of March was to be spent in New York City at theatres the Keatons had frequented often. The first was Proctor's 23rd Street, beginning the week of 14 March and extended over to 20 March for a special Sunday concert. Buster was described as 'the most natural and entertaining child comedian on the vaudeville stage,'[34] and 'better every time he comes to town and is now a downright good comedian.'[35] The next week, beginning 21 March they traveled up the Proctor's Albany,[36] then they were back at Tony Pastor's 14th Street Theatre as a special added attraction. The Keatons 'again proved their worth as vaudeville top-notchers by repeating the success of many former engagements here. Little Buster Keaton's talent in character comedy becomes more apparent at every appearance.'[37] Buster, by himself, was now the name in bold on the Keaton family ads in the stage papers, the *Mirror* and the *Clipper* on occasion (it flipped back and forth between 'Buster' and 'The Three Keatons').

April started with the Keatons headlining at the Music Hall in Yonkers New York, along with the Dot Carroll Company in repertory.[38] At a new venue next, Hyde & Behman's Theatre, located at 365 Fulton Street, Little Buster Keaton 'fairly brought down the house with his antics and imitations and he is without doubt one of the cleverest youths that ever came to Brooklyn.'[39]

Another reviewer focused on Buster first: 'Ten year old "Buster" Keaton, a precocious youngster, whose daddy tossed him about like a rubber ball, and who sang and gave life-like imitations in miniature of the late Dan Daly and other stage celebrities, seemed to outclass the top-liners in popular favor. The little fellow responded to encores until nature gave out.'[40] Then at yet another new venue, the Trent Theatre in Trenton, New Jersey, Joe, Myra and Buster were the featured act, with Buster the focus of the critics: 'he is cute from the soles of his flat comedy feet to the red wig upon his knowing little head. He makes up in exact counterpart of his six-foot father and the two do what probably is the best knockabout comedy work ever seen in this city.'[41] Then, the final week of the month, beginning 25 April, the Keatons were back at the Dockstader Theatre in Wilmington, Delaware, now called The Garrick, headlining.[42] The Keatons then revisited the Chase Theatre in Washington, D. C. 2 May,[43] where Elsie Janis was again on the bill and, this time, was noted as also performing imitations – of Dan Daly, Anna Held, Vesta Tilley, Elfie Fay, and Eddie Foy[44] – which may have presented Buster some competition. Then in Lancaster, Pennsylvania, known for its large Pennsylvania Dutch community, they played the Roof Garden beginning 9 May, where the Keatons were featured.[45] 'Little Buster Keaton is a whole show in himself,' wrote one reviewer, 'His funny makeup and quaint sayings keep the audience in a roar of laughter. He is the star of a performance that should not be missed by anybody who loves pure wholesome fun.'[46] Between times, an amusing story was featured in several papers, including the *Clipper*, regarding an argument about who was the best prize fighter. Some chose Fitzsimmons and others Jeffries, but 'the little comedian, who had been listening intently to the different arguments, finally voiced his opinion, and that ended the discussion. "You're all wrong," he said, "Santa and God are the best of all."'[47] By this time the act was making $225 a week.[48]

At the Bon Ton Theatre in Jersey City, New Jersey the week of 16 May,[49] the Hermann the Great Company (sans Hermann) was the headliner, with Mrs. Adelaide Hermann having taken over her husband's magic act. The Keatons had played alongside her before and Buster, later in life, liked to relate a story about wrecking her act. Mrs. Hermann was just finishing up and had many white doves flying around the stage. Her costume for the night was a plain nineteenth, century dress with a hoop skirt. She was still dilly-dallying with the birds when the Keatons took the stage. Theatres had a drop curtain for acts to utilize if they didn't have their own, which was the Keatons' situation. Joe, at the end of the act, would saunter up to the footlights and pretend they were the brass foot rail found in saloons, and Buster would do the same. Their exchange would be about what drink Buster wanted – a scotch, rye, gin? To which Buster's answer was always 'no.' Finally, Buster offered that he wanted only water:

> Grabbing me by the back of the neck, he would turn me around and walk me towards the curtain, meanwhile grumbling, 'So it is water you want?' Then he would hurl me into the painted water scene [on the curtain]. As I hit the curtain, it would give quite a bit. While sliding to the floor, the drop's wooden strip sometimes would flap up, and I would be trapped in it. The stagehands then would pull up the curtain a few inches to help me free myself. That Monday matinee at the Bon Ton everything went off as usual until I was sliding down the curtain. Near the bottom I felt a bump as I hit some object of substantial proportions that I couldn't see. The stagehand pulled up the drop dumping me on the stage. This revealed the highly respectable widow Hermann in the most exposed position of her stage career. She had been bending over to stuff the last of her doves in a box near the curtain when knocked flat. The startled birds promptly flew out of their boxes going in every direction. Sitting on the stage, as ribald laughter erupted in the audience, I looked around and saw that the lady magician's hoop skirt had been thrown over her head, displaying her bottom which, even by the standards of that well-padded era, was enormous.[50]

After this engagement, the Keatons announced in the *Mirror* that they were open the 23 and 30 May, 6, 16, 20, and 27 June.[51] Of course, this was unusual, especially considering that Buster was at the top of his popularity. The probable reason was that Myra was pregnant and may not have wanted to travel far from their comfortable rooms on the second floor of the Ehrich boarding house. Joe announced the pregnancy 18 June, 'going to enlarge the troupe next season.'[52] No ads appeared in either the *Clipper* or the *Mirror* the first two weeks of June, but the *Mirror* finally announced the act had an engagement with J. W. Gorman's 'Tuxedo Specialty Company,' first at Lake Grove Park in Auburn, Maine the week of 13 June, then Gorman's Merrymaking Park in Lewiston, Maine, and Gorman's Riverton Park in Portland, Maine. Finally receiving some notice in Portland, the reviewer offered that the group was still three in number, so Myra had made the trip despite her condition:

> The headliners are the Three Keatons, a trio of funny people who do acrobatic stunts on tables and chairs and all manner of laughable things. One of the three, a little chap hardly three feet tall, has been making a great hit everywhere he has appeared. He couldn't be any funnier if he was six feet tall. Quite rightly he has been dubbed 'the miniature comedian.'[53]

The week of 4 July, the Keatons moved over to Canobie Lake Park in Salem, New Hampshire, still with the Tuxedo Specialty Company. One of several fires the Keatons experienced over their years in vaudeville occurred there at the Canobie Park Hotel. Most of the Tuxedo company performers lost everything (the hotel was a total loss), but Joe somehow had the foresight to save the family's trunks. He was alerted to the fire while the vaudeville acts were going on and 'dashed into the hotel with his makeup on and ran up two flights to his room. He dumped as many things as he could find into two trunks, which he threw down the stairs.'[54] He only left behind Buster's suitcase, one he had been given by Walter McKay and one that had several of his best suits of clothes inside. Meanwhile, Buster had volunteered to stand in for another performer, who was absent due to the fire, and performed 'a remarkable clever turn, eliciting much applause.'[55]

Their last engagement week for the summer was at Sheedy's Freebody Park Theatre in Newport, Rhode Island beginning the week of 18 July. This seems to be an engagement outside of the Tuxedo Specialty Company, which probably disbanded after its performers lost their belongings in the fire. The Keatons were headlining, with Buster labeled 'the Comedy Cyclone' and 'The Phenomenal Juvenile Irish Comedian,' his photo in costume adorning the ad.[56] The *Mirror* reported 30 July and every week until 3 September that the Keatons were 'resting and getting new gags for next season' back in New York. Harry Stanley Keaton, named after the manager of the Mechanic Hall in Salem, Massachusetts, H. C. Stanley,[57] was then born in New York City on 25 August 1904, and the Keaton act peered into its immediate future with some concern about being able to keep its engagements, at least in the month of September. The home folks in Perry, Oklahoma took note of the Keaton birth: 'Daddy Joe writes his parents here and that the new comedian is the finest yet. "Six hours old and needs a haircut. He's busy on the milk wagon now. He's a corker. Everybody concerned doing well.'"[58] Notices followed in the *Mirror* and the *Clipper*, but in an occasional newspaper as well. Little Harry came to be known as 'Jingles' early in life, without the nickname's origin being known or at least remembered.[59] Buster's supposed response appeared in the *Mirror*: 'There ain't no joy in life for me,/I'm sighing all the day:/My nose is out o' joint, because/the baby's come to stay.'[60]

As the Keatons' Boston Keith's engagement approached, it was clear that Myra wouldn't be recovered enough to perform, so Bostonians were informed of the fact by 11 September.[61] The act was still titled 'The Three Keatons,' for obvious reasons, and only a brief hint of the absence of Myra is alluded to in the descriptions and reviews: 'The Three Keatons, including the midget "Buster" are back again and the little fellow and his big companion are as funny as ever.'[62] Having started the Keith Circuit again in October, the Keatons moved on to Keith's, Providence, Rhode Island. One reviewer poured on the praise:

> The audience laughed themselves tired at the antics of 'Buster' Keaton, the midget comedian, everything the little fellow did or said bringing forth a shout of laughter as usual. He has added quite a little that is new to his act and made even a bigger hit than on his previous visits. There is absolutely no doubt but that 'Buster' is the funniest little comedian on the stage today.[63]

Then in Philadelphia 8 October at the Keith's Chestnut Street Theatre, the Keatons 'provided 20 minutes of rough and tumble fun, the youthful member doing the burden of the work, and indeed the most entertaining bit of it.'[64]

Then at Keith's, Union Square, the Keatons were still hot and 'carried the comedy honors. "Buster" was in unusually fine feather and kept the house in roars with his odd little tricks. [. . .] Joe and "Buster" are now wearing black wigs and "hatstraps" instead of the red ones they formerly used.'[65] The *Mirror* 22 October sported a montage of Buster photos on the cover, indicating he had indeed made the big time.

The Maryland Theatre in Baltimore, a new venue for the Keatons, was home for the week beginning 24 October. They were a bit down on the bill, but still garnered some favorable reviews, with Buster being described as 'a microscopic scrap of jollity who was slammed around promiscuously like an old rubber doll and who always bobbed up again serenely.'[66] Then they were at the Grand Opera House Pittsburgh, where a scientific sensation Enigmarelle, was the headlining act. Enigmarelle was an automaton in the shape of a man brought over from England that walked, rode a bicycle, smoked, wrote, and performed other human-like acts.[67] It was one of Buster's favorite acts and he recalled 'how the operator set the metal giant going with push buttons, then took him apart – wheels, gears, levers and all – to prove he was kosher, then did a reassembly job so that Enigmarelle could take his bow at the footlights, shift gears, and stomp offstage.'[68]

Playing the Arcade Theatre in Toledo, Ohio beginning Sunday 6 November,[69] Buster was still being referred to as a midget comedian, albeit the funniest on the stage, possibly due to an uptick in cities that now had child protection laws and enforcers. At Cleveland's Theatre in Chicago, they headlined and were able to expand the engagement a week,[70] then completed November at the Temple Theatre in Detroit, Michigan. The Three Keatons 'do an acrobatic act that has not yet been duplicated. The star of the trio is a young lad who is thrown about the stage in a way that would astound a football player. The youngster is a humorist as well and gives several imitations of well-known vaudeville characters.'[71]

Beginning the month of December, the Keatons kept an engagement at Shea's Garden Theatre in Buffalo, New York. The Saturday before, however, Buster was featured in *The Billboard*,[72] with a photo in costume and a short blurb. It was being reported that this would be the Keatons' last engagement in Buffalo for a while because they had booked engagements in Europe, beginning in the spring. Joe had been toying with this idea on and off, but the family would not travel overseas until 1909. Next was Shea's Theatre Toronto[73] and then the last engagement of 1904 was spent at Keith's Prospect Theatre in Cleveland, Ohio.[74] Back home in New York to spend their first Christmas together as a family of four, the Keatons looked forward to an engagement at their old stomping grounds, Tony Pastor's, in the new year.

The year 1905 opened with the Keatons being engaged by the Keith's circuit once again, for two times around the circuit, as Joe bragged about in his 10 December ad in the *Mirror*. In that same ad, he suggested that Jingles would be part of the act, 'keep your eyes on H. Stanley Keaton,'[75] and indeed that came about this year, as did further confrontations with the child protection officers. Buster's fame would continue to grow.

At Pastor's the first matinée performance of the year was standing room only and caused the management to put the house policeman to work: 'An overflow house gathered before 2 o'clock. From that time until the afternoon performance was over the house policeman was busy keeping lines in waiting order in the lobby, and by 8 o'clock the box office was again closed.'[76] The Keatons, listed as 'The 3 Keatons with Buster,' were featured as an extra attraction and 'had laughter and applause well in hand from the moment of their appearance, and the cleverness of the little chap was as noticeable as of yore.'[77] Back then at Hyde & Behman's Theatre in Brooklyn, New York 9 January,[78] the act received fantastic reviews and a nice description of the act at this point:

> Perhaps the biggest hit of the night was scored by 'Buster' Keaton, of the Three Keatons. The other members of the team are the father and mother of this clever youth. 'Buster' works behind a makeup of the traditional Milesian kind, and the antics of this three-foot comedian kept the big house in almost tumultuous laughter during the entire act. He had a persistent habit of getting in his father's way, and each time his irate parent would gently push him aside, sometimes pushing him the full length of the stage. Each time the human rubber ball would arise, and approaching his athletic pater, would meekly say: 'I'm so sorry I fell down.' In a manner that would get upon the risibilities of an incurable dyspeptic. The numerous inimitable pieces of business that he works in, his clever side allusions and his intelligent imitations further emphasize him as a marvel of precocity, and the Keaton family assuredly have in this gifted juvenile a prolific breadwinner for years to come.[79]

Joe reprinted this review verbatim in his ad in the *Mirror* 21 January and included a new photo of the family that presented baby Jingles. Following this glowing engagement week, the Keatons played the Trent Theatre in Trenton, New Jersey,[80] then Proctor's Theatre in Newark,[81] Proctor's 23rd Street[82] and Poli's Theatre in Springfield, Massachusetts. The local news reported that the week's bill in Springfield 'continues to please good audiences, the knockabout comedy of the Keatons being the best laugh-producer. Little "Buster" Keaton, who is only nine years old, seems to suffer no lasting effects from his being tossed around like a football.'[83]

Moving up to Proctor's Albany beginning 12 February,[84] the Keatons, uncharacteristically, weren't mentioned as part of the bill that week in the write-up for the *Mirror*, which probably had to do with the debacle that occurred there. While playing the week, unfortunately, the child protection officers, now a more common feature in cities other than New York, came calling, this time taking Buster, Joe, and the manager of Proctor's, Howard Graham, to court. The first court date was most likely 17 February, with proceedings adjourned until Buster could be brought in. This second court date was on 18 February. Martin D. Conway was Howard Graham's lawyer and Harold Alexander defended the Child Protection Society, as did its employee, Superintendent Walker. Buster showed up decked out in a sack coat, vest, and a white shirt with a standup collar. His pants were tucked into rubber boots, his overcoat had a belt, and his hat was a black derby. He wore a gold watch chain across his vest that was adorned with a diamond locket. In other words, Buster was trying to look as old as possible. He told Judge Brady that he was 11, when he was really only eight. He needed to be 16 to escape scrutiny. Superintendent Walker was asked if he attended the performance in question, which he answered in the negative, but claimed having a representative there. Mr. Conway argued that Mr. Graham had acquired the proper permits beforehand but was interrupted by Walker who insisted that the permission was for a speaking part only, but Buster had been performing an acrobatic turn. Mr. Conway insisted that speaking had been all Buster had done.[85] Proceedings were adjourned again until Thursday, 23 February,[86] at which time Graham was on his own, as the Keatons had moved onto their next venue. One report argued that Mr. Graham intended to take the case to the highest court possible so that a final decision on such cases could be secured, but this was not the outcome.[87]

The Keatons had traveled on ahead to Poli's Theatre in New Haven, Connecticut, where they began an engagement 20 February as headliners. The Keatons had 'a reputation as the best comedy trio ever put on any stage in America,' with Little Buster as an especially pleasing attraction.[88] It may have been this engagement that Buster remembers in a 1964 interview with Fletcher Markle for Canadian Broadcasting Company. He remembered the prevalence and importance of falls in the Keaton act:

> I used to do a thing coming out of the set house door of the stage, and we're grabbing the piece of scenery here and holding the door here and my own hand on my neck. And from the front, it looks like somebody has got me by the neck. And I'd yell blue murder and shake the scenery and everything and with my feet going in all directions. And my old man comes up there to free me. And he used to kick over my head, and his

foot would come down there and knock me loose from there. And as I'd slid back across the stage this way, he saw that it was me who had a hold of myself and he'd chase me right out of the theater, see.[89]

At this particular venue and engagement, however, Joe's high kick missed, and his kneecap caught Buster in the back of the head. He was out cold for a long period: 18 hours in this telling and 22 hours in a few others.

The final week of February was spent then at Poli's, Hartford, Connecticut.[90] The Keatons were touted in the paper, first with a headline: 'Keatings [sic] Do a Remarkable Knockabout Act.' The review itself, still misspelling their name, offers

The three Keatings were the comedians and the way little 'Buster' Keating was thrown around the stage by his father was ludicrous in the extreme. How he escapes being hurt is a mystery. He is dragged and thrown all over the stage, but strange to say he would almost invariably land on his feet, and when he did happen to fall he seemed to be made of springs, the way he would snap up, smiling and ready for more of the same thing. Besides all this he is quite a comedian. His imitations of Press Eldridge and Dan Daly being especially clever. Joe Keating does some neat acrobatic stunts and, taken altogether, it is the most entertaining act seen at the house this season.[91]

It appeared the court proceedings had not affected the Keatons' overall popularity, either with the audience or the theatre owners. Meanwhile, as of the 11 February edition of the *Mirror*, Joe had been suggesting in his ad that Jingles would be available as part of the act in 1905 and, in fact, his name had been part of the ad since the beginning of the year. Clearly, the just 6-month-old child was dangerously close to his performance debut date.

For the week of 6 March, the Keatons played the Jacques Theatre in Waterbury, Connecticut. Although labeled 'The Three Keatons and Buster,' suggesting that Jingles was now part of the act, there was no indication from the many laudatory reviews they received that the toddler was ever onstage at this location. Buster especially was heralded almost every day in the local paper. Before the week's engagements even started, he was

Buster Keaton, the diminutive comedian whose sensational success has been the talk of the public almost from the time he was able to toddle out onto the stage. Buster is a youngster compared with whom a solid rubber ball is dead in the point of bouncing and standing hard usage. He is thrown around the stage like a sack of meal, but always lands on his feet, no matter how difficult to attain such a position may be.[92]

Headliners this week, there were 'no better exponents of the art of causing laughs,' and 'the name of "Buster" Keaton has passed into usage as the standard for all juvenile comedians.' According to this reviewer, '"Buster" acquired his name because of the quantity of buttons which his actions cause to disappear from the wearing apparel of the audiences.'[93] By 7 March, after the Keatons had been playing in Waterbury for only one night, Buster began the review:

'Buster' Keaton cornered the laugh market at the Jacques yesterday afternoon so successfully that it will be many a long day before those who witnessed the initial performance of this week's bill will recover from the effects of the paroxysms of merriment into which the actions of the little man threw them. [. . .] The act in which 'Buster' and his parents appear is a roaring mélange of funny stunts, and the tiny tot's 'I'm sorry I fell' fairly prostrated the audience with delight.[94]

The week of 13 March, the act traveled over to Bridgeport, Connecticut to play the week at Poli's Theatre,[95] where they occupied the top third of the ad, and benefited from a nice graphic employing their name, which was printed diagonally down the right side. On the left, in a box, were the words 'The Juvenile Jollier' lined up next to 'Buster' Keaton, printed under the larger diagonal 'KEATONS.' Of course, Buster dominated the only review of the week published the day before they began:

The two Keatons that were the cause of it all are good, but they have to go backstage when their young hopeful Buster, aged eight, takes the floor. He is a pinnacle of diminutive merriment, agility, drollery, and real ability. His father actually throws him all over the stage, but that doesn't phase Buster, for he always lands on his feet. The fun generally waxes so strong and furious that the audience demands more from 'Buster,' and there he starts on his long suit – imitations of grownups in the theatrical profession whom he knows, Press Eldridge and other well-known comedians.[96]

They then began a week at Hathaway's in New Bedford, Massachusetts,[97] then Hyde & Behman's in Brooklyn again 27 March,[98] then Keith's, Boston. By 6 April, the *Boston Globe* was reporting on Buster's popularity, especially with children:

> Juvenile theatregoers are crowding Keith's every afternoon this week to see 'Buster' Keaton. The spontaneous merriment that this little spright causes and the childish wholesomeness of all his work, is exceedingly attractive to both young and old. There is no aping the style of older comedians, but just the lovable ginger of animal spirits of a healthy youngster.[99]

He was awarded with a largish ad in the paper that said, in large print: 'LITTLE BUSTER KEATON is scoring the hit of the current week's show, which is one of the strongest of the season. This is at KEITH's. Of course, though that is probably superfluous information, since the whole town is talking about it.'[100] The next Keith's theatre in the circuit was Union Square in New York City, which the Keatons played beginning the week of 10 April. Just two days before, Buster had appeared on the cover of the *New York Clipper*, accompanied by a short article on page two: 'Young though he is he ranks with the funniest of his older brother professionals, and none can create laughter better than he.'[101] The writer noted that Buster often talked to his father about ways to improve the act and that he was sometimes featured on the cover of the theatre programs. The piece ended with the assertion that the Keaton family were fully booked until January 1906 and would be undertaking a European tour thereafter, being booked at the London Coliseum beginning 15 January 1906 for four weeks, then at various music halls and theatres throughout Ireland and Scotland through August. In fact, once again, this overseas tour did not occur and the circumstances around its planning and/or being canceled are not clear.[102] The *Mirror* reported on the Keatons' success here, as well as on the fact that they had added many new bits to the act: 'Several new and amusing tricks were introduced, including one in which Mrs. Keaton reveals herself very suddenly in a makeup similar to those worn by "Buster" and his father. It is a slick trick and won a big laugh. "Buster" has added an imitation of Henry Lee's impersonation of Mark Twain that brought down the house.'[103] The act then played Keith's Million Dollar Theatre in Philadelphia, Pennsylvania beginning 17 April.[104]

After a successful week in Philadelphia, the Keatons played the Grand Opera House in Pittsburgh, Pennsylvania,[105] where the *Pittsburgh Press* mentioned that Jingles was 'not much over a year old' (he was 9 months) and that he was being carried onstage every night, already conducting 'himself with the composure of a tried veteran.'[106] Sure enough, several small pieces appeared at this point, which focused on the youngest Keaton, including one entitled 'The Newest Keaton': 'he has been before the footlights since he was three weeks old. His brother brings him on in a buggy and his father says the lad will be given a few stunts to do as soon as he can walk.' Joe offered,

> '[Jingles] enjoys the best of health and I really believe he has the stage fever already. When waiting in the wings to be taken on the stage by his brother, he expresses his delight by kicking and crowing in the most vigorous manner. We bring him to the theatre early in the afternoon and he generally takes a nap on an improvised bed, arranged on a trunk in the dressing room for him.'[107]

Certainly, Jingles' true debut on stage with the family act was nigh.

Back at Dockstader's Garrick Theatre in Wilmington, Delaware beginning 1 May, Joe may have wanted to debut his baby Jingles at this location, given the fact that the theatre was the apocryphal spot of Buster's earlier debut, and in fact, the newspaper ads for the theatre labeled the Keaton act 'The Four Keatons' as of 2 May. A review contained high praise for the now 10-year-old performer:

> The youngster, Buster, if his salary is in proportion to the attention paid him by the audience, gets a big end of the roll when Saturday night comes round. There is undoubtedly the making of a good comedian in this little fellow. He knows how to make fun without being rude, and when to let go after he has once caught on. There are heads much older in the business who have yet to find this out.[108]

Meanwhile, Papa Joe made the papers for a different reason; he was nearly robbed of his big diamond ring that week, one 'of large size and glittering wealth.'[109] Leaving the Garrick Theatre on that Tuesday night 2 May, Joe walked down the alley to King Street, where a 'highwayman' was waiting with a club and swung at him. Being an acrobat, of course Joe ducked and received a mere glancing blow on the head, crushing only his stiff hat, one that had to be replaced the next morning. Joe gave chase but was soon outdistanced and gave up the pursuit.

With the rumor of a European tour still in the air, Joseph Z. Keaton, wife and son Bert (Jessie) decided to make the trip east to visit for a few weeks, leaving Perry on Saturday 11 May on the Frisco (a train route).[110] Indeed, the Keatons' next engagement was not until the week of 29 May at the Bon Ton Theatre in Jersey City.[111] Jingles was noted as joining the act in a go-cart.[112] Between the end of the Bon Ton Theatre gig, until the Keatons played in Muskegon, Michigan the last week of July, the family experienced some leisure time in New York City. Sitting one day in the Paradise Gardens with his friends, Joe told a story that had occurred the week before, when he had taken the family to the New Jersey woods: 'On the ferry boat returning to New York, he had leaned over to adjust the strap of "Jingles's" carriage, when that lively youngster doubled up his little fist and planted it squarely in his papa's optic,'[113] resulting in the black eye that had been the original reason for the story.

They would not play another engagement until 23 July at Lake Michigan Park Theatre in Muskegon, Michigan.[114] Undoubtedly the cost was the prohibitive element and the reason their summer dates were fewer than usual. Muskegon would soon become the Keatons' most significant residence until Buster left vaudeville and moved to California. This week in 1905 would be their second taste of the area (the first was in June 1902), one that would leave a lasting impression such that Joe would percolate on the idea to begin a sort of actor's colony there. The *Mirror* reported that they spent the time in Muskegon '[breaking] in their act and [catching] a number of big fish.'[115] In Canton, Ohio 30 July they played Meyer's Lake Park Theatre, where they were deemed 'an enormous expense,'[116] then on to the Farm in Toledo, where C. M. Edson noted that 'houses [were] packed.'[117] Something happened there of a problematic nature, however, because Joe noted in his 19 August ad in the *Mirror*: 'Last week we played the FARM Theatre, and earned the position given us, and the Management accepted Press Matter without offence. And strange nobody had a fight that week, and once more a pleasure to play the Farm.'[118] A short article in the *Toledo News-Bee*, makes some suggestion regarding what it was all about. Entitled 'Embryo Actor Was Raised in a Trunk,' the piece focused on little

Jingles, but the first paragraph revealed the issue: 'The probabilities are that the next time the manager of a Toledo vaudeville theatre sends word to his booking agent to sign the Keaton family for a week he will find when the contracts come on that he has engaged the four Keatons, instead of the three Keatons, as it is now billed.'[119] Clearly, Joe was already charging for Jingles's presence onstage during their performance, despite the fact that all the boy did was ride in a go-cart pulled by Buster (if he was awake) and take a bow. Joe later published a piece in the *Mirror* that seemed to work as a means of placating the management:

> Joe Keaton writes that he and his family had the time of their lives during their engagement at the Farm, Toledo, last week. In the bill were Reno & Richards, who have a burlesque baseball game in their act, and as they were the closing number, the entire company volunteered to help as supers. 'Buster' was the umpire, and he and the others [. . .] introduced so many funny stunts that the act on several evenings ran forty minutes.[120]

In other words, it's as if Joe is suggesting that the Farm received not just more of the Keatons with this voluntary expansion of the final turn, but more of everyone, therefore, it had received more than its money's worth. Whatever the intent on Joe's part, the Farm's manager, Joe Pearlstine, had obviously decided to take the thing in stride, for 'nobody had a fight that week.'

In August, the Keatons played the Temple Theatre in Detroit,[121] where the Keatons 'were a show in themselves, and young Buster, as well as Buster, Jr., amused the audience to side-splitting mirth with their cute antics.'[122] At Shea's Buffalo, the act was noted as presenting something new with Jingles,[123] although no one recounted exactly what that was.[124] After a week at Shea's Toronto, the Keatons began September back on the Keith's circuit playing Cleveland, as part of the opening bill of the season.[125] Just south to Youngstown, Ohio, they played the Grand Opera House,[126] then the Maryland Theatre in Baltimore where they were billed as 'The Four Keatons,' who 'in a jumble of acrobatic eccentricities, give a clever exhibition, topped off by bringing Baby Keaton before the curtain to coo at the audience.'[127] The week of 26 September, the Keatons played the Million Dollar Theatre in Philadelphia,[128] then Keith's, Union Square beginning 2 October.[129] The *Mirror* offered that 'Joe, Myra and "Buster"

Keaton were an especially attractive feature and scored heavily with their acrobatic nonsense. "Buster" was in fine trim, and, although he is growing taller all the time, he is as funny as ever. He gave imitations of Charlie Case, Dan Daly, and Sydney Grant, and they were all well done.'[130] The Keatons as a family act, had appeared on the cover of the *Mirror* 7 October, with a descriptive paragraph published just inside. Initially, the piece focused on Jingles, who was described as under Buster's management:

> As he did not appear at every performance, 'Buster' decided that the baby's salary should be in proportion to his value as an attraction and credited him with ten cents a week as a starter. Since his debut, however, 'Jingles' has improved so much that his astute manager, in order to encourage him, has gradually increased his pay until he is now receiving one dollar and twenty-five cents a week. Even with this encouragement, 'Jingles' has the airs of a prima donna, and at times refuses absolutely to go on.[131]

Still, Buster was the star of the show and received the most praise in the piece, and was a great hit with children, for obvious reasons:

> His popularity increases with every return date. He is especially a pet of the children, and in many of the Keith houses the management makes it a point to invite the children to come and see him perform. The vaudeville players make a pet of him and never tire of giving him points on how to improve his work. He has reciprocated by studying the specialties of some of the best-known vaudevillians and gives imitations of them that are remarkably accurate.[132]

From New York, the act then traveled on to Keith's, Providence, Rhode Island,[133] then Keith's, Boston. The *Boston Globe* was advertising Buster's merits and his upcoming visit a full two weeks beforehand on 1 October.[134] It's safe to say that Buster had no competition, at least with the kiddies, on this bill. Joe reported in the *Mirror* that 'the entire audience remained to give "Buster" and his parents their full share of approval.'[135]

The week of 23 October, the Keatons were playing Hathaway's in New Bedford, Massachusetts.[136] Buster was given a shout-out for his performances this week when it was reported that 'in connection with being a clever acrobat, slapstick artist, monologuist and comedian, [he] has now added matinée idol to his many achievements. Last week at New Bedford he shook hands with the greater part of the population and was elected one of the season's great successes as a genial host.'[137] His popularity was beginning to know no bounds. The act then played Hyde & Behman's in Brooklyn,[138] then Proctor's Griswold Theatre in Troy, New York.[139] Back in Boston, Massachusetts at Howard's Atheneum again 13 November,[140] the Keatons were the headliners – no surprise given all the great popularity of Buster in an earlier visit that fall: 'Buster's new tricks are no less ludicrous than the old ones and there is a perfect whirlwind of merriment when he holds the stage.'[141] This was followed by a week at the Empires in Paterson[142] and Hoboken, New Jersey.[143] From New Jersey, the act moved back into New York City for a couple of weeks, first at Tony Pastor's, where they headlined, 'with Little Jingles Keaton thrown in for good measure.'[144] From Pastor's, the Keatons played Proctor's 23rd Street Theatre, where they shared the bill once again with Captain Bordeverry, the French sharpshooting specialist, whom Buster had introduced an imitation of in his act. This imitation was reported to be 'as funny as anything the little fellow has ever done. Colonel Bordeverry was so amused with the travesty that he loaned "Buster" one of his small rifles for the entire week.'[145]

Back in New Jersey at the Trent Theatre in Trenton 18 December,[146] the Keaton family spent Christmas performing at the Grand Opera House. On the bill was Will Rogers, 'sun-browned cowpuncher from the cattle ranges, known as the 'Lariat King,'[147] who was to become one of the hottest draws in vaudeville after his skill with the lariat led to a contract with the Ziegfeld Follies in 1915. Along with his roping antics, Rogers began to add in commentary on topics of the day in a sort of down-home, cornpone manner, which lead to a radio show and newspaper column. Eventually, Rogers began to make films, the first one in 1918. His career was cut short when he died in a plane crash on 15 August 1935. Joe was contacted for a sort of obituary of Rogers after this fatal accident.[148] Meanwhile, via the industry rags, Buster was a subject of focus in the Christmas issue of the *Mirror* in a short piece adorned with a nice caricature of the youngster in costume and the Keatons as a family did their best to wish their audience and colleagues a happy holiday. In Buster's piece, the writer noted that he 'is a born mimic and has only to see a full-grown actor go through his performance once in order to be able to reproduce his mannerisms to perfection.'[149]

The new year of 1906 was to begin in Newark, New Jersey at the Proctor's Theatre, beginning 1 January. This year would bring the third and last Keaton child, a daughter Louise, who would be born in late October. It would see the Keatons joining forces with George M. Fenberg in August, to be part of the Fenberg Stock Company for the rest of the year. This allowed late-pregnancy Myra to work when she felt like it and would open up an opportunity for Buster to do something besides comedy, when he was allowed to be part of the repertory company plays, namely *Little Lord Fauntleroy* and *East Lynne*. This year would also show that either Joe felt he and his family were too busy and too famous to visit Perry, Oklahoma (his father's home) or that the parties were at odds. The elder Keatons had visited Joe and family in 1905 for four weeks in New York City, but this year, there would be no visit and Myra, despite being pregnant, would not seek assistance from Joe's kin. Joe's father, Joseph Z. Keaton, was reportedly in Detroit Michigan for about eight weeks at a hospital where he was being treated for Bright's disease, known nowadays as nephritis or inflammation of the kidneys. No mention was made of Joe, Myra, and their children and in fact, no announcement of Louise Keaton's birth made the Perry, Oklahoma papers.

At the Newark Proctor's at the year's start, *Variety* noted that 'Little Buster Keaton, with his comical parents, is a big laugh getter here.'[150] The next week, the act had traveled up to the state capital of New York, Albany, to the Proctor's.[151] Joe reported that 'Jingles closed the big Proctor Show at Albany 8 Jan week – and they are still talking: "you have to talk baby talk to them up there."'[152] From Albany, the Keatons played Poli's, Worcester, Massachusetts.[153] The 18 and 19 January, it was being reported that Joseph Z. Keaton, Joe's dad, had successfully returned to Perry, Oklahoma from an eight-week stay at the Grace Hospital in Detroit under the care of Dr. Shelton. He was considered near death at checkin, yet he returned from Michigan with a new lease on life and completely cured.[154] His youngest son Bert had accompanied him. At this point, and due to the fact that no mention was made of the more famous son in any of these stories, it is unclear what the health of Joe's relationship with his family really was.

From Worcester, they played Poli's, Springfield, Massachusetts,[155] then Poli's, Hartford, Connecticut. The children in the audience were titillated by 'Berzac's donkey and the antics of Buster Keaton.'[156] A. Dumont reported that the theatre experienced 'immense audiences' and that 'the attendance has been so enormous that the building inspector has issued orders that hereafter only 100 standing room only tickets may be sold.'[157] They began February at Poli's Theatre, New Haven,[158] where Little Buster Keaton was 'the favorite of the week,'[159] then Bridgeport's Poli's, where they were expected to be a huge hit, with the reviewer predicting that 'Little Buster Keaton will be as merry as ever, and his faculty for falling on his feet when his irate parent throws him recklessly about the stage will doubtless evoke the same shrieks of merriment as of yore.'[160] One reporter noted that 'the latest edition of the Keatons, little Jingles, will be added in this city. Jingles is small, but he will make as much mirthful comedy as the other three.'[161] That may have been the marketing verbiage, but far from the truth at this point. At Jacques Theatre in Waterbury, Connecticut, the next week, the Keatons continued their streak of great reviews,[162] then in North Adams, Massachusetts at the Richmond Theatre, Buster was again touted in the press as important due to his impersonations, if nothing else:[163]

> The Four Keatons including Buster, an extremely clever acrobat and character comedian, are deservedly the headliners. No youngster was ever handled apparently so roughly and came out with bones and skin intact as this Buster. His makeup, and facial expression with the equally clever work of his father kept the audiences yesterday in roars of laughter and Mrs. Keaton adds some dainty musical numbers. Even the baby, 'Jingles,' appears for a moment. [164]

Back in New York City the first week of March, the Keatons' played Proctor's 58th Street Theatre. Joe had been dodging the Gerries every few months by sneaking back into New York City, where he resided, to play at one familiar venue after the other, so far without repercussions.[165] The *Mirror* reported that '"Buster" Keaton, assisted by his parents, Joe and Myra, was on par with Mr. Corbett[166] as far as popularity was concerned, and was recalled again and again. His imitations were especially well liked and his tricks with his father kept the house in roars.'[167] In Reading, Pennsylvania the next week the Keatons played the Orpheum Theatre for the first time,[168] then the Portland Theatre in Maine following, receiving a warm welcome and great reviews as usual. Joe decided to stage a publicity stunt here, at the behest of the Portland Theatre management.[169] The supposed kidnapping took place at 11.00 am on Wednesday 21 March on Preble Street in downtown Portland. Joe had taken his son out that morning to have a look at the construction site of the new Keith's theatre, which Jingles seemed to be very interested in – the father imagining, of course, that someday soon, the four of them would be playing there. Joe was distracted by something in a store nearby and left Jingles in his go-cart to go inside the store for a few minutes and that's when the kidnapping took place. The kidnapper grabbed Jingles and actually hailed a cab, driven by a man named George Evans, who took the pair to Union Station. Meanwhile a pack of men and boys had seen the heist and were hotly in pursuit. Joe was alerted and called Manager Moore and Business Manager Gerstle from the Portland Theatre. Moore got in a cab with Joe and they made their way to the station, while Gerstle went on ahead. At Union Station, the boy had already been discovered by Officer Quinn sitting on a bench with a handful of candy – all alone. Reportedly, the kidnapper had entered the smoking room at the station and had not returned, possibly noting the crowd of people that soon surrounded the boy. Joe was interviewed afterwards and offered that he believed this to be a particular man who had been following them from city to city for some time.[170] Other biographers have asserted that the Jingles kidnapping was staged; it was the idea of Portland Theatre's Manager Moore and the actual kidnapper was a prop man from the theatre.[171] However, no one counted on the group of bystanders on Preble Street taking off after the offender, which had to have caused a moment or two of anxiety on the part of the planners. Weren't the Keatons popular enough without such stunts?

After all this excitement, the Keatons headlined the Howard Atheneum in Boston beginning 26 March.[172] On that Sunday, 1 April, still in Boston, the Keatons added another night by performing at the Bowdoin Square Theatre on Bowdoin Square in the West End of the city, with several other big acts.[173] In Syracuse, New York at Keith's Grand Theatre the next day, Buster's picture appeared in the *Syracuse Journal*.[174] Then they joined the Harcourt Comedy Group for one week again, up in Brockton Massachusetts, this date being corroborated for Harcourt in the *Clipper*,[175] then followed with a week at the Bijou Theatre in Jersey City beginning 16 April, a week punctuated by a series of special nights, all to the benefit of the Police Mutual Aid Society. The first was the annual policemen's performance, which featured a play written by and enacted by the police themselves. Some of the new technology used in solving cases was featured, such as the Bertillon system[176] of identification. Actual policemen from the local contingent played the various parts, including Police Captain Kelly. The crowd viewing this spectacle was humongous: 'Stretching down from the gallery under the dome, through the balcony, the orchestra circle and the parquet to the footlights, men in all departments of the busy life of a cosmopolitan city were seen accompanied by splendidly gowned women.' The Four Keatons 'simply drove the audience into convulsions of laughter, while admiration for talent displayed by each was evinced by the applause that punctuated the funny incidents.'[177] At the end of this engagement, Buster's images appeared on the cover of *The Billboard*, with a brief paragraph description inside. Shown were three photos including Buster as a baby, Buster in costume and Buster in his 'grown-up' suit, complete with derby hat. The caption noted that he was 'acknowledged to be the best comedian of his age and inches on the stage.'[178]

Then, it was back to Dockstader's Garrick Theater again. One reviewer noted that 'The youngster is a favorite with local audiences; in fact, he began his career at the Seventh and Shipley Street house under Manager Dockstader.'[179] The first week of May, the Keatons took a couple of weeks off, then traveled south for the first time in a while. Certainly, Myra must have needed this respite, being about four months pregnant. In the meantime, their first engagement that month was at the Bijou in Atlanta, Georgia, beginning 14 May, the final week of the season. One reviewer wondered 'how the younger Keaton manages to survive a performance after being used as a football fully twenty minutes.'[180]

The Keatons now began the summer season, their first venue being a totally new one, the Casino at Electric Park in Montgomery Alabama. The group was under the management of George Homans, who arranged the entertainments for the Jake Wells's circuit of parks during the summer.[181] A large audience welcomed the bill that Monday night and another one braved the bad weather to attend on Tuesday: 'The myriads of electric lights at Electric Park reflected upon the crystal bosom of the lake, converts the place into a fairyland. No wonder the people like Electric Park.'[182] From Montgomery it was the Bijou, Birmingham,[183] where the Keatons met with high praise:

> Buster Keaton, propelled about the stage by the nap of his neck by Daddy Keaton, captured a large audience at the Bijou theatre last night when vaudeville was inaugurated. [. . .] It's a wonder to the uninitiated how the youngster keeps from getting killed. He is thrown about, kicked and cuffed, pitched around and mixed up generally in a rough and tumble manner that would apparently kill him half a dozen times during the performance, but he turns up smiling each time none the worse for wear.[184]

However, while things went smoothly this first night, all turned to chaos one of the other nights when the regular house band went to Tuscaloosa for the evening. The 'scratch band' that had been hired, simply wasn't up to the challenge and so, the drummer girl, Ethel McDonough, who struggled through her turn because of the fact, decided to make things easier for the other turns, many of which relied on musical accompaniment for their success. McDonough took over for the band conductor and was able to lead the 'wobbly musicians' so well that this fresh start seemed to fix the problem. When the Keatons came on, however,

> McDonough realized that the handling of the drums and effects was the most important thing, so she took the drummer's chair and helped the Keatons with all the tricks known to the drummer's trade in a most effective way. Toward the finish of the act, Myra Keaton took up the leader's baton, and between her and Miss McDonough not a cue was missed, and Joe and Buster concluded their turn with music that was entirely satisfactory.[185]

Significant in this episode is not just the fact that the vaudeville bunch were troubleshooters and problem-solvers, but how important music was to the acts in general and to the Keatons' act in particular. The success of such a knockabout act can be attributed to the rhythm of music and it's this factor that made the difference between Buster ending the act without incident and getting badly injured.

For the first week in June, the Keatons traveled to Mountain Park Casino in Roanoke,[186] the Casino at Rivermont Park in Lynchburg and a week later Ocean Park Casino in Norfolk, Virginia. The Keatons received much of the print attention:

> Old Man Keaton and the Kid, well known as Buster, do a comedy turn that is laughable from start to finish. Buster is a human football, and the way his father throws him around the stage causes actual fear out in the audience until the spectators understand how it's done. Mrs. Keaton plays well on several musical instruments.[187]

With only one Jake Wells's engagement as part of the Homans troupe to go, Joe felt it okay to print a defamatory poem by Jack Norworth in his ad 16 June, one which frankly presents the reality of traveling as part of this group over the summer:

Geo. Homans asked us in New York to make his Southern Tour.
He said the Hotels were immense and that the air was pure.
He also said that Southern Folks would meet us at each station,
And give us fruit, it wasn't work t'was just a nice vacation.
Since we arrived down here we found the atmosphere is punk,
And every hotel where we stop is an awful case of bunk.
The audience wear handcuffs and there ain't an act can stir 'em,
And now we think Geo. Homans handed us a pack of Durham.[188]

Joe then added a postscript: 'The only fruit the natives ever gave us were Lemons.' But, there was still one venue to go, the Summer Playhouse at Idlewood Park in Richmond.[189]

Free now of Homans and Jake Wells, the Keatons traveled back home to New York to spend three weeks off there. Myra was now five months pregnant and probably appreciated the rest, even though Joe had been making a few weak efforts to get dates. They started up again beginning the week of 30 July, when they played the Coliseum in Cleveland, Ohio, opening up the fall season.[190] Buster was noted as carrying 'off the individual honors' for the first night of the engagement and 'seemed to enjoy the rough and tumble treatment to which he is subjected as well as ever, and his imitations were enthusiastically received.'[191] He himself remarked on the topic, '"lots of people sit in the audience an' shudder when papa throws me around, but I never get hurt. Instead, I like it first-rate. You see this pad in my trousers? Well, that's where I usually land. Now lift that coat. Pretty hard to get a bruise through that, don't you think?"' In the same interview Buster gave to the *Plain Dealer* that week, he hinted at what was next for the act: '"In a couple of weeks papa an' me are goin' to go out in a stock company for a short time. He thinks it would be good trainin' for me. Mama says probably in some plays they'll want to put curls on me an' make me play little girl parts, but just let 'em try it! Not for Buster! Not for Buster!"'[192]

The week of 6 August, then, would mark their first week of performances with the Fenberg Stock Company, with whom they would appear for the rest of the year. The Keatons would find their time with another stock company, although necessary due to Myra's condition, regrettable, because of the lack of freedom, relatively low pay, more time on the stage and small-town venues. Upon exiting the 20-week contract 17 December 1906, Joe vowed he would never subject his family to such conditions again and that they would play only big cities and large venues. However, there were some dark clouds on the horizon he hadn't counted on.

Chapter 5

The 'Three Keatons' Become Five and Enjoy Buster's Fame

■■■■■■■■■■■■■■■■■■■■■■■■■■■■

George M. Fenberg, successful manager and director of the Fenberg Stock companies, toured four repertoire companies numbered 1 through 4, Eastern, Western, Northern, and Southern respectively. The Keatons were hired for number 1, the Eastern Company. Fenberg was known to carry 'more scenery than any other stock company on the road.'[1] According to E. E. Meredith, there were many benefits for the performer who had gained a position with a repertoire company: 'They are sure of a long season, a fair salary, and get week stands, and [. . .] they are never forced to go far West or into the South where the jumps are bad and accommodations poor.'[2] It has been suggested that Joe was able to get his usual wage, $250 a week, with Fenberg, thus the attraction. By 1904, Fenberg Stock had earned the 'reputation of being one of the most sterling organizations now before the public. This attraction plays a week [. . .] at popular prices, producing five matinees' beginning on Tuesday.[3] Buster would shine at those matinées, which were often geared towards a young audience, whom he awarded with candy for their attendance.

The Keatons were asked to fill in between the second and third act of that play, and the venues would not be of the same caliber that they had become used to. However, his old friends the Colby family (of Colby and Oliver) had been with Fenberg on and off since early 1904 and probably recommended the company to Joe. He only signed on for 20 weeks, or half the season, with his last day being 17 December, so he realized he probably wanted the experience to be as short as possible. In the meantime, the engagement with Fenberg began in Peekskill, New York at the Colonial Theatre. After a week here beginning 6 August, the troupe visited some 20 cities and venues throughout the fall and winter. Members of the company at start up were Harry R. Vickers, business manager, Lawrence Brooke (who left early), Tommy Shearer, the singing and dancing comedian, B. W. Carpenter, illustrated songs, D. J. Hamilton, E. Evarts, Oliver D. Bailey, A. O. Miller, Charles Stevens, the leading man replacing Brooke, who had recently performed with legendary American actor (and father of playwright Eugene) James O'Neill, Virginia Zollman, the leading lady, Jane Tarr, Mabel Hawthorne, a clever soubrette, and Jane Wood. The orchestra was led by Marie McNeil, who doubled as a cornet soloist.[4]

It wasn't long before Buster was called upon to play a child part or two in the plays, *Little Lord Fauntleroy* and *East Lynne* in particular. In fact, this was announced by 18 August in the *Mirror*, which, with the lag time required to get something published, meant that he was taking such parts already in either New Rochelle or Worcester. Of course, this was in addition to what he was doing with his own family act. But due to Myra's pregnancy, a bit more focus was on him than usual, because the Keaton act now consisted of Joe and Buster only: 'Mrs. Keaton is ill at present, so Joe and "Buster" are working as a team and doing very nicely indeed.'[5]

The weather in New England that fall was brutal, around 100°F in some places. This most likely affected the audience turnout in each location, something that may have given Joe a negative impression of the company from early on. Peekskill, for instance, noted in the *Mirror* that 'Fenberg Stock [. . .] opened the season here: attendance was fair considering the weather and performances.'[6] In New Rochelle, New York, the local paper featured a photo of Buster with his derby hat and a caption announcing the 'Three Keatons' in their town the next week.[7] Opening night in Woonsocket, Rhode Island, was 'witnessed by a crowded house.' As the headliners, the Keatons received lots of press coverage: 'Buster is precocious as ever – none the worse apparently for being thrown around the stage like a bag of meal twice a day for three hundred days a year. Little Jingles, who doesn't look over two years old, is a marvel of self-possession and captured the hearts of all the ladies in the audience at once.'[8] In New London, Connecticut at the Lyceum Theatre, Buster was being advertised as playing the role of Little Lord Fauntleroy in the play of that name at the Saturday 15 September matinée. As part of his own act with Joe only ('Mrs. Keaton was unable to appear'), they 'kept the audience in an uproar for nearly half an hour.'[9] On Friday night, he received special praise for a parodic interpretation of the song 'Waiting at the Church,' 'with a diminutive church to illustrate it.'[10] The song, written by Fred W. Leigh and Harry Pether, had been made very popular by British music hall performer Vesta Tilley, who sang the thing in a white wedding dress. It's essentially about a bride who is left at the altar. The chorus provides some idea of how hilarious it would have been to see 11-year-old Buster singing this:

> There I was waiting at the church, waiting at the church, waiting at the church,
> When I found he'd left me in the lurch.
> Ler, how it did upset me!
> All at once he sent me round a note.
> Here's the very note.
> This is what he wrote –
> 'Can't get away to marry you today –
> My wife won't let me!

Waterville Maine reported Buster in the starring role of *Little Lord Fauntleroy* again, this time providing him an entire article in the newspaper about his imminent visit to the town to alert his potential audience.[11] In Bangor, Maine, one of Joe's tall tales made the paper, the one in which he's playing poker on board ship, losing, and losing with Buster kibbitzing from the sidelines. Another hand is played, and the bid is raised, then raised again. Finally, Myra comes in and tells the boy he must go to bed, with Buster's response being, 'All right, Mother, just as soon as I see father play those four aces.' And the bidding ceased, as did the game.[12] A description of the Fenberg Stock company's offerings suggested that the Keatons would be presenting a new act 7 October, but this may simply have been the act with only Joe and Buster (therefore new).[13]

In Maine's state capital city, Augusta, Buster was again playing the role of Little Lord Fauntleroy at the matinée, with 'every child attending the matinee [receiving] a box of candy upon entering the theatre.'[14] After Lowell, Massachusetts, the Fenberg Stock Company played Lewiston, Maine. The Keatons arrived numbering four individuals and would leave numbering five. In the meantime, Buster was playing Little Lord Fauntleroy again at the Saturday matinée. Meanwhile, Myra went into labor and gave birth to a baby girl on Tuesday 30 October at 4.00 am, probably at the Atwood Hotel where they were staying. Supposedly, Joe bet everyone in the company and everyone else he could think of that the baby would be another boy, but seemed just as proud of his daughter, announcing her birth in the act that night. The Keatons named their daughter Louise Dresser Keaton, after their frequent co-star in vaudeville, and arguably the most beautiful woman on the stage at that time.[15]

From Lewiston, the troupe traveled over to Biddeford, Maine. By the time they made Salem, Massachusetts, the Keatons were reportedly 'back in the harness again,' meaning Myra was back on stage. Little Louise Keaton, 'the new arrival, is doing splendidly, and even this early has shown signs of talent that is to come.'[16] From Salem, the troupe was on to Concord, New Hampshire and from there, they traveled to Nashua, New Hampshire, where they were announced 'the most expensive act ever presented at popular prices and they will positively be seen at every performance.'[17] Also, at this venue, Buster took on another role, of Little Willie in the play *East Lynne* from the novel by Mrs. Henry Wood. The original story was considered sensational, in the traditional sense of the word, and had so many plot lines, that the reader had to pay strict attention to what was going on to have any understanding at all.[18] It was considered a guaranteed money maker, and companies would insert it into their agendas whenever they were in need of bumping up the number of attendees. Since Fenberg Stock was playing the Christmas season by this point, it's not surprising that the play suddenly appeared on the schedule.

Little Willie was the tubercular son of the misdirected main character, Lady Isabel. The child's death scene, in the arms of what he believes is his nanny Mrs. Vine, but is really his mother in disguise, contained some of the most oft-quoted lines of the play:

> Madam Vine (*rising*): O Heaven! My punishment is more than I can bear. He has gone to bring that woman here that she may mingle her shallow sympathy with his deep grief. Oh! If ever retribution came to woman, it has come to me now. I can no longer bear it. I shall lose my senses. O William! In this last, dying hour, try to think I am your mother.
>
> William: Papa has gone for her now.
>
> Madam Vine: No, not that woman there, not that woman. (Throws off cap and spectacles) Look at me, William. I am your mother! (*Catches him in her arms. He says 'Mother' faintly and falls back dead in her arms*) Oh! He is dead! He is dead. O William. Wake and call me mother once again! My child is dead! My child is dead!

Of course, Buster had a great story about his experience with this play and the particular actress who played Lady Isabel, Alice Irving, who took herself too seriously. Buster had to be part of his family's comedy turn after the second act, so he had his costume for the turn on underneath the white nightgown he was to wear as Willie. He even had the slapshoes on. During the scene described above, Irving gets carried away and when she collapses in grief her elbows hit Buster in the stomach and his feet, with the slapshoes on, shot straight up in the air. The audience started laughing and didn't stop until the play was over. Buster recalled the aftermath: 'When we leave the theatre, there's Fenberg waiting and looking like War Declared. He barely opens his mouth, and Joe hollers, "One word to the kid, just one word, and I'll slug you. Go get that cut-rate Sarah Bernhardt and leave him alone!"'[19] Clearly, their time with Fenberg Stock was coming to a close. Although they advertised their last day with Fenberg as 17 December, the first night of the Lynn, Massachusetts engagement,[20] it appears that the Keatons were in residence in Lynn until at least the first weekend, when Buster would have given his final performance as Little Lord Fauntleroy.[21]

Louise's name had been added to the family ad in the *Mirror* with the first December issue, so like it or not, she was now part of the act. Now, though, the Keatons were scheduled back on the Keith and Proctor circuit, to begin 7 January,[22] so they had almost two weeks off to enjoy the holidays as a family of five. The year 1907 would prove to be a challenging one for the Keatons due to happenstance, poor decision making, and a changing vaudeville business plan. Joe and his children would finally be caught by the Gerries this year – late in the year at least – and they would find themselves unable to play in the big New York cities for two years. The business model for the vaudeville theatres and agents was changing drastically. Some were joining forces, like Keith and Proctor, who had come together in June 1906.[23] Keith and Proctor would become the Keith-Albee circuit and then Klaw and Erlanger would try to merge with the Shuberts in direct opposition to Keith-Albee, in what would be a failed attempt, that in late 1907 would result in K & E being forced out of vaudeville altogether. These mergers certainly did not bode well for the health and happiness of performers. In fact, in March 1907, Keith-Albee decided to blacklist acts (a decision made in March 1907) that signed contracts for even one performance outside their circuit, a stipulation that would directly affect the Keatons. Klaw & Erlanger and the Shuberts, who were the opposition in that all their bookings went through the agent, William Morris, stole some of the better acts aways from Keith-Albee initially, due to offering higher pay, but these acts, the Keatons included, would find themselves high and dry when the Klaw & Erlanger effort ended up in court.

In late 1906 Keith and Proctor took it upon themselves to shake things up by being the first to do away with continuous performances, which they did in their two new houses, the remodeled Fifth Avenue and the new Harlem location. Here the two-a-day performance rule would be instated. Another change, which was to prove problematic for the Keatons, was that the intermission was removed from the Twenty-third Street house, meaning smoking would now be permitted throughout this house, as well as the Fifth Street and Harlem Opera House locations.[24] They had been scheduled to start the year with a week at the Fifth Street Theatre 7 January, but Mayor McClellan's office would not sign off on a permit for Buster to work in any house that allowed smoking.[25] This made their first engagement of the year move to Keith's, Boston beginning the week of 14 January. This turned out to be a happy week, because the Keatons were finally on the bill with Harry Houdini, maybe for the first time ever. What is certain is that Joe and Harry were well acquainted and shared some correspondence (which can be dated to about 1901).

That week in Boston, Houdini managed a list of tricks that, even without descriptions, took the breath away: escape from a great boiler into which he was riveted, from a gigantic rolltop desk and from a specially constructed, glass-lined cabinet.[26] Then it was another week off due to a New York Keith's cancelation (probably their Albany, New York date). The Keatons had finagled a family photo for the cover of the *Mirror* 19 January, hoping to start the year off with a positive note.

The week of 28 January, the Keatons performed at Keith's, Philadelphia, Pennsylvania.[27] Then at Keith's, Newark, New Jersey, where they were 'a great success.'[28] It was Jingles, however, who received especial mention this week:

> It was the exhibition of the infantile cuteries of the previously unknown Keaton baby that made the 'hit.' Shortly before the close of the act, this toddler, occupying a seat in a small go-cart, was wheeled into view, quickly divested of his baby dress, and his plump and dimpled little body, encased in a tightly fitting and scarlet-coloured suit of fleshings, exposed to the admiration of those in front. While it was thus made apparent that Joe and Myra, the papa and mama in this interesting family, had been holding something in reserve to prove that they are no believers in race suicide, Baby Keaton also made it evident that as a chip off the old block he is able to do his share towards keeping the family pot boiling. He does not

shirk from the footlights but takes to them as confidently as the proverbial duck to water. Although a mere toddler, yet he shows a mimetic faculty that enables him to hold successfully the centre of the stage against his relatives.[29]

They followed this with a week at Keith and Proctor's Union Square Theatre, which was allowed, because it was one of the New York City houses that did not allow smoking.[30] The *Mirror* reported that

> Joe, Myra and 'Buster' Keaton made their first appearance in New York in several months and were given a rousing reception. 'Buster' was in his best form, and introduced a lot of new tricks that pleased his admirers immensely. He is improving all the time, and though he is growing taller, he is still in the 'cute' class in which women and children are especially interested. Joe and Myra supported him as cleverly as usual, and the act went with a rush from start to finish.[31]

This success was followed by a week at Keith's, Manchester, New Hampshire. A couple of days before this gig, the Keatons found a family photo and portrait of Jingles featured in the *Clipper*.

The week beginning 4 March, the Keatons were back in Boston, playing at the Howard Atheneum.[32] They booked a random Sunday 10 March at the Bowdoin Square Theatre in the city again.[33] The very next day, they were in Binghamton, New York playing a week at the Armory,[34] then traveled to Jersey City for a week at Keith and Proctor's,[35] and then back with Lew Dockstader at the Garrick Theatre in Wilmington, Delaware. One reviewer noted that the Keatons

> are too well known here to need any special reference, but it may be said that their act really sems stronger than ever. Certainly the elder Keaton uses fully as much force as he ever did in throwing Buster about, and as usual the youngster managed to land in the soft places, or at least places that should be soft. Vaudeville has few if any family companies that can offer more or better comedy in a given time than the Keatons.[36]

After receiving this predictably warm reception in Wilmington, the Keatons traveled to the Maryland Theatre, Baltimore where they received a rare negative review: 'The Four Keatons, in another knockabout act, are funny too, but last night two of them remained on view too long, and so they wore out their welcome.'[37]

The week of 8 April, at the Grand Opera House in Pittsburgh, they again received a negative review: 'The Four Keatons, well known here, are good, but they allow their act to drag by using too much of the same thing.'[38] Was Joe taking note of these reviews? The act then traveled to Valentine's in Toledo,[39] then Keith's, Cleveland,[40] and the week of 6 May, Keith's, Columbus, Ohio. The Keatons, who reportedly were referring to themselves as the 'tickling triumvirate,'[41] received some impressive ink in the *Dispatch*, which did well covering almost the whole family:

> The Three Keatons (with Jingles, the three-year-old and Louise, aged six months, brought in as finales) were good in a certain knockabout way, and it is marvelous that Buster has any bones left unbroken. Myra Keaton plays the saxophone well, and Jingles is a darling and will soon enable the father to bill the family as The Four Keatons.[42]

They were scheduled to play the Temple Theatre in Detroit the week of 13 May but were turned away due to a new child protection bill having been put in place there,[43] so their next engagement began 20 May up in Toronto, Canada at Shea's Theatre,[44] followed by Shea's Buffalo, New York beginning 27 May.[45] The Three Keatons

> were really the Five Keatons, for 'old man Keaton' rings in the two latest additions to his family, and they are both 'chips off the old block,' and do some Keatonesque stunts. Joe Keaton is an all-around original entertainer, and Myra and the inimitable Buster are great in their way. It is a treat to witness the 'act' of Mr. Keaton's two and one half-year-old child.[46]

And so began the summer season. Beginning the week of 3 June, the Keatons played the Casino Theatre at Lakeside Park in Akron, Ohio.[47] The Keatons made a great impression here, with one reviewer labeling them 'the funniest feature' of the week. They were 'excruciatingly funny, and the kid was funnier. The makeup of both was enough to make a Weary Willie green with envy, and the stunts done by the two were about the most comical ever seen on a local stage. The song, "No, No, No, Never, Nox," by the "Kid" brought down the house.'[48]

The Keatons then played Meyers Park Lake Theatre in Canton, Ohio,[49] followed by Fairview Park Theatre in Dayton.[50] Manager Redelle ordered free matinée performances both Wednesday and Thursday that week, a decision which seemed to uptick attendance at the evening shows as well. Of course, the Keaton children were a huge hit: 'The Keatons, with Buster and Jingles, touched the hearts of the assembly because it is seldom that children with such marked ability are seen anywhere. The act given by the Keaton family is one howl from beginning to end. Joe Keaton, the father, and Myra, the mother, are very capable, and it is no wonder the Keaton children are so talented.'[51]

They needed a break and decided to take it back in Perry, Oklahoma at the home of Joe's father. So, whether or not he had been estranged from his family in the past couple of years, things had been patched up between them enough for a short visit. After all, his parents had not yet seen the new baby. They arrived in Perry on 24 June and had booked an engagement over in Oklahoma City at Delmar Garden beginning 8 July for two weeks. At this point, Joe had made a huge business mistake that would taint the rest of the year's engagements as well as those on into the future. He signed with the new Klaw & Erlanger operation, against Keith-Albee. Klaw & Erlanger were linked now with the Shubert houses, all of whom signed their talent through the William Morris agency. After Myra's confinement, 'Joe, Myra and Buster resumed their vaudeville dates and finished out the season successfully, in spite of several handicaps. They have a fine list of bookings for next season.'[52] It's probable that Joe realized the Keith circuit had instated a rule in March that banned all acts signing with Morris from ever playing them again, but he must have decided that with all the missed dates they had experienced due to the new smoking rules, something had to give. He couldn't have foreseen, however, that Klaw & Erlanger would be forced out of vaudeville entirely by December. Then, in a 15 June article, the reporter offered that the two new additions to the Keaton clan had caused Joe to go with K & E: 'Since that time [their visit to Oklahoma City four years prior] the family has increased and now Buster has a rival, yet a baby barely able to walk but with an intelligence for fun-making that has caused the Keatons to be a continued feature on the Klaw & Erlanger circuit.' After their return to Perry following the two weeks at the Delmar Gardens, they would 'open on K & E time as a headline act.'[53]

Hints had been provided since Louise's birth that the Keatons had begun employing a nanny/nurse to accompany them on their travels, but a mention in the Perry newspaper ascertained the fact: 'They are accompanied by the governess who teaches young Buster and has charge of the two-and-a-half-year old son and the baby sister seven months old.'[54] While Buster himself has recalled only one day of public school education in his life – somewhere in New Jersey – how much he learned from the supposed governess is up for debate. It is more likely that the woman, whoever she was, worked mostly as a child-minder, for wrangling two small children under the age of 3 was beyond the ability of two working parents and a working oldest son. In any event, Joe was calling the act 'A Man with a Wife, Three Kids, a Governess and a Table' now in some publications.

The home folks had hoped for another benefit performance by their native son and family (and the local paper suggested there would be one), but they would have to wait until mid-August, near the end of their stay. They were soon heading over to the state capital, Oklahoma City, to perform at Delmar Gardens for a two-week engagement, boasting huge crowds both weeks of the Keatons' residence. The manager Sinopoulo had negotiated for some time to acquire the Keatons for his theatre and was more than happy with the response: 'The Keatons have made several changes in their act. They continue in favor and Little Jingles, who appears at the matinée only, straightaway won his audience. Buster and his father continue in their rough and tumble acrobatics that have pleased so well and Mrs. Keaton is heard in a pretty interpolated saxophone solo.'[55] After these successful two weeks, the Keatons returned to Perry to spend three more weeks with Joe's father 'on vacation.'

Joe had a lengthy article entitled 'Joe Keaton the Boomer' published in the *Perry [Oklahoma] Republican* 26 July, which told about his early days in Oklahoma during the various land claim opportunities, with a few Joe Keaton tall tales thrown in. Finally, before the family headed for St. Louis, the site of their first venue on the Klaw & Erlanger circuit, they participated in their usual night of entertainment for the locals, but this time, it was not a benefit. Despite the ridiculously sultry weather, the attendance was good for what would be about an hour of merriment in the local opera house Thursday 15 August:

> Better than ever are the Keatons. Jingles, the latest member of the family to appear before the footlights was an outrageous hit. The act proper in the large theatres runs but twenty-

three minutes. Last evening was given a full hour of fun and nonsense including the regular routine of work varied with parodies and travesty on local topics.[56]

Meanwhile, the Keaton act received some refurbishments over the summer: 'Everything receiving finishing touches around Winter quarters. All new side wall – one little top – table has a new coat of paint.'[57] And costumer Guttenberg came by to visit (and update their wardrobe). Now being a part of 'Advanced Vaudeville,' Joe felt they needed to look the part.

While the Keatons were to begin with Klaw & Erlanger at the Garrick Theatre in St. Louis the week of 1 September, they added a week's engagement beginning 18 August at the Moline Theatre in Illinois, where they opened the season for that venue.[58] The day after their first performance, a caricature of the Keaton family appeared along with a review of the entertainment, which showed Myra in her nightgown holding a screaming Louise and bare-footed, with Buster and Jingles just visible in bed behind her, their startled faces peeking out from the covers. Joe is nowhere to be found. A sign on the wall reads 'What is a home without Dad? Signed Buster and Ma.'

Not only were the Keatons beginning their tenure with Klaw & Erlanger, but Klaw & Erlanger as part of 'Advanced Vaudeville' was inaugurating its presence at the Garrick in St. Louis this week. 'Advanced Vaudeville' meant the highest possible class of entertainment in the genre, another factor that probably convinced Joe to sign up. The supposedly superlative bill included Hardeen, the handcuff king and brother of Harry Houdini. 'Advanced Vaudeville' also employed the tactic of announcing the week's bill at the last possible moment, believing 'that this method will add to the interest that may be aroused in the bills.'[59]

The Shuberts were also a part of this effort and so the Keatons' next venue was the Shubert Theatre in Kansas City, Missouri the week beginning 8 September,[60] From Kansas City, they moved on to Louisville, Kentucky at the Mary Anderson Theatre,[61] and later the Duquesne in Pittsburgh, beginning 23 September. One reporter noted that 'Advanced Vaudeville' had 'now settled down to a smoothly running basis.'[62] Then beginning the week of 29 September, the Keatons' venue had changed to the Forrest Theatre in Philadelphia, but so had most of the bill. Louise Keaton made a big hit, as did the rest of her family:

Miss Louise Keaton made her bow to Philadelphia yesterday. It was only for an instant – in the arms of her mother at the close of the family stunt – but she is destined to give the others a run for popularity if the chorus of feminine 'Ohs' and 'Ahs' that greeted her mean anything. Miss Louise, be it known, has not yet reached the tender age of one year, but she surveyed the situation with the air of one born to a stage career. Joe Keaton, head of the family, repeated his familiar but always funny table act, and incidentally served as foil to Buster Keaton, who has grown to be quite a big boy. Young Keaton, with a makeup an exact replica of that worn by his father, contributed a bunch of nonsense to the act that was doubly absurd coming from the mouth of a youngster. Jingles, the other child, a sturdy boy of three years, danced a breakdown that caught the audience, while the mother of these remarkable children effectively rendered several solos.[63]

In Boston, they played the Tremont Theatre,[64] then the People's Theatre in Philadelphia.[65] For some reason, Joe used the text of his *Mirror* ad 19 October to reflect back on George Fenberg, for whom he appeared to bear a grudge, using pejorative language and mentioning that Mr. Fenberg never thanked Buster for his 14 weeks of hard work (it was really 20) and that he, Joe, had to wait until the entire contract was fulfilled to be paid anything.

The Keatons' next week of engagements began 28 October at the Academy of Music in Montréal, Canada,[66] then they were on to Springfield Massachusetts and the Nelson Theatre,[67] followed by the Franklin Square Theatre in Worcester, Massachusetts.[68] After the Keatons left Worcester, however, the bottom fell out, in more ways than one. On Sunday 17 November, Joe had agreed to a one-night appearance at the Grand Opera House in Brooklyn of the whole family, Jingles and Louise included. The engagement was even announced in the 23 November *Mirror* as a 'Keaton Festival': 'This was the only appearance of the Keatons in New York this season, and Joe arranged to have the whole family on hand. [. . .] When Jingles and his baby sister appeared on the scene, there was a tumult, and the entire family had to come before the curtain several times to bow their thanks.'[69] Unfortunately, the Gerries would be in attendance that night.

After the performance, Joe was taken into custody the next morning at Ehrich House.[70] The William Morris office provided the funds for bail, some $300, and then both Joe and the theatre manager, John Springer, appeared in court that day, Monday 18 November. The case was postponed then until 28 November, even though Joe didn't want it, because he would be missing a week of engagements.[71] Because William Morris had posted his bail, however, Joe had no choice. On 28 November then, Justice Zeller in a Special Session of Court fined Springer $150 for allowing underaged children to perform on his stage and Joe $75. Agent Moore was the Gerry officer in court that day. Interestingly, the underaged children were identified as Joseph Jr., 14, George, 3, and Vera, one.[72] Buster was actually just twelve. Harry and Louise were obviously having their identities protected. Not mentioned in the paper was the fact that Joe was now not allowed to play in the vicinity of New York City until Buster was 16, but he would break that requirement in exactly one year. This experience would be just the first knock.

The second came the same week, on Wednesday 13 November, when Klaw & Erlanger announced that they were suddenly out of the vaudeville business entirely. In a conference with the United Booking Office (the Keith-Albee faction) held the first week of November, Klaw & Erlanger agreed to leave the vaudeville business within 90 days of that date, with UBO then taking over all of the 'Advanced Vaudeville' unexpired contracts:

> To the performers the settlement of the conflict means much. The large salaries caused by opposition will soon be a thing of the past, and besides, work will not be so plentiful. Big acts that have little or no time booked ahead will have small chance of engagements for several weeks to come, as the United Offices will probably have all they can attend to in placing acts already booked by both sides.[73]

In essence, Klaw & Erlanger had overextended themselves. They spent more than $1 million ($32.5 million today) bringing in acts from Europe that didn't draw any audiences, and paying American acts huge salaries as well, money that K & E also never recouped. About 125 acts were on contract at the time of the dissolution, forcing UBO to be very creative in the coming months in placing them all.[74] The Keatons, having dumped the UBO to take the higher salary at K & E, were simply out of luck. Joe had to find another circuit to sign on with. That circuit was the Majestic, which would take the Keatons south and west once again. Their first date would be 2 December in Birmingham Alabama at the Majestic Theatre. Their balloon burst, they traveled down to Birmingham with their proverbial tails between their legs. The Keatons 'easily took off the honors of the evening.

The ridiculous way in which Father Keaton throws Buster Keaton around the stage and the positions in which the youngster lands was the cause of laughter of the genuine variety.'[75] Another reviewer mentioned 'Buster Keaton's rendition of "Under the Spreading Chestnut Tree,'" makes a decided hit:'[76] This was, in fact, 'The Village Blacksmith,' a poem by Henry Wadsworth Longfellow:[77]

> Under a spreading chestnut-tree
> The village smithy stands;
> The smith, a mighty man is he,
> With large and sinewy hands,
> And the muscles of his brawny arms
> Are as strong as iron bands.

The poem consisted of seven more stanzas.

Such an outpouring of praise should have been a salve for the Keatons' recent wounds. The Keatons then moved on to the Majestic Theatre in Little Rock, Arkansas.[78] From Little Rock, they moved over to Fort Worth, Texas to the Majestic Theatre. Though last on the bill once again, the Keatons remained popular. One reviewer noted that their very long act, 'so long that it would be tedious if any less funny,' was the best thing on a very good bill. While the audience enjoyed the knockabout acrobatics, Buster made a big hit again with his recitation of 'The Village Blacksmith.' This long and trying year would end in Houston, Texas's Majestic Theatre, with the Keatons previewed in the newspaper as 'secured direct from the Klaw & Erlanger forces in New York, [they] will make their first appearance in a glomeration of eccentricities and absurdities for driving care away.'[79] At least the year could now end on a semi-happy note.

As 1908 dawned, the Keatons found themselves still in Houston, Texas, finishing up their week at the Majestic. They would begin their time with the Orpheum circuit in El Paso, Texas. After the Orpheum Circuit, the act would revisit some familiar venues, get booked into several Proctor's houses again and chance another few dates in and around New York. Notable this year was Joe's desire to buy a home somewhere, a desire that started with the idea of a New York artists' colony and ended with a similar place in Muskegon, Michigan, where the Keatons finally planted roots. Little Louise would experience a life-threatening accident from which she survived, and Buster would be 13 in October, but his fake age put him at fifteen. Joe would receive a letter from London that finally persuaded him to try an overseas engagement in 1909. Right now, though, they were playing Houston, then traveled west to El Paso, located on the far west border of the state, beginning an engagement there at the Orpheum Theatre 8 January (strangely, a Wednesday) and ending 14 January (a Tuesday).

Martin Beck or no Martin Beck, the Keatons were back on the Orpheum circuit. The first night was reviewed with the Keatons in the top spot, despite not being the headliners:

> The father and oldest son, Joe and Buster, are the funmakers in their knockabout stunts that are about the cleanest and funniest act that could possibly be thrown together. Starting out with the statement that 'It just breaks father's heart to be rough,' father Joe proceeds to slam Buster around the stage and through the scenery in a way that would make an ordinary kid yell murder. Mother Keaton, besides taking care of the little Keatons, does a saxophone solo that is better than the average and, while she is at this, Joe and Buster do an eccentric dance that includes numerous falls through the scenery.[80]

From El Paso, they traveled on to Los Angeles's Orpheum.[81] Even though they received lukewarm reviews here, the Keatons were asked to stay a second week.[82] In taking that second week at the Orpheum in Los Angeles, the Keatons had dropped a week at the Orpheum in Salt Lake City, Utah. The act then moved on to San Francisco's Orpheum beginning Sunday 2 February with the matinée.[83] Waldemar Young wrote his piece after the first day of performances and, perhaps, likened the Keatons' act to 'art' for the first time:

> Joe and Buster keep the house literally in an uproar. Myra's contribution to the act, aside from Buster, consists of one instrumental solo, which serves simply to allow Dad and the lad to get their breaths. Then they resume their acrobatic tomfoolery – and again comes the surging roar of laughter. For a slapstick act it is wonderful in that it almost becomes art.[84]

Accompanying the review were several caricatures of the performers on the bill, including one of Buster. Perhaps this heralded a demand for a second week at the venue for the Keatons, because they did continue on the week of 10 February, with a different bill.[85] The week of 16 February, the Keatons simply moved across town to the Oakland, California Orpheum,[86] where the ink on the Keatons was again lukewarm: 'They proved to be very acceptable, eccentric comedians the little chap, Buster, being especially amusing.'[87]

From Oakland, it was time to start the journey back east, stopping at Denver, Colorado's Orpheum Theatre.[88] From Denver, it was on to a familiar old venue, Kansas City, Kansas, a town they hadn't played since the medicine shows. Appearing at the Orpheum,[89] Buster received a lengthy 'interview,' which ended with the intimation that the Keatons might be brought up on charges of playing on Sunday. In fact, the managers of four theatres in the Kansas City area were all defendants in a case involving the so-called Blue Laws[90] of the state of Missouri, which prohibited performances of any kind on Sundays, going through the courts at this time and had made the papers just two days[91] before the Keatons' arrival in town for their engagement. Oddly, performances continued to be put on Sunday afternoons, perhaps in flagrant protest of the laws.

In the interview, Buster talked about the physicality of the family act and expressed being extremely tired and wondering how much longer he could continue at the pace they had been working: '"I'm wearing out,"' he noted, saying that if he continued to do so much sliding on the stage, his body would wear down such that he would disappear: '"If I live long enough, I'll get to be just a point and there won't be enough of me left to hang clothes on."' The interviewer noted that Buster's makeup 'gives him a look about as cheerful as a tombstone, and when, on top of that, or rather down under that, he gets solemn sure enough, the extreme limit of funereal melancholy has been surpassed.' His father 'seizes him by the back of the coat and slides him clear across the stage. He knocks Buster down and then jerks him up. This display of affection is followed by a kick. At last, he gives Buster such a violent kiss, that the victim is completely disabled, and slides clear off the stage into the wings.' Connecting this then to the blue laws infraction, the interviewer asked '"What will you do, Buster, when you are taken before Judge Wallace on the charge of acting on Sunday?"'[92] Fortunately, this never became a worry.

The week beginning 16 March, the Keatons played Sioux City, Iowa's Orpheum Theatre. On Wednesday night, they took part in a special vaudeville performance for a group of merchants attending the Shenkberg

Banquet, held at the Mondamin Hotel. Buster presented a monologue and sang 'Somebody Lied to Me:'[93]

> George Washington so history says, would never tell a lie;
> I wish there were more Washingtons I do, I hope to die.
> When I was but a little boy, somebody felt my head:
> Says he 'you'll be a President someday' that's what he said.
>
> Chorus:
> Somebody lied.
> Somebody lied, you see;
> There never was a President that ever resembled me.
> Somebody lied.[94]

In April, the act was off to the south again, playing the Colonial in Norfolk, Virginia. The Keatons closed the show: 'Little Buster Keaton, who makes up like his father, imitates his father and does a lot of stunts his father cannot do.'[95] Obviously, he sang the favorite tune 'Somebody Lied' here as well, because a sheet music seller advertised it for sale 15 April, hoping to capitalize on Buster's success.[96] From Norfolk, it was a short trip over to the Colonial in Richmond, Virginia. They were touted as 'the big laughing act' of the week:

> There are strenuous times on the Colonial stage from the minute Buster Keaton makes his first entrance until he bows himself off. Talk about knockabout teams, this one is it. A football game is childish and innocent amusement, only fit for girls, in comparison with the work of Buster and his daddy. The latter says he hates to be so rough. He then takes up his offspring bodily and throws him across the stage some twenty feet. But Buster doesn't mind. He wears a suit that many a boy would like to borrow when he goes home after playing 'hooky' and meets the stern countenance of his father, who is waiting, not at the church, but in the vicinity of the woodshed.[97]

Jingles was still performing only at the matinées, and although she wasn't a permanent fixture there as yet, Louise was known to make an appearance in the afternoon from time to time.

Back east again, they played the Empire Theatre in Paterson, New Jersey beginning 20 April. The Keatons closed the show again with 'one of the strongest and best acts in that position ever seen at the Empire.'[98] Then it was over to Hoboken's Empire Theatre,[99] and on to Poli's in Scranton, Pennsylvania, a town invested in mining and rail transportation located in the northeastern part of the state.[100] Notably, Holden's Mannikins, an act that might have interested Buster, was a strong favorite: 'Every move of the tiny figures is as life-like as if they were of flesh and blood and the scenic effects are beautiful beyond description. The allegorical spectacle toward the close is one of the handsomest examples of miniature stage craft ever devised.'[101] The Keatons again received high praise, which was largely focused on Buster: 'From the time the trio make their appearance on the stage until the act is ended, there is a continuous series of surprises and a good share of them are furnished by Buster, a diminutive specimen to whom the most difficult acrobatic feats appear to be no effort.'[102]

For the week beginning 11 May, the Keatons traveled east again to Hartford, Connecticut and the Poli's Theatre, again headlining.[103] They then appeared at the Poli's in New Haven the last week of the regular vaudeville season.[104] The teaser presented a couple of days before the engagement featured a photo of four of the Keatons, all save Louise, dressed alike in their stereotypical Irish makeup and costumes.

Then, back in New York at their Ehrich House residence, tragedy occurred. The Keatons were moving their operations to the second floor of the building when little Louise took a walk out a French window, which had a low sill and fell to the street, cutting her tongue very badly with her own teeth in the fall. Most of her teeth had to be removed. Myra was in the room at the time and able to get the baby off in a horse and buggy to St. Mary's hospital, where she received 'the tenderest care. Mrs Keaton was prostrated by the accident, and had to have medical attention.'[105] Louise managed to heal from the incident without much repercussion, and according to Joe, was saying 'daddy' by the second week in June.[106] The accident was mentioned in an article about the Vaudeville Comedy Club members' recent activities, 'Joe Keaton's Baby Hurt by Fall from Window,'[107] and a week later in 'Vaudeville Jottings.' Buster remembered that Louise suffered no ill effects from the accident. However, this complicated the schedule of the Three Keatons, and they laid off the final week of May, deciding then what to do about the summer.

Joe had obviously been thinking this over even before the baby's accident. One report offered that he had purchased 'several splendidly located lots' owned by the Vaudeville Investors' Company near Coney Island, which he might build a house on, or simply hold for investment purposes.[108] Although the *Mirror* only covered this in June, the *New-York Tribune* ran a story about the Coney Island development in January, calling it an actor's colony and listing at least 16 artists who had already purchased lots, Joe Keaton among them. The land was called the McLaughlin Park Tract in the Gravesend section of the 31st Ward near Coney Island. Preliminary work on the property, such as the installation of water and gas mains, electric light conduits and a complete sewage system began the second week of January.[109] However, it's clear that Joe decided not to build on his New York lot for some reason but took the idea of an actors' colony to a place a bit more to his liking, Muskegon, Michigan.

The Keatons had 'discovered' Muskegon and environs in summer 1902, when they played the Lake Michigan Park Theatre there for the first time. The theatre had been built in 1898, and by this time was a respected venue on the summer park circuit. They had revisited in 1905, adding some time to their stay, which allowed them the opportunity to enjoy what the area had to offer, fishing and other outdoor sports, including baseball. So, with Louise still on the mend and the prospect of searching for summer park work looming large, Joe decided to take the family up to Michigan in early June 1908 and spend three months there. Bluffton, a small town nearby that offered some pretty lots on the lake in the Edgewater area, ended up being the heart of the artists' colony that began to develop that summer, with the assistance and commitment of Joe Keaton himself. After he purchased his lots at 1579 Edgewater, he began building a house, and then decided to spend some time evangelizing about the place to his fellow vaudevillians. Theatrical agent Lew Earl also purchased property early in the game, and helped to found the colony as well. That summer, the Actors' Colony, as it was officially called, incorporated, with Joe Keaton as president, Paul Lucier vice-president and William Rawls secretary-treasurer.

Eventually, colony residents would share their entertainment skills with their Muskegon neighbors at the Lake Michigan Theatre and then organize their own show, where acts could try out new bits before they tried to foist them on the large-city audiences of the circuits. Over the next few years, Joe's evangelism netted him some profits; he would buy up land and then convince his confrères to buy and build, with the result that at one time nearly 200 artists called the place 'home' during the summer months. Lew Earl made the place his permanent year-round home and as such was named honorary mayor. The dock and dock house were soon built on Earl's property, too.[110] The summer of 1908, however, was the time when all of this was just starting. The Keatons would be back on the road 14 September, but until then, they set about making Bluffton their first home.

The summer was winding down into the beginnings of autumn by the time the Keatons wended their way back to their New York digs. While summers in Michigan might be idyllic, due to the cooler temperatures and natural surroundings, winter could be brutal and the Keatons certainly didn't want to have to remain there as the temperatures plummeted. Happily, they were back on the United Booking Office circuit again,[111] meaning any ill feeling their signing with Advanced Vaudeville had caused initially was now put aside, probably because the United Booking Office knew it needed these top-notch moneymaking acts. Their first week of engagements began then on 14 September at the Proctor's Theatre in Newark.[112] They then played the Trent Theatre in Trenton again,[113] following that with a week at the Hudson Theatre in Union Hill, New Jersey.[114] Returning to the Orpheum in Reading, Pennsylvania 12 October, the Keatons closed the show and 'were there, as usual, with the goods. [. . .] They are in a class all by themselves. As eccentric comedians, they have no superiors.'[115] Joe and Myra were now producing their two youngest at the end of the show, afternoon and evening, for the pleasure of the ladies in the audience. Buster pleased the folks with his rendition of 'Highland Mary:'

> Ye banks and braes and streams around
> The castle of Montgomery,
> Green be your woods, and fair your flowers,
> Your waters never drumlie;
> Where summer first unfolds her robe,
> And there the langest tarry,
> For there I took my last farewell
> Of my sweet Highland Mary.[116]

And five more verses. All three children offered their typical Saturday matinée performance, at which they handed out candy and signed photos.[117]

From Reading, the Keatons moved to the Majestic in Johnstown, Pennsylvania.[118] Then, after quite a journey, the Keatons arrived in Dayton, Ohio to begin a week at the Lyric Theatre,[119] where they garnered an article all to themselves in the local newspaper that worked to demonstrate the familial bliss that was the Keaton family motto: 'We are a happy family and our act has achieved success because we all do the very best we can at all times, and because we work with and for each other.' In the article, Joe is described as 'just a plain, big, good-hearted father' and mother and sons are also 'good, plain people.' They work hard for each other, in hopes that one day they will be independent and can buy a little house to settle into. And that's all there is.[120] From Dayton, it was back to Poli's, Wilkes-Barre, then the Richmond Theatre in North Adams, Massachusetts,[121] and a week at the Jacques Theatre in Waterbury, beginning 30 November.[122] From Waterbury, they played Poli's, Bridgeport, Connecticut,[123] then decided to take some time off for Christmas in New York City.[124] Back at work 27 December in Reading, Pennsylvania again, at the Orpheum, the Keatons were 'the laughing hit of the bill.'[125] A day before they returned to the road, Buster had once again appeared on the cover of the *Mirror*. A new portrait bust appeared on the right, showing a youngster growing into a man, with him pictured in his Irish stage costume on the left and above him. Inside, he garnered a fairly long article, which started by repeating the old apocryphal bio, then added a yarn from Joe about Buster's 'spankless' pants, 'the patches so thick you can't hurt me.'[126] Joe threw in a reminder that Buster would be 16 on 4 October 1909, and therefore, finally free of the Gerries. In fact, he would be only fourteen.

1909 finally turned over and found the Keatons still in Reading. This year would bring more success, for the most part. The Keatons would continue many years of resting and relaxing in their new summer home in Bluffton, Michigan, then *finally* take a boat over to London to try their hand there in what would be an ill-fated engagement. Buster would turn a fake 16, but at least this fooled the Gerries, and the Keatons re-entered New York City proper that October.

The first engagement of the year was back in Wilmington, Delaware at their old stomping grounds, Lew Dockstader's Garrick Theatre, beginning the week of 4 January.[127] It was noted that 'the Keatons have made many friends in the twelve years they have been coming to Wilmington, and they are always sure of a welcome.'[128] From the Garrick, they moved over to the Hudson Theatre in Union Hill, New Jersey,[129] then to the Orpheum Theatre in Harrisburg, Pennsylvania. Being a new-to-Harrisburg act, of course Buster received great reviews:

> Buster Keaton is a wonderful boy and if there was not an entertainer at the Orpheum theatre this week other than Buster, vaudeville patrons in this city would have a feature that in itself would be worth the price of admission. [. . .] Following

each of his mischievous turns he has a laugh that is contagious to every part of the house and despite the well-meant kindness of a kissing Father, he is thrown about in a merciless fashion that makes the house ring with laughter.[130]

Another review, reprinted in the *Mirror*, related that 'Nothing funnier has ever been seen at the Orpheum or at any other vaudeville house than the Keatons – Pa, Ma and Buster, who, though not billed as the topliners were, through the discriminating appreciation of Manager Hopkins, assigned to the most important place on the bill, the closing act at the performance last night.'[131] From Harrisburg, the Keatons went south and west and rejoined the Majestic Circuit, now called the Interstate Circuit, with dates in Birmingham, Little Rock, Arkansas, Fort Worth, Dallas and Houston, Texas. In Birmingham,[132] instead of 'The Man with the Table,' one review noted the Keatons' act was entitled 'It Breaks Father's Heart to Be Rough.' Obviously, this reviewer had never seen the act before: 'A man and boy dressed as clowns provide all sorts of fun with the "knock down and drag out" work and the boy was thrown over and off the stage in a manner that was calculated to suggest to the minds of the spectators that it was about time to call in the society for the protection of children.'[133]

In Houston, the Keatons had been placed at the end of the bill, probably because no one could really recover from them, and, for the first time in a while, one of Buster's impersonations was mentioned in the press, one of another performer on the bill, Fred Zobedie, the balancing act specialist. In addition, one writer mentioned that 'he sings, too, in that clownish way of his, three songs, in a laugh-producing manner.'[134] From Houston, the Keatons were back playing the Orpheum theatres in Atlanta,[135] Easton, Pennsylvania,[136] and then at Poli's, Worcester 5 April.[137] For the next week's engagement, the Keatons had traveled to the Broadway in Camden, New Jersey. Being Easter week, everyone on the bill expected big audiences.[138] One review revealed a new song for Buster: 'Buster's topical song "Father Brings Home Something Every Day," from buns and bundles to measles and tomcats, provoked convulsive laughter and kept the bright and natural born boy comedian busy turning out verse after verse.'[139]

From Camden, the Keatons traveled up to Syracuse, New York to play the Grand Theatre starting 19 April,[140] then the Empire in Hoboken.[141] This would be their last performance before a full three weeks in Muskegon. Joe reported in the *Mirror* 8 May that three Gus Edwards's songs, two beyond 'Father Brings Home,' had afforded them great success in the Wilmer and

Vincent houses they had played this spring. The two others were 'Sunbonnet Sue' and 'Merry-Go-Round Rag,'[142] this last being from Edwards's musical by the same name, which had a run on Broadway at the Circle Theatre in 1908 and would have been a piece for Myra.

A largish ad, 'Buster with the Three Keatons, the same old riproarers' in *Variety* 15 May gave Joe's address as c/o Bullhead Pasco, Lake Michigan Park, Muskegon, Michigan, and announced that their three weeks' stay there would begin 17 May.[143] And, it was indeed Bullhead Pascoe who received the renowned letter from Alfred Butt to Joe during that time, asking him to come and play the Palace Theatre of Varieties in London.

Chapter 6

London Disappointments and Buster Becoming a Fake Sixteen

■■■■■■■■■■■■■■■■■■■■■■■■■■■■■

In the early summer of 1909, the Keaton family were enjoying their new holiday home in Bluffton, Michigan, when a letter came to Papa Joe from an overseas address, delivered at Bullhead Pascoe's. It was an invitation from legendary theatre manager Alfred Butt of the Palace Theatre of Varieties in London. Joe decided tentatively to accept, but the Keatons had a few engagements already lined up at the summer parks, Lakeside Park Theatre (Akron), Meyers Lake Park (Canton), Rock Spring Farm Theatre (East Liverpool) – all in Ohio – and put off going until 1 July. These engagements completed, it was time to go to London.

The young and brash Alfred Butt ran the Palace according to his own rules, his aim being always to provide the audience a 'bright, clean, novel and interesting show, without objectionable features.' Supposedly, he especially liked to hire American acts, and engaged more of them than any other house in London.[1] This is where the Keatons came in.

Vaudevillian Walter C. Kelly, known for his characterization 'The Virginian Judge,' which eventually became a silent film, assured Joe, despite reservations he had heard from other acts and performers, that the gig would be a good one and that they would be able to stay abroad for several months. Little did he know, but the £40 Butt had offered the Keatons in his letter was the bottom of the barrel. Joe knew he would be making less than his usual $250 a week, because £40 was only equal to $200, but he had no idea how much Butt had low-balled him from the outset – or he would never have accepted the offer. So, the Keatons purchased second-class tickets for $250 and left on the Norddeutscher Lloyd's S. S. *George Washington* out of New York Harbor on 1 July.[2] They arrived in Plymouth 8 July at 1.35 pm[3] and would have taken the boat train into town, landing at Paddington Station. Kelly met them there and gave them the name of a hotel to stay at, the de Provence Hotel at Leicester Square, which turned out to be a fleabag. After the Keatons had settled into their questionable digs, Joe called on the theatre the next morning: 'I found an elegant big theatre, standing alone and occupying an entire block. I saw nineteen acts billed, but no Keaton! Not even a photo out. The smallest salaried act on the program was billed, but not the Keatons.' Joe asked the stage manager if, in fact, the Keatons were on the bill: 'Are you ashamed to bill us?' Joe's orchestrater Fred Helf had sent him off to London with a fine set of scores to guarantee their act would go off smoothly, however, the Palace orchestra director, Mr. Fink, would have none of it. Joe then asked the stage manager for the props he needed: brooms, a chair, a pistol, a gong, but all he got was a complaint from the fellow: 'Why don't you carry your own props?'[4] Well, at least they had toted the infamous table all the way from New York. In addition, the condition of the stage itself would prove to be a barrier to the success of the act. It ran up a hill and was full of traps and splinters, which would have been torture for Buster to slide along. Their first night on the Palace stage was 12 July and they did appear on the bill in the paper, *The Daily Telegraph*. Here, in an ad for the Palace, the were listed as appearing at 8.45 pm, which was eighth on the bill, out of 15 acts. Walter Kelly was in a more prime spot at number thirteen.[5] Something Joe failed to complain about in his ad was the fact that the Keaton act was cut dramatically. Butt was quoted as saying that American comedy acts were too long and should be cut to 15 minutes only,[6] thus the huge number of acts on the bill. The Palace ad showed that the act after the Keatons, Merian's Dogs, began at 9.00 pm, thereby ascertaining the fact that this policy was in effect for them also.

Despite not having even one rehearsal on this stage, they had the audience laughing after the first minute. William Gould, writing for *Variety*, noted that after sauntering into the Palace on 12 July to see the Keatons opening:

> They went very well with the gallery; in fact, I never heard before the gallery so insistent for an encore. They applauded and hollered 'Encore!' for fully three minutes, but the stalls were quite 'reserved.' The reason for that was that Humpski and Bumski had been on two turns before the Keatons, doing fifteen minutes of Jimmy Rice's stuff. I predict that the Three Keatons will be a riot in the provinces or in any of the London halls, barring the Empire, Alhambra and Palace.[7]

Of course, not knowing or understanding what Jimmy Rice's stuff had to do with anything makes it impossible to understand most of this review, but it's clear that it had something to do with a heightened sensitivity on the part of those audience members 'in the stalls,' in regards to the violence of the Keaton act, not something that would ever worry an act in the States. Despite the abundance of applause they did get, however, the Keatons weren't permitted a bow, Butt vocalizing, "'It isn't on the level.'"

The second night, the Keatons were so early on the bill that there was no one in the audience to appreciate them. The morning after that, Joe was called into Butt's office and reprimanded for treating his own son so cruelly (in the act). Joe then purchased return tickets on the first boat sailing,[8] but they played out the week, as evidenced by one of Joe's rhymes in a *Variety* ad: 'In dear old London, it is a fine old Town./The PALACE, oh! the Palace, where the Keatons went to Clown./We opened on a Monday./On Saturday we shut./We certainly had a lively time,/Butt – Butt – Butt.'[9] To add insult to injury, the day before they sailed, 20 July, Joe's father, Joseph Z. Keaton of Perry, Oklahoma, died without his knowledge.[10] They left Southampton on the White Star Line's S. S. *Oceanic* at 9.45 am (tickets were less expensive at $200) and were back in New York 28 July.[11] Now, however, all that was left was to pick up the pieces, play the houses and for the audiences where they felt truly appreciated. In fact, they would be back playing the Keith's circuit for the fall season, beginning 23 August. In the meantime, they christened the new Muskegon house 'Jingles' Jungle' and did their best to assuage their abused feelings by fishing, playing pinochle, or baseball with their friends in the artists' colony.

On the road again for the fall season 23 August, the Keatons played Keith's Philadelphia, the Temple Theatre in Detroit, Bennett's in Hamilton, Ontario, Canada, Bennett's, Ottawa, and Bennett's, Montréal. The Keatons' act was still lasting 25 minutes and kept the Ottawa crowd 'doubled up with laughter.'[12] Just over the Canadian border, the Keatons played Shea's Theatre in Buffalo, New York beginning 27 September. The Keatons 'are back again, with four and even five in the family this time, and their act apparently pleased the audience. At any rate, it called forth vociferous applause.'[13] Beginning the first week of October, the Keatons were supposed to play Keith and Proctor's Fifth Avenue house, from which they had been banned for about two years, due to the child protection mandate against the Keaton children. This triumphal return had, in fact, been announced and expected since at least 15 May, when a piece appeared in *Variety*.[14] Of course, Joe had been announcing Buster's 16th birthday as taking place 4 October 1909, so the act was supposed to be celebrating with an engagement at this particular venue. Joe found out that his agent Eddie Keller had booked the gig knowing they would be first on the bill, overrode this agreement, and booked another week with Shea's, this time in Toronto. The week of 11 October, however, they were back at Keith's Theatre – in Boston, Massachusetts.

Then beginning 18 October, they played Oscar Hammerstein's Victoria Theatre, perhaps the most legendary venue in all of vaudeville and it came about for the Keatons by chance. When the Hammerstein's Theatre engagement became a reality, the 16th birthday ads returned in the trades. One of these appeared in the *Mirror* 16 October and it read in huge letters, '"The Funny Family" 3 Keatons Joe, Myra and Buster Hammerstein's Theatre GOOD-BYE MR. GERRY.'[15] The celebrations were back on. The Keatons were third on the bill and it was noted that Buster was now past the oversight of the Gerries:

> With his father and mother surrounding him, Buster captured the house instanter and scored a personal success upon his merits as performer and comedian. The manner of closing the act had a tendency to limit the applause, but in the earlier stages there were storms of laughter for the redoubtable Buster's bumps. The Three Keatons won all the way.[16]

All in all, this engagement superseded and exceeded anything they had planned for 4 October at the Fifth Avenue.

The week of 25 October, the Keatons proudly strolled back through the doors of Proctor's Theatre in Newark, New Jersey, then Keith's, Providence, Rhode Island. Joe reported in the *Clipper* that at Providence 'they were received with salvos of applause, and the act made one of the biggest hits of Joe Keaton's long stage career.'[17] Subsequent engagements included the Auditorium Theatre in Lynn, Massachusetts, Poli's Theatre in Wilkes-Barre, Pennsylvania, Poli's Theatre in Scranton, Pennsylvania, and Maryland Theatre in Baltimore, ending the month of November. The Keatons 'are about as novel a troupe as has been seen for some time in this city. Father and mother are good comedians, while their eldest shows that his head is hard and that he can stand many a knock. He takes his kicks and spankings with a stoicism that is generally absent in the youngster.'[18] The week of 6 December, the act was in Brooklyn, New York playing a new theatre for them, the Greenpoint, then, on 6 December, they were announced as being part of a group of entertainers beginning to rehearse a production of *Dick Whittington* produced by the Shuberts and staged by Frank Smithson. The first rehearsal took place at the Casino Theatre and the cast included Louise Dresser, Irene Dillon, Edward Favor, Alexander Clark, and Cook and Lorenz.[19] The show was an English pantomime with nine scenes that that ran from an Elizabethan London to a modern department store.[20] Joe indicated, in a piece for *Variety*, that as of middle December, he hadn't seen a contract yet: 'He began canceling his vaudeville time, but stopped it.'[21] In fact, the Keatons did not take part after all. So, then, after Brooklyn, the Keatons played the Bronx Theatre beginning 13 December. The Keatons, without the two youngest, 'were a big scream. Buster improves with every show, and the youngster will undoubtedly be a better comedian as a man than he is as a boy, which is saying something. But Joe Keaton isn't a bad little comedian himself, though he will have to work on a home trainer if Buster grows much more.'[22]

As Buster describes it, the act developed into a sort of ballet of domestic utensils, rather than simply the old routine of Joe throwing Buster around the stage. The broom was perhaps the most often used such utensil. The act might start with Joe on the stage, breaking into some well-known ditty, such as 'Maud Muller,' when Buster would enter and choose one of the 13 or 14 brooms placed on the set. A fight would ensue:

> Our most popular fighting routine was one in which I whaled away at him with a broom while he retaliated by skidding his hand off my forehead. We started with tiny taps exchanged in fun. These were followed by harder blows, then slams to which we gave out our all. In the middle of this fight the orchestra leader, reacting as though all this never happened before, got to his feet, tapped his baton, and had the orchestra start playing 'The Anvil Chorus,' to which we kept time by hitting one another.[23]

Meanwhile, Joe was using a lawyer, Denis F. O'Brien, to try to get his money back from the Vaudeville Investors' Company, the group that promoted real estate near Coney Island to be used as an actors' colony. Joe had invested $2,600, and he wasn't alone. O'Brien was also working for other artists, including Billie Burke, who had $3,000 invested. According to an article in *Variety*, the Vaudeville Comedy Club president Will M. Cressy used meetings to solicit investors, then dumped his own holdings before the slump. Things didn't look good for the others: 'A proposition lately made by Mr O'Brien for the clearing up of all entangled matters concerning his clients' relations with the Vaudeville Investors' Co. was rejected.'[24] Later, a follow-up article that appeared in *Variety* 5 February 1910 reported that O'Brien had finally succeeded in getting title to four lots from the Coney Island Boulevard and Realty Co. for *Myra Keaton*, not Joe.[25] What she then did with the property is not known. In any event, the Muskegon colony, with which Joe was more closely involved, proved to be the better investment.

Taking the week of 20 December off for Christmas, the Keatons had booked the week following in Proctor's Albany, however, one or more of the young children came down sick and Joe had to uncharacteristically cancel.[26] And so ended the busy, chaotic, and somewhat disconcerting year of 1909.

The year 1910 would prove to signal the eventual end (still seven years off) of what had been a long and successful vaudeville career. The concern of the London audience (the stalls) for Buster's rough treatment in the act back in summer 1909 led to some changes that week, which then continued back home in the States thereafter. Buster was growing up and as such, it was 1) difficult for an aging Joe Keaton to manipulate him as he had been doing, 2) Buster's voice was beginning to change, so his comic renditions of popular songs were often replaced by a re-invigoration of the celebrity impersonations. A couple of new bits were employed in the act, that allowed some acrobatic fun without all the rough housing. The theme for the act, called recently The Fun Family (The Phun Phamily) but also The Tumblebug Family, or just The Tumblebugs, was still that Buster had to be reprimanded, but this was carried out in a less rigorous way.

Joe started the year with a big Keaton ad in *Variety*, featuring the Knott pencil sketch of Buster in costume and a long poem about him. More and more, Buster had crept back into the limelight, after it had become apparent that he was the one with the most talent in the group, and his younger siblings were offering him no competition. With the Albany cancelation, Joe managed a booking in Yonkers to begin the year 3 January at the Warburton Theatre. Billed as 'The Tumble-bug Family' the Keatons encountered a blockade as soon as they started. Mislabeled 'Buster,' young Jingles was denied the ability to perform at the Warburton by Charles H. Warner, who informed Mayor Lennon of Yonkers of the fact: "'There is no objection to a child of that age speaking a piece on the stage, but in this case Buster is supposed to imitate his elders in their acrobatic feats, and that is contrary to the statute.'"[27] In their reduced form, one that would eventually become permanent, the Keatons, 'Joe and Buster – were easily the best laugh-makers of the evening; their act was of the rough-and-tumble variety, but Myra Keaton confined herself to playing good solos on a saxophone.'[28]

From Yonkers, the Keatons traveled to the Colonial Theatre in Norfolk, Virginia beginning 10 January. The local reviewer noted that 'The three Keatons really have developed into five Keatons. Buster is still there and he is a bigger scream than ever. The other two little tots will contribute their share.'[29] So, despite the continued problems with the child protection authorities in different places, the younger kids were still part of the act and would be the rest of the year, except for a few summer dates. The next week the Keatons played the Chase Theatre in Washington, D. C., then the Orpheum Theatre in Allentown, Pennsylvania, Keith and Proctor's Fifth Avenue Theatre, the Hudson Theatre in Union Hill, and the Orpheum Harrisburg starting 14 February. The Keatons had a bit of an incident before the week started in Harrisburg. The train they were traveling on was hit just as the Keatons (and others, of course) were arising from their berths for the day. The jolt was so strong that Buster acquired a contusion on his face and sprained his back; Joe had three teeth loosened.[30] The whole family showed up for their first appearance at the Orpheum on the first night, despite their injuries. 'Father is a Judge' was the song Buster offered that week: 'That father was a learned man we never had suspected/That he is full of knowledge of course the Democrats detected/They put him up for judge and strange to say he was elected/And he hasn't done a day's work since.'[31] One reviewer described his voice as 'also funny, rasping like a phonograph when the needle is not working well.'[32] This was certainly a strong indication that Buster's voice was changing and his future as a singer was limited. By 16 February, it was reported that there had been a run on the box office for almost every performance that week.[33]

The next engagement was at the Broadway Theatre in Camden, New Jersey, beginning 28 February, where the Keatons received the ravest of reviews:

> Such a warm reception as was accorded the Keaton family, Joe, Myra, Buster, Jingles and the cute little baby, was something good to witness, a most richly merited tribute to as popular and prolific a vaudeville troupe as has ever played in Camden, a team of five that furnishes one continuous rip-roaring ripple every tick of the watch during the twenty-five minutes the convulsively funny and strenuously slam-bang sketch, 'Twisted and Tangled' in being unraveled.

The comic antics of Jingles and Louise (stage name 'Joy') were also touted as a nice addition to the act, one that pointed to a rich future career in comedy for both.[34] Noteworthy is the new name applied to the Keatons' act, which was now 25 minutes long, as 'Twisted and Tangled.'

At the Alhambra Theatre in New York City, a review of Monday evening's performance noted that 'The dexterity or expertness with which Joe Keaton handles "Buster" is almost beyond belief of studied "business." The boy accomplishes everything attempted naturally, taking a dive into the backdrop that almost any comedy acrobat of more mature years could watch with profit.'[35] Then they played the Colonial Theatre with a nice review appearing in the *Clipper*: 'The Three Keatons held up the comedy end of the bill in capital style, and the diminutive Buster again demonstrated the fact that he is rapidly approaching the very front rank of comedy actors.'[36] This review is remarkable, considering a different review, this time in the *Mirror*, that revealed the Keatons were first on the bill:

> Three Keatons opened and in this hard position, they just about passed muster. Probably due to this fact, Buster did not seem to work with his accustomed exuberance and Joe was heard to make several remarks 'under his breath' which to the average 'professional' would lead one to think he was not tickled to death with life in general and his spot on the bill in particular.[37]

Perhaps the Keatons' predicament at the Colonial was ameliorated a bit by their engagement at Hammerstein's Victoria Theatre once again. The *Clipper*'s reviewer reported that 'The elder Keaton still retains his suppleness, while Buster Keaton, as the receiving end of the slambang comedy stunts, seems to thrive upon the hard work, and comes up smiling from falls that would leave dents in the anatomy of hardened performers.'[38] From New York, the act then traveled up to Keith's, Providence, Rhode Island, then took part in the Friar's Frolic Sunday 17 April at the New York Theatre. They then played the Star Theatre in Brooklyn. According to one review, Buster had returned to comic imitations, 'made more effective by comic side issues of his own.'[39] While in the vicinity, the Keaton family were the guests of honor at the Brooklyn Chapter of the Elks. Joe was given the 'stage' at one point, which allowed him to regale the audience with a complete history of his own stage career and then, of course, Buster's as well. The boy was described as 'full of fun and tricks, but fond of study when he is not speeding in his three-horsepower automobile that looks like a toy but has a speed of eighteen miles an hour.'[40] There can be no doubt that young Buster was welcoming various mechanical objects into his life in an increasing volume as his finances permitted.

The Keatons continued on in Brooklyn the week beginning 25 April but at the Gayety Theatre. Despite heavy rain that week, the Keatons helped to make it a big success, achieving 'a big hit with their clever tumbling and comedy work.'[41] At the Gayety Theatre in Pittsburgh, Pennsylvania, they were labeled 'The Three Tumble Bugs' and considered a special added attraction, then played the Star and Garter Theatre in Chicago, Illinois, their first engagement in Chicago in seven years (except for a brief stint at the Cleveland Theatre). With a few weeks to go before their Muskegon vacation, the Keatons were in the olio that was part of the Golden Crook Extravaganza Company, described as 'a good beauty show,'[42] then played Lakeside Casino at Summit Beach in Akron, and finally Meyers Lakeside Casino in Canton, Ohio. Complaining in a joking way about 'dry' Canton, Ohio, Joe achieved a small note in the paper entitled 'Joe Keaton Was Dry,' announcing his long summer break:

> Dear Sam – I spent Sunday in a little Ohio town that was so dry there were bullfrogs three years old that hadn't learned to swim yet. I play Myers [sic] Lake, Canton, Ohio, week of May 20 [actually the 29] and then take some earthworms and grubs and beat it for Muskegon, Michigan. All well. Three Keatons.[43]

Home to Muskegon, Michigan, beginning 6 June, where. Joe would spend his time fishing, drinking, and telling stories; Myra would play her favorite card games, especially pinochle. The fall vaudeville season began for Hammerstein's Victoria Theatre *and* the Three Keatons the week beginning 5 September. The 'always welcome Keaton family' performed their usual knockabout act, 'which is in a class by itself as a sure laugh producer.'[44] From there, they played the Grand Theatre in Syracuse, the Trent Theatre in Trenton, then turned south as the weather became cooler, playing the Forsyth Theatre in Atlanta, where Buster encountered Enigmarelle again – described as 'an electrical wonder, able to walk and write and ride a bicycle.'[45] From Atlanta, it was on to the Orpheum in Nashville, Tennessee, where the Keatons [here Keatings] received a lengthy and complimentary review in the local press:

They were a symphony in crashes, combined with a melody in smashes and a general threnody in roughhouse, hurly burly all the way. Father, mother, and son opened the terrific hand to hand conflict, only to be followed by another pair that completed the full house, good enough to beat the average pat hand any day in the week. [. . .] The two little Keatings who broke in upon the scenery captured the house, but it looked as if they might just as well be in bed asleep. Father and son Keating, who held the spotlight longest, drew an ovation, the boy especially being a very fine feature.[46]

This description of the act and the role of Jingles suggests he was still playing a negligible role.

Back at the Gayety Theatre in Brooklyn, the week beginning 24 October, the Keatons then played the Star Theatre, also in Brooklyn, where they were an added attraction, followed by a week at the Gayety Theatre in Pittsburgh. The Keatons were deemed the hit of the show, with the remark that 'the father throws his children around like so many bags of chaff, and they seem to like it. The audience couldn't stop laughing and encoring for a long time.'[47] An additional element was that election results were read from the stage. Then, it was down to southwestern Ohio to the Queen City, Cincinnati, to play at the Columbia Theatre beginning 14 November. Thanksgiving week, they played Poli's Theatre, Hartford, where the Keatons introduced 'a few new stunts of horseplay that are just as funny as any of their old stuff. The appearance of the smaller members of the family is responsible for much of the laughter that is accorded the act.'[48] Engagements the rest of the year included (in order) Poli's, Worcester, Hathaway's, Lowell, where their knockabout work was such that it kept the audience 'wondering if one of them will be killed,'[49] Hathaway's, New Bedford, Massachusetts, and Poli's, Bridgeport, Connecticut, where Thursday night was a special event for the newsboys (those working for the *Bridgeport Evening Farmer* and the *New York Evening Journal*).[50] Midweek, Poli's manager, L. D. Garvey, was starting to advertise the Saturday matinée and the fact that Santa Claus would visit. So, naturally, the youngest Keaton children received more ink than usual: 'Jingles and Louise are but knee high to a grasshopper, but they can sing, dance and tumble about and they are a big scream.'[51] With Christmas day falling on a Sunday this year, the Keatons were able to enjoy it without working two shows. The final week of the year they played Poli's, Scranton.

As the year 1911 progressed, the familiarity of the Keaton knockabout act continued to result in a little less popularity of it now and then – a decrease that can be measured by the journalistic coverage of the vaudeville theatres and the placement and size of the Keaton name in theatre ads. Noticeable this year, and really, most of last year, is the fact that the Keatons are named far down on the list of performers in newspaper descriptions. Joe has either economized or become bored with publishing witty ads in the industry mags. His ads in *The Clipper* vanished several years prior and those in *Variety* and the *Mirror* became non-existent in 1910 (except for four ads he posted in one month only – April). Also this year, both younger children began to disappear from the act entirely, starting with the summer months. Also the Keatons' marketability grew less over the course of the year, and due to these and other changes, Joe swapped hard liquor for his daily imbibements of beer, with negative results.

From Scranton, they traveled to Poli's, Wilkes-Barre to begin the new year, beginning 2 January. The Keatons 'gave their ever new stunt in which Buster is hauled and mauled and thrown about the stage. Several new stunts were introduced and the younger children furnish considerable comedy.'[52] The act's next few engagements included Proctor's Park Place Theatre in Newark, New Jersey, Poli's in New Haven, Connecticut, and then, Poli's, Springfield, Massachusetts. The last week of the month, they played the Empire Theatre in Pittsfield, Massachusetts, then were back touring the Shea's houses in February including Buffalo and Toronto, then the Temple theatre in Hamilton, Ontario and the Dominion Theatre, Ottawa, where the bill included Braham's Educated Flea Circus, that had been trained to drive and draw cabs and ride bicycles.[53] The next week, starting 6 March, the act was in Montréal playing the Orpheum Theatre, then returned to the New York area, playing the Majestic Theatre Paterson, where a critic offered that, 'the entire stage is covered with the tumblers, in which the youngsters enter quite as heartily as their elders.'[54] They 'keep the audience bubbling over with good nature and shaking with laughter.'[55] Back at Hammerstein's Victoria Theatre beginning 20 March, the act then followed this week with several engagements at Keith's Theatres, including Keith's, Philadelphia, with George M. Young noting that

> the bill played through to a much better average than promised from its appearance on paper. A lot of this was due to what the Keatons did in the third position. They put over the biggest laughing hit heard in Keith's in a very long period – and that's

doing something with the Monday audiences here. It was a sure clean-up – what Will Rogers would call a 'humdinger,' for the Muskegon fisherman and his brood. 'Buster' has developed into about the funniest knockabout tumbler that vaudeville can boast of and 'Papa' has worked in almost enough new tricks to make a new act of the old one.[56]

Keith's, Boston, where they were billed as "Buster" Keaton and Company, followed.[57]

After playing the Alhambra Theatre in New York during their sixth anniversary week, the Keatons played the Broadway Theatre, Camden, New Jersey during Easter week, where they headlined for a change. A photo of Jingles even highlighted the initial description of the bill in the newspaper. Calling themselves 'The Tumblebug Fun Family' on this bill, the Keatons were noted to have recently recovered from the whooping cough, but still received 'a great hand.'[58] About this time, Sime noted in a review of Keller Mack and Frank Orth's sketch 'The Wrong One,' that Buster had sung one of the pair's tunes during this engagement, a song entitled 'O'Hara,' suggesting that he was still singing in the act, despite his changing voice.[59]

The act's next two engagements were at the Colonial Theatre again, and the New Brighton Beach Theatre in New Jersey. One critic noted Buster's eyes for what might be the first time in a review: 'young Buster has a pair of eyes that fairly talk, and he is as bright and nimble as a squirrel. Pop Keaton and Buster kept the house in an uproar, and it did seem frequently as if an ambulance would have to be called to pick up the dislocated joints of the pair as they tumbled and fell about the stage. It was a good exposition of how to bring up a son.'[60] On 31 May, Joe and Myra Keaton celebrated 17 years of marriage, for which Joe gave Myra a diamond solitaire, six years after he had given her a wedding band for their eleventh. Joe had only had $4 on their wedding day, two of which went to the parson.[61] Indeed, their fortunes had changed.

The week of 5 June was the opening week of Hammerstein's Rooftop and the Keatons were on the bill. The rooftop consisted of an area atop both the Victoria and Republic theatres referred to as 'The Farm,' which this year was decked out as a suffragette refuge, with 'Votes for Women' advocates as laborers. Women could be seen 'working' as blacksmiths, sheep-shearers and other types of labor during the intermissions.[62] On Monday night, 'the Keatons, judging by the hearty laughter which greeted the comedy acrobatic work of "father" and "Buster," could rightly claim every auditor as a personal friend, and Mrs Keaton, in a natty male costume, rendered her saxophone solo finely.'[63] With this engagement satisfied, the Keatons headed home to Muskegon for the summer, performing one or two times at venues near home, such as the Temple Theatre in Detroit. Here Buster was described as contributing much to the family act, 'with his tumbling, his boyish voice, which is just changing, and his bubbling humor.'[64] Another report ascertained that the act consisted only of 'father, mother and son,' thereby supporting the belief that the younger Keatons were not part of the act this summer.[65]

The first engagement of the new season for the Three Keatons began 27 August at the Orpheum Theatre in Brooklyn, New York. According to Buster's datebook, which he began keeping in 1909, the Keatons had an engagement at Keith's Theatre in Portland, Maine beginning 18 September,[66] followed by a week at Keith's, Boston, Massachusetts, where the Keatons met up with their old friends Harry and Bess Houdini.[67] From Boston, the Keatons traveled back to New York again to play Hammerstein's Victoria Theatre, where one critic reported that 'Joe and Buster Keaton bumped and thumped over the boards, while Myra Keaton inserted a saxophone solo, registering a success that at the finish called for a half-dozen bows.'[68] The following week, beginning 9 October, the Keatons played Poli's, Hartford, where the two younger Keatons now appeared before the ending of the turn once again: 'There are a couple of the younger members of the family who show themselves before the act is over and they run the older ones a close race in the way of producing merriment.'[69] They continued at various Poli's houses the next few weeks, including New Haven, Springfield, Massachusetts and Worcester, Massachusetts, but ended up at their favorite place, Hammerstein's, Victoria again. Three professional baseball players tossing a ball around appeared to be the main attraction, featuring Chief Bender, Jack Coombs, and Cy Morgan. The Keatons 'mauled and hauled each other around the stage with the usual laughing results.'[70]

Bridgeport, Connecticut's Poli's Theatre was the site of the next Keaton venue for the week beginning 6 November. One reviewer noted that Buster was now wearing a strap across his back that facilitated his father's throwing him around the stage – given his larger size[71] (Joe had actually implemented this in 1900). The younger Keatons were present and labeled by one writer 'The Busterettes.'[72] The week of 13 November, the Keatons played Proctor's Theatre, Newark, but received press only the week after in a column entitled 'Gossip of Theatrical Affairs.' They hadn't had a long biographical piece written about them for a while and this one seemed to regurgitate the old stories, including about Buster's first moment on stage and his assuming different ages depending on his audience.

Back at Hammerstein's Victoria Theatre the next two weeks, and the Orpheum Theatre in Brooklyn the week following, Buster is analyzed as a person by one writer:

> 'Buster' Keaton or Master Joseph F. Keaton, Jr., as he is known in his own personality, is not the clown in real life that he appears to be on the stage. [. . .] He has a brisk, businesslike personality that indicates that he is confident to take care of himself and endure the hard knocks of life as imperturbably as he endures the (apparent) hard knocks to which he is subjected by his father in their knockabout act.[73]

After playing The Colonial Theatre and the Alhambra again in December, Joe published one line in *Variety* 23 December: 'I'll go on the wagon – maybe. Joe Keaton.'[74] It seems to indicate, albeit jokingly, what had started to become a real problem: Joe's drinking. At some point in recent history, Joe had traded a beer addiction for a hard liquor addiction and the results would become more and more dire as time went on, leading to the eventual end of the Keaton act and of the Keaton marriage. At this point in late 1911, it was just beginning to rear its ugly head.

Finally, Christmas week was spent both in Wilkes-Barre and New York City.[75] In New York, the Vaudeville Comedy Club hosted several 'laugh' nights for the holidays, with Joe taking part at least once. Notably Joseph M. Schenck was listed as part of the Board of Control for the organization.[76] Buster was not a member yet, but with Joe an active one, it would not be surprising if one or both of them knew Schenck, well before he would enter Buster's life in a big way in 1917.

Between this moment in December 1911 and the end of the Keaton act in early 1917, the degradation of the Keatons' life on the road, as knockabout stars and as a family is not an unfamiliar story. The year 1912 started in Wilkes-Barre at Poli's with a negative review: 'Their act is the same as

Frank, Burt, Lizzie and Myra
Cutler, circa 1880s.

Frank Luke Cutler
wearing a familiar-
looking hat, circa
1880s.

Above: Joe, Myra and Buster Keaton in costume, April 1901. First family photo featured in *New York Dramatic Mirror*. (Courtesy of the Museum of Modern Art, New York)

Left: Joe, Myra and Buster Keaton in costume, circa 1901. (Courtesy of the Museum of Modern Art, New York)

Joe, Myra, and Buster Keaton in costume with the table, circa 1901. (Courtesy of the Museum of Modern Art, New York)

Joe, Myra and Buster Keaton *New York Dramatic Mirror* ad, 20 December 1902.

BUSTER KEATON.

BUSTER KEATON.

Above: Buster Keaton in Irish costume, four views, circa 1903, Feinberg studios. (Courtesy of the Museum of Modern Art, New York)

THE KEATONS.

Left: Joe, Buster, Myra and Harry 'Jingles' Keaton, Christmas 1904.

Above: Buster and Harry 'Jingles' Keaton, two views, circa 1905. (Courtesy of the Museum of Modern Art, New York)

Right: Buster Keaton as Little Lord Fauntleroy, Fenton Stock Company, 1906. (Courtesy of the Museum of Modern Art, New York)

Cartoon of the Keaton Family that appeared in the 19 August 1907 edition of the *Dispatch [Moline, Illinois]* in advertisement for their appearance at the Moline Theatre.

Buster Keaton with the all-important broom, circa 1917. (Courtesy of Robert Arkus)

Right: Comique Films ad, circa 1917.

Below: *The Butcher Boy*, Buster's first film. Al St. John holding his leg up, Arthur Earle holding the girl, Josephine Stevens, Roscoe Arbuckle near the pitchfork tines, Buster far right.

Left: *Rough House* ad, 1917.

Below: Scene from *His Wedding Night,* left to right, Alice Mann, Roscoe Arbuckle, Arthur Earle, Buster, unknown, Al St. John, 1917. (George Pratt Collection, George Eastman Museum, Rochester, New York)

Scene from *His Wedding Night*, Roscoe Arbuckle, far left, Al St. John driving car, Buster on the roof, 1917. (George Pratt Collection, George Eastman Museum, Rochester, New York)

Scene from 'Oh, Doctor!' Buster on left, Roscoe Arbuckle on right, 1917.

WITHIN THE LAW; OH DOCTOR.!

Above: Lobby card from 'Oh, Doctor!' Left to right, unknown, Al St. John, Alice Lake, Roscoe Arbuckle, Buster, Alice Mann, unknown, 1917. (Courtesy of Robert Arkus)

Left: Publicity photo from *Coney Island*, left to right Alice Lake, Roscoe Arbuckle, Buster, 1917. (Courtesy of the Museum of Modern Art, New York)

Above: Scene from *A Country Hero*, left to right (front row), Al St. John, Roscoe Arbuckle, Buster, 1917.

Right: Scene from *Out West*, Roscoe Arbuckle third from left, Buster sitting on the bar, 1918. (George Pratt Collection, George Eastman Museum, Rochester, New York)

Scene from *Out West*, Roscoe Arbuckle with hands raised behind the bar on the right, Buster directly to his left, 1918. (George Pratt Collection, George Eastman Museum, Rochester, New York)

Scene from *The Bell Boy*, left to right, Roscoe Arbuckle, Buster, Alice Lake, 1918. (Courtesy Museum of Modern Art, New York)

Lobby card from *Moonshine*, left to right, Alice Lake, Buster (on roof), Al St. John, Roscoe Arbuckle, 1918.

Scene from *Good Night, Nurse!* Left to right, Buster, Roscoe Arbuckle, Kate Price, Alice Lake, 1918. (Courtesy Robert Arkus)

Lobby card from *The Cook*, left to right, Al St. John, Roscoe Arbuckle, Buster, Alice Lake, John Rand, 1918. (Courtesy Robert Arkus)

Scene from *Back Stage*, left to right, Molly Malone, Roscoe Arbuckle, Buster (in drag), Al St. John, 1919. (Courtesy Robert Arkus)

Scene from *The Hayseed*, left to right Roscoe Arbuckle, Molly Malone, Buster, 1919. (Courtesy Robert Arkus)

Scene from *The Garage*, left to right, Dan Crimmins, Roscoe Arbuckle, Buster, Molly Malone, 1920.

Lobby card from *The Saphead*, left to right, William H. Crane, Beulah Booker, Buster, 1920.

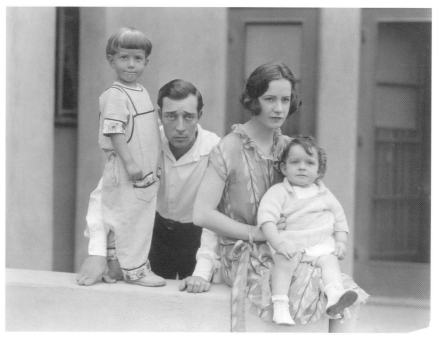

The Four Keatons circa 1920s, left to right, Jimmy, Buster, Natalie (Talmadge), Bobby. (Courtesy the Museum of Modern Art, New York)

ever. It is tedious in parts, horseplay throughout, yet so ridiculous that it wins favor with the audience. If it were cut in half, it would be more satisfactory.'[77] Perhaps this heralded the challenges to come. In addition to the houses they had been playing the past two to three years, the Keatons were being scheduled at all new venues for them, including places like the Savoy in Atlantic City, New Jersey, the Bushwick in Brooklyn, and the National in Boston, all venues on the Keith's circuit but a bit lower down the scale. At the Savoy the end of February and into March, the Keatons shared the bill with Lou Anger, who would figure large in Buster's life in about five years. He performed as a German soldier (just two years before the onset of World War I): '[He] discusses various topics current among the army and other spheres of life in a persona monologue, which has a rich flavour of comedy mingled among its tales of daily troubles.'[78] Other venues this year included the Bijou in Philadelphia (where they were first on the bill), the Savoy in Fall River, Massachusetts, then summer in Muskegon beginning in May. Joe's brother Jesse (Bert) married Catherine Hurley 29 June in Perry, Oklahoma in a private ceremony, then caught the train to Muskegon to spend their honeymoon near his brother and family.[79]

After a lovely summer, they began playing first Hammerstein's, Victoria, then the New York City Keith and Proctor's houses to start the fall season, including the Fifth Avenue. Other venues included Keith's, Indianapolis, Keith's, Cincinnati (the two youngest Keatons still mentioned as performing), the Columbia, St. Louis, the Orpheum, Brooklyn, the Colonial and Alhambra, New York City, Poli's, Hartford, Connecticut, where it was noted that the Keaton act had changed considerably since their last appearance,[80] and finally, the Savoy in Atlantic City again, where they were heartily welcomed: 'If there is any combination that can think up more ludicrous things to do, beat the Keatons in cleverness and cause more merriment, it is yet to be heard from.'[81]

Having completed the year, the Keatons barely grabbed a few lines of text here and there, having to go on first or maybe third, instead of sixth or seventh, and moving into the new year hoping to continue at least that much. The Keith-Orpheum circuit, under the management of Joe Keaton nemesis Martin Beck, was the circuit to be on, because it guaranteed sometimes 40-plus weeks of engagements, but dealing with the humiliation of being the curtain-raiser had to be starting to irritate Joe, more than a little bit.

In 1913, the Keatons played a lot of familiar venues. At Poli's, Bridgeport, Connecticut, one writer remarked that '"Buster" Keaton, the young man who has been the recipient of some 15 million jumps in his short stage career, is still being thrown about carelesslike by his dad,'[82] and at Poli's, Wilkes-Barre, the two youngest Keatons are still being mentioned as part of the act. At the Bushwick in Brooklyn 10 February, Joe Keaton was rumored to have had a tiff with entertainer Joe Boganny: 'Mr. Boganny said Mr. Keaton had gotten Buster's coat with the holding strap in England [meaning he had stolen it from Boganny]. Then Keaton broke loose.'[83] Boganny responded with a letter also published in *Variety* trying to set the record straight, stating that no riff occurred, that he may have said the theft occurred in Europe, but it may have occurred in the States, and that there were no fisticuffs involved: 'I also met Mr. Keaton in a saloon outside the stage door one day whilst I was having a glass of beer there, and there was none of that boisterous stuff anywhere.'[84] Joe's response, printed in the 7 March edition, branded Joe Boganny a true stealer of other people's 'business,' George Rena's 'misfit army' comedy, Joe Jackson's bows, Todd Judge's comedy, Burt Melrose's fall and

> Buster Keaton's coat with the handle on the back. And I did crack him at the Bushwick theatre, Brooklyn, and the only reason I didn't soak him in the barroom was because he disguised himself and I didn't know him. [. . .] P. S. The coat with the handle on the back belongs to me since 1900, at Tony Pastor's.[85]

Following hard upon this was the organization of the *Clipper* Registry Bureau, designed to provide a means of 'copyrighting' gags, tricks, dances, and other innovative performance. Joe had registered a 'comedy trick' sometime 25 February to 3 March,[86] perhaps moved to do so by his current tirade. But, strangely enough, two things happened following this episode. Already the first week of May, Joe had joined with Joe Jackson (also named in the tirade as a victim of theft), Bert Melrose and, yes, Joe Boganny, in an act called 'Joe Boganny's Lunatic Bakers,' that played the Majestic in Chicago and was noted as putting 'some real life in the bill. The act is full of fire and always on the jump. They were a big hit.'[87] Later that summer, Buster and one of his neighbors, Edward Gray, formed a sham vaudeville act for the Elks Club benefit named 'Butt and Bogany,'[88] lunatic jugglers, the name obviously based on Joe's two nemeses, as well as the name of Boganny's act. Vaudeville certainly makes strange bedfellows, so to speak.

That spring, they had played the Union Square Theatre in New York City, where it was evident from the ad in the newspaper that their act had been cut five minutes, then Keith's Bronx Theatre, and moved up to the Orpheum, Montréal, where 'the chief characteristics of the turn by the Three Keatons [. . .] were noise and dust.'[89] Summer in Muskegon began in April this year, with a notable episode involving 'The Dixie Pirate,' a watercraft that took part in the water carnival on the lake mid-August causing a stir. Its operators were Lew Earl assisted by Joe and Len Potter, and its claim to fame was orienteering across the lake without a compass.[90]

The new season was spent performing pretty much the old venues, such as the Colonial, Alhambra and Orpheum in New York, the Orpheum in Brooklyn, Keith's, Boston and Washington, D. C., Hammerstein's, Victoria and Union Square back in New York, the Grand Pittsburgh, the Colonial in Portsmouth, Virginia, the Forsyth in Atlanta, the Colonial in Norfolk and the Lyric in Richmond Virginia for Thanksgiving week and the Temple Theatre in Detroit for Christmas week. Most reviews mentioned that Buster had become a man, and several that the Keatons were doing the same old thing, but just as many called them 'the laughing hit of the bill.'[91] The act had become familiar but was still garnering enough good laughs and amusement to keep them popular, no matter where they fell in the lineup: 'The Three Keatons tumble about on the stage indiscriminately intermingled with brooms, tables and chairs.'[92]

The new year 1914 found the Keatons playing the National in Boston. This same year, Charlie Chaplin would make his film debut in *Kid Auto Races in Venice* for Keystone, the first Chaplin film to be released (7 February) and the first to feature the Little Tramp persona. Roscoe Arbuckle also worked at Keystone and was in some ways the Grand Old Man of the studio, having started there in 1913. Buster had grown up, but he hadn't yet given into his ambitions. Despite the difficulties of performing the same strenuous act with his father aging and his having grown in height and weight, it continued in pretty much the same vein week after week and day after day. The two youngest were no longer in the act, a decision finally having been made to send both Harry and Louise to boarding school, Harry to Barbour Hall Junior Military and Louise to Ursuline Academy. The focus for the Keatons had turned to Muskegon, a place they now spent the summers and more, truly their first and only real home.

And so, they continued on the Keith circuit in many of the same locations and venues. Remarkable this year was a note that the Keatons had played their 29th week in five years at Hammerstein's Victoria,[93] At the Fifth Avenue Theatre, another venue they had played at least once a year and probably more, the Keatons' act was described at this point with great affection: 'Joe Keaton continued attempting to make the rather larger Buster behave, but Buster slips "Pop" a few of the medicines he's been brought up on, and with Myra, why, they just swept things clean for satisfaction.'[94]

In Knoxville, Tennessee at the Bijou, the Keatons were still very much appreciated, as they were at many venues, new and old: 'Their rough and tumble comedy was quite amusing and Mrs. Keaton rendered a much-enjoyed saxophone solo, with orchestral accompaniment.'[95] At the Palace in Chicago, a location they hadn't visited for several years (except for Joe with Joe Boganny), the act received more ink than it had in some time. One critic noted 'The Three Keatons are the gem of the show. There is neither rhyme or reason in their extravagant comedy, but among entertainers pure and simple, they are the sort of 'artists' that defy any scientific explanation, who follow no method except for that of being unutterably funny.'[96] Then Percy Hammond, noted journalist and theatre critic for the *Chicago Tribune*, wrote,

> Equipped with many implements of violence, they assault and batter each other gravely for an hour, indulging meantime in all the acrobatic 'falls' known to variety. They apotheosize the slapstick and exalt the inflated bladder, because they are genuine clowns and there is more comedy in 'Buster' Keaton's quaint stares than there is in a hundred 'sketches' of the kind that infest the vaudeville theatres every week.[97]

The Keaton act was a familiar one, yes, but somewhere along the line, it had become true art, but could it maintain that status and for how long?

In April, the act traveled to Kentucky and played the Ben Ali in Lexington, the Keith's in Louisville and the Grand Opera House in Paris, all new venues, except that the Keatons and one other act, Paul LaCroix and Company, failed to perform in Paris: 'At the last minute the "Three Keatons" refused to work, as they claimed their contract called for a performance at the Ben Ali only.' Colonial Amusement Co.'s apology in the paper to the citizens of Paris offered that it would have canceled the show and refunded their money had the cancelation come earlier, and would get a written guarantee of the acts to perform the next time the Keith's acts came to town.[98] After another summer in Muskegon, the fall season found the Keatons still on the Keith circuit, but in some new venues, such as the Prospect Theatre in Brooklyn, the Majestic in Cedar, Rapids, Iowa, the Empress in Decatur, Illinois, the Orpheum, Montréal, the Dominion in Ottawa, and the Majestic in Waterloo,

Iowa. At the Prospect in Brooklyn, a writer offered that 'Buster Keaton and Papa Joe now look alike as peas, the former having grown so that if he keeps on he will be head and shoulders above his dad in another year. The Keatons are working closely along their former lines with a few new ways of doing some of their "bits." They were a laughing hit.'[99] Then Christmas week, back at Hammerstein's, Buster was trying something new, a bit part in someone else's endeavor, namely 'Sully's Cabaret Barber Shop,' called 'an ad lib concoction.' The story involved a particular barber shop patronized mostly by actors, managers, booking agents and the like. Sully thinks he is an actor. A theatre is offering him a chance to find out whether or not he is any good and 'every performance different stars will introduce specialties.' Buster played 'a fresh customer,' who wanted a haircut with his hat on.[100] Joe was also in the cast. This turn was put on in addition to each performer's regular act and played 14 performances in all. A cast photo appeared in the 1 January 1915 edition of *Variety*, with Buster sitting in the front row.

The first week of 1915, it was announced that Buster and Joe were to be part of the new Winter Garden Theatre revue, to replace 'Dancing Around.' The Shuberts (owners of the Winter Garden) wanted to start calling Buster Joe Keaton, Jr., but it's not certain how long this inclination lasted. Others in the 'show' included Joe Jackson and W. C. Fields.[101] In Harrisburg, Pennsylvania mid-January, the Keatons found their name in the headlines for the Orpheum and received a lengthy piece alongside it, a nice change and way to begin the year.[102] In February at the New Palace Theatre in Fort Wayne, Indiana, the reviewer offered an accurate assessment of the changes that had come to the Keaton act by this point:

> A few years ago, Daddy Keaton could throw Buster around livelier than a political candidate can throw the bull, but Buster failed to run true to his mother's belief and grew up just like any other boy. As a result, his father cannot heave him across the stage in the hilariously funny manner he used to, but that doesn't mean that the Three Keatons are not as funny as ever they were. Buster's increase in bulk has not been his only gain. He has grown considerable gray matter under his hair and thinks of new stunts, trick novelties, etc., to include in the performance just as well as his father ever could. As a result, no two performances by this combination ever are alike, and that's what worries Father Keaton trying to keep Buster outguessed.[103]

In March, after playing the Orpheum in Madison, Wisconsin and the Columbia Theatre in St. Louis, the Keatons went to Muskegon for the month of April, so that Myra could have an operation.[104] In May, all three Keatons played the Palace in Chicago, where the critic noticed that Buster, 'a youth with the features of a poet whose violent and casual antics give the lie to every lineament of his soulful physiognomy,' was 'the most important and turbulent of the Three Keatons.'[105]

Back in Muskegon, Joe's 48th birthday 6 July was celebrated with a shebang. Three hundred vaudeville actors joined in a parade, with the birthday boy and Myra seated at the head on top of Minnie, one of Gruber's elephants. The parade was followed by the Actor's Colony picnic at Bay Mills, with decorations and music by a brass band.[106] They returned to life on the Keith circuit that fall, but little did they know that their days with that organization were numbered. Perhaps Buster's accident 14 October at the Majestic Theatre in Chicago was a sort of harbinger of bad luck to come. Buster had run a nail into his foot after the matinée, and tried to perform in the evening show, but 'became so weak he had to be removed to the hotel in a taxi. Fever developed and the remainder of the Chicago week was canceled. Buster was sufficiently improved to accompany the act to Milwaukee.'[107] Besides Milwaukee, they also played Memphis, Tennessee, New Orleans, Louisiana, and the Forsyth in Atlanta during Thanksgiving week, where they were touted as presenting 'the season's swiftest, most surprising comedy stunt, which apparently was irresistible. The audience laughed and yelled and screamed at the antics any attempt to describe would be pitiful.'[108]

The dawning of the year 1916 would bring stark change to the Keaton family and to the Keaton act. They would soon be ending their last full season in vaudeville on the Keith circuit. Venues during the second half of the 1915–1916 season included Youngstown, Ohio's Hippodrome, the Keith's Theatres in Louisville and Dayton, Ohio, where the critic was nonplussed by the Keatons' act, which he found a 'slow-going, pouncing-pounding-punching act. Perhaps [others] could even feel the harmonious and beautiful fun in it. But this writer is less fortunate, or perhaps less artistically appreciative.'[109] In April, they played the Royal in New York and eventually ended up at the Palace in the same city, where the drama was to take place. Somehow, Joe and Martin Beck had tolerated each other over the last few years that the Keatons had played the Keith circuit religiously. That was to end the night of 24 April. For the matinée, the act was scheduled third on the bill, but by evening, with Beck having been backstage brooding around all day, they were moved to the curtain-raising act, when most attendees are milling around trying to find their seats. This is a position on the bill Joe had tolerated now and then over the years, but by this point in their career, he couldn't let it slide. Being third on the bill had already placed the Keaton name low in the ads in very small print and caused them to receive little if any ink in the newspapers. Being placed in first position was the last straw. A critic from *Variety* was in house that day and described that

> the Palace programme was thoroughly shaken up between the Monday shows, and, barring a slight stage wait during the first section, the change developed the entertaining possibilities and apparently strengthened the programme in its running form, for as it played Monday night everything on hand looked at its very best. The shakeup brought Helen Ware and Elinor and Williams up with the early entries and replaced them in the second period with Beatrice Hartford and Pilcer and Douglas. The opening was entrusted to the care of the Three Keatons Monday night, the acro-comics giving the second spot to the Royal Poinciana Sextet. [. . .] The Keatons were popular favorites with the few present at the early hour, [but] the real value is lost, however, in such an early position, and a spot lower down would have doubly benefited the act and the show.[110]

With this humiliation ended the Three Keatons' relationship with Martin Beck and the Keith circuit. On 13 May, they would open on the Loew's circuit[111] at the American Roof in New York City, where they headlined and were welcomed with a reception,[112] but even this relationship wouldn't last long. The act worked the Loew's circuit until they took a break to go to Muskegon in July. They had worked uncharacteristically through May and June in venues such as the Bijou in Brooklyn, the Lyric in Buffalo, where they found their name highlighted in the papers, the Orpheum in Detroit, where their act was described as 'a mélange wherein clever tumbling, music, comedy and strange contraptions figure.'[113] They headlined throughout these engagements. On 1 June, Buster and Joe took part in an evening of the entertainers entertaining the entertainers down the street in Buffalo at Shea's, recently a frequently played venue.[114] Detroit was the last engagement of the season, so the Keatons made their way to Muskegon with all speed.

A December 1915 article noted that the Keatons were usually spending a full three months a year at their house in Muskegon[115] and indeed it was becoming a hotbed of activity for more than just them. The Muskegon Club House was dedicated by the mayor, chief of police, and a couple of aldermen on 9 August. Joe had donated the land and Myra was voted president of the Woman's Auxiliary. The clubhouse was to be called the T-C-Y-C (Theatrical Colony Yacht Club) and was a 'bungalowish-yacht clubhouse [. . .] built by members.'[116] But as peaceful and energizing as their time in Muskegon was, Joe faced the new vaudeville season with trepidation. He had to sign with the dreaded Pantages circuit, which would take the act to venues far north and west, limit it to 15 minutes, and demand that they perform three times a day. The Pantages was the bottom of the barrel in terms of vaudeville contracts, so it can be argued that the days when Joe was thinking big and signed with K & E to be part of 'Advanced Vaudeville' were long and forever over. Joe was now 49, Myra 39 and Buster almost voting age (21). How much longer could they continue given these conditions?

It has to be said that the Three Keatons' reviews never became totally negative, and, in fact, were largely positive all the way to the end.[117] On the Pantages, they played Calgary, Edmonton, Victoria, Vancouver and Winnepeg in Canada, Great Falls, Missoula and Butte, Montana, Spokane and Tacoma, Washington, Portland, Oregon and Oakland and San Francisco in California. By the time they played Christmas week in Oakland, although nerves were frazzled and bodies tired, no one really knew that their vaudeville tenure would end the first month into the new year.

Chapter 7

Comique Films and Roscoe Arbuckle
Film's Initial Attractions

■■■■■■■■■■■■■■■■■■■■■■■■■■■■■■

The year 1917 dawned with the Keatons playing their final performances as a family on the Pantages Circuit. It's doubtful that any one of the three of them really understood that they were experiencing their last month (week, really) of performing in vaudeville together this year. The first week of the year, beginning right on 1 January, the were playing the Pantages Theatre in Oakland, California.[1] The Keatons were now calling themselves 'Fun's Funniest Family.' Then the week of 8 January, they had an engagement at the Pantages Theatre in Los Angeles.[2] Unfortunately, it was reported that illness kept them from appearing the first night of the week,[3] but, the fact was that Buster and Myra had left Joe high and dry. After Los Angeles, they were due to play Salt Lake, City Utah (and then Odgen, Utah) and the newspapers were already heralding their imminent arrival, so, clearly, no one knew that the breakup was about to occur. The industry rags were strangely silent on this development, until one short piece was published in the 21 February edition of the *Clipper*, which suggested that Joe was trying desperately to get the group back together: 'Joe Keaton, of the Five Keatons, has returned from a tour over the Pantages Circuit to persuade his family, consisting of his wife, two daughters and a son, to join him again. The Five Keatons were together for twenty-two years.'[4] First, it's odd that Joe would have this printed in the *Clipper*, which he hadn't utilized since 1905 or so. Second, he refers to the act as 'The Five Keatons.' The group with this name barely existed while it was together and for sure permanently returned to 'The Three Keatons' when the two youngest – a son and a daughter, not two daughters – left the act to go to school.

As Buster tells the story, he and his mother left Joe in Los Angeles without a word, leaving his bags and some money (Myra always took care of the finances) and took the train to Detroit, where Myra stayed for a month and then joined Joe, who had traveled back to Muskegon by then. Buster's datebook put him back in New York 18 January,[5] where he had to figure out what he was going to do next.

Buster went to see Max Hart, a well-respected theatrical agent and Hart immediately took him to the Shuberts, thinking he would be perfect for *The Passing Show*. *The Passing Show* had been devised in 1894 and put on yearly in the summer ever since. Written by Sydney Rosenfeld, in its initial incarnation, the show was a burlesque of other shows or performances that had been put on during the previous winter.[6] This original show took place in the Casino Theatre, but in 1912, the Shubert Brothers adopted the idea, added the year in the title in order to differentiate it from the Casino Theatre version and made it into a huge summer event. By 1916, the show ran for 140 performances and included music by George Gershwin and featured stars such as Ed Wynn, Fred and Adele Astaire, and Marie Dressler. It was designed to compete with the Ziegfeld Follies. The first six weeks of the show were on Broadway, and then it went on the road. Buster was to be paid $250 a week in New York and $300 a week on the road.

Obviously, Buster was in the mood for something newer (to him) than *The Passing Show*. On 17 March, he ran into Lou Anger, a German-dialect comedian that the Keatons had shared the bill with a few times. Anger was accompanied by former Keystone Studios comedian Roscoe Arbuckle, for whom Anger was now working as studio manager, and introduced him to Buster. Arbuckle asked Buster if he'd ever been in films and, finding the answer to be 'no,' invited him around to his studio the next Monday morning (according to Buster's datebook, 19 March). And so, he went round to the Colony Studios, 318–320 E. 48th Street,[7] at the agreed-upon time. Arbuckle had left Keystone a few months previous, signing a contract with Selznick, which required him to move to New York to make films. He shared the facility with both Norma and Constance Talmadge, significant silent film actresses of the time. Norma was married to Joseph Schenck, who had entered the film industry as a producer. Schenck would be part of Buster's life for many years to come. Arbuckle's studio was then on the third floor, with a stage about 100 by 125 feet. Schenck had spent $100,000 on equipping the building, $35,000 of which was spent on lighting.[8] He had chosen this eastern location after being unsatisfied with any studio offered him in Los Angeles.[9]

Once inside the large loft building, and after Arbuckle explained the hows and wherefores of the film business and the technology needed to succeed in it, Buster was hooked. He was hired at a mere $40 a week and began his new career with Arbuckle's first film on the new contract, *The Butcher Boy*, which they began filming a couple of days after (21 March) Buster's first visit to the studio.[10] Another attraction for Buster was Natalie Talmadge, younger sister of the two Talmadge actresses, who was acting as a secretary and script girl. Buster described her as 'a meek, mild girl who had much warmth and great feminine sweetness.'[11] She would later become his first wife.

Roscoe Arbuckle's new production company was named Comique Film Productions (pronounced "Cu-mee-kee). Interestingly, he told *Motography* that 'he is not going to have any stock company of players. His entire cast was to consist of three people, himself, Al St. John [his nephew] and a girl – The rest of the players will be picked up as needed and dropped again after they have served their purpose.'[12] Obviously, meeting Buster Keaton changed those plans a bit. Arbuckle would be directing most of his own films, but also wanted to develop new talent and eventually move into producing as well.

The first Arbuckle film under the new contract was due 1 March, but the 21 March date existing in the Keaton recounting suggests a delay already, due to Roscoe's tardiness in arriving on the east coast. As Jim Kline noted, Arbuckle films usually followed a template of sorts:

> First the basic setting is established (a general store, a hotel, a hospital, a garage or an outdoor setting or event), then the characters are introduced, usually consisting of Roscoe, a girl, and a rival or two for the girl's affections. Then all hell breaks loose as Roscoe and the others battle for her attention. Sometimes after the first reel, the action switches to another setting and repeats itself.[13]

This format was followed and adhered to in many of the films under the new contract. A writer for *Photoplay* noted that slapstick comedy relied on successful gags, with a gag being 'a bit of "business" – a situation that will shake a laugh out of the casual looker, because of its incongruity, its abrupt contrast, or its physical humour. It may be a subtle piece of work or a sudden bit of rough stuff.'[14] Roscoe was quoted as saying 'one of the most important factors in screen comedy is speed. By that I do not refer to speed in the slang sense of the word as applied to vulgarity, but to speed of plot and action. Keep things jumping and your audience will be with you every moment.'[15] Part of the problem was that Arbuckle strongly believed that film audiences were comprised of individuals who had the mental capacity of a 12-year-old. Buster felt differently – that audiences were intelligent, and that the performer should not be afraid to challenge them. During their collaborative films, it would take a while before Buster could convince Roscoe to consider this philosophy, but he eventually did.

Notice of the addition of Buster and leading lady Josephine Stevens, both novices in the film industry, appeared in the industry rags the first week of April. The newspapers ran a good-sized article on Buster himself, focusing on the habit of Joe Keaton at six foot plus throwing his much smaller son Buster around the stage in the vaudeville days and comparing that with what Roscoe at a similar height compounded by his 280-pound weight might inflict on him, alluding to a scene with molasses as an example: 'According to Buster, heretofore noted for his conservatism, the physical disparity between the lanky Joe Keaton and Fatty Roscoe Arbuckle is only exceeded by the latter's ability to slam him about the harder.'[16] By 14 April, the release date of 23 April for Arbuckle's first short under the new contract was announced, with the expectation that 200 prints would be released nationwide.[17]

The first film they worked on was *The Butcher Boy* (1917). As Kline described, it has two acts, this time with each in a different setting. The first act takes place in a general store, where Roscoe is the butcher and all-around clerk, and Al St. John is a co-worker but also a rival for the hand of the owner's (Arthur Earle's) daughter, played by Josephine Stevens.[18] Buster is introduced as a customer, who comes to the store for molasses, but stops at a barrel of brooms first, withdrawing one, pulling out a few straws and then subjecting a second one to that treatment before returning to his original reason for being there. Since the broom bit is not particularly funny, perhaps it was Buster's brief homage to his family's vaudeville act, one in which he and Joe did a whole segment of the turn with brooms. As Kline suggests, '[Buster's] deadpan expression, slow, methodical movements, and subtle curiosity about his surroundings are with him in that first moment on screen and contrast profoundly with the flailing antics of the other cast members.'[19] Keaton doesn't embrace this demeanor permanently, however, until he begins producing his own films, for he often smiled and laughed his way through certain scenes in the Comiques.[20] The next couple of big gags, not including Luke the dog's stint as a pepper grinder in one scene, includes Roscoe and Buster's set of molasses gags, in which Buster places the money for the molasses in the same bucket that he asked Roscoe to fill, Roscoe's emptying the bucket in Buster's hat to retrieve the coins, then dumping the molasses back into the bucket. The sticky molasses then plays a role in creating Buster's 'stuck' hat (already a porkpie hat,[21] by the way) and finally his stuck shoes. The other big gag in Act I is the flour bag fight, with Roscoe, Buster and Al, as well as most of the other stock characters, taking part. Ben H. Grimm, reviewer for *Moving Picture World*, called this 'one of the best comedy battles yet staged. The main ammunition is flour, and what doesn't happen in that store when the flour bombs begin to fly is hardly worth mentioning.'[22] A pie, a traditional comedy missile, comes in at the end (this time containing molasses) and steals the final moments. In Act II, when Stevens is sent off to Miss Teachem's Girls' School (Teachem is played by Agnes Neilson, who becomes a Comique regular), both Roscoe and then Al decide to enroll in drag to be near her. There are significant exteriors used in the second act, which include the exterior of a Victorian house, that doubles as the girls' school and a yard with trees on a waterfront, in which the chase scenes occur, and the henchmen hang out. In this second half, Buster becomes, along with stock actor Joe Bordeaux, one of these henchmen assisting St. John's character, but he still has a good moment when he throws in a gratuitous neck roll[23] during this chase. Both Roscoe and Al in drag are hilarious, especially when close-up shots are used to highlight Al's particularly unfeminine table manners. In the end, he is vanquished, and the store owner's daughter ends up with Roscoe, as expected. Grimm praised Buster's 'excellent comedy falls,' and reviewer George W. Graves called his performance 'a praiseworthy one.'[24]

By 28 April, Comique Films had decided that a short entitled *His Wedding Night*, written by Herbert Warren and William Jefferson, would be the second title in the series.[25] However, *Moving Picture World* announced 12 May that *A Reckless Romeo* would be Arbuckle's second Comique release instead. This was a film left over from the Keystone period that was never released and so, doesn't star any of the new 'company' of actors.[26] In the meantime, *His Wedding Night* was moved to the fourth position, with a new story, entitled *The Rough House*, now sitting in third place. Already, Buster would share directing duties with Roscoe on the film. In this one, Roscoe plays the son who, with his mother and sister, are running a holiday home, which turns out to be quite a chaotic place. In Act I, the focus is on Roscoe, of course, who is lying in bed smoking, when the bed catches fire. Kline argues that the next bit is pure Keaton – when Arbuckle carries one teacup of water at a time from the kitchen to the bedroom to try to quench the fire, but of course, it gets quickly out of control. Buster comes in here, as a gardener with five o'clock shadow and a cap, who is working in the yard and whose hose comes to the rescue. Buster enters a bit later in the kitchen as a delivery boy in a billed cap. He starts flirting with Josephine the maid and this upsets Al the cook, who's also chasing her, which results initially in a broom fight, similar to one Buster used in the Three Keatons' sketch. Buster kisses her before he leaves the room to fight. Their 'fight' ends with Buster throwing a large kitchen knife at Al, like a knife thrower in a circus would throw one, with it landing in Al's mouth, who then tries to throw it back. Then Roscoe is atop the dinner table with Buster and Al chasing each other around it, causing it to spin. Buster and Al are then both kicked out and continue their fight in the yard, eventually being joined by a cop. The maid is fired when she's caught by the two women cavorting with Roscoe, so Roscoe has to do it all – cook and then deliver a fully set table in a wrapped-up tablecloth in another use of reverse camerawork (the knife in Al's mouth being the other). He serves dinner to the 'Rough' ladies, played by Alice Lake and Agnes Neilson, who are entertaining two men (one of which is Glen Cavender), who proceed to rob the house as soon as Roscoe's chaotic dinner gives them the opportunity. Al and Buster are given a choice at the police station: sign up to be a cop or serve time. They become cops. In this guise, Buster gets hung up on a chain link fence in a chase and needs both Al and Joe Bordeaux to get him down. Eventually, however, the ineffective cops catch the criminals, and all is well. *Moving Picture World* wrote that Arbuckle had hired the largest cabaret in New York City, Churchill's White Light restaurant, to act in a number of scenes,[27] but this scene doesn't exist in the final film, because Florenz Ziegfield took Joe Schenck to court at the last minute, claiming that it had been ripped from his current show entitled *Trenches on Broadway*, particularly the 'One Man Bar' scene.[28] No evidence of this scene now exists in the film and, in fact, such a scene wouldn't easily fit into any part of the existing plot. Roscoe wrote about the scene in an article for *Motion Picture* magazine:

> The cabaret consisted of eighteen or twenty members of the chorus, seven or eight featured artists, the full restaurant orchestra, a full staff of waiters, and enough extras in evening-dress to give the appearance of one of Broadway's showplaces at its merriest. That same scene cost me just an even ten thousand dollars, but no one except the members of my company and the cabaret members ever saw it.[29]

Another bit of the film that was advertised but doesn't appear in the final version concerned a beach scene. The mother-in-law was made more oppositional: 'The climax is Fatty's decision that two is company and three a crowd. Suiting the deed to the thought, mother-in-law takes an involuntary ocean plunge.'[30] As one particular ad for the film states, 'the name is descriptive, the story is there but you forget it in the rush of action.'[31] Arbuckle began cutting the film 4 August[32] and then *The Rough House* was released to theatres 25 June. The vegetables used in the film as missiles of one sort or another were sorted out following the shooting, with the good ones donated to East Side (New York City) families.[33]

One reporter attempted to describe Roscoe's particular method on *The Rough House* set:

> In preparing the scenario before starting to 'shoot' the scenes, Roscoe Arbuckle carefully figures on the fitness and personality of his two mainstays, Al St John and 'Buster' Keaton, writing parts which will give their comedy propensities fullest scope. Then during the making of the picture when it frequently happens that the situation takes a twist unanticipated by the scenario writer, instead of eliminating it or reconstructing it so that he may 'hog' the scene, 'Fatty' allows the incident to work itself out to the logical conclusion, the glory going to whoever is entitled to it.[34]

Roscoe was also believed to sing bits of opera during the breaks between filming, such as the sextette from *Lucia*: 'The obliging Mr. Arbuckle conveys the information that Verdi, Gounod, Puccini and their confederates are antidotes he knows for too much custard pie.'[35]

Finally, *His Wedding Night* was released to theatres 20 August.[36] Strangely, nearly the entire plot was included in an *Exhibitor's Herald* article 28 July, focusing on Roscoe as a soda jerk in a pharmacy (Koff and Kramp druggists), attracted to the pharmacist's daughter, who is also desired by Al's character. Roscoe asks the daughter, played by Alice Mann, to marry him and she accepts. Al finds out, seeks help from the pharmacist, but is thrown over in favor of Roscoe. Then a kidnapping ensues, as the article suggests, 'which ends in comical disaster for the kidnappers.'[37] And here's where Buster comes in. Initially, he's the delivery boy for the wedding dressmaker, bringing a box with the dress to the drug store on a bicycle. Alice asks him to model the dress, so that she can make any adjustments on it that she needs. As Kline notes,

In the film's most Keatonesque moment, Buster ducks behind a changing partition, then makes a spectacularly theatrical reappearance as it falls, and a spotlight suddenly hits him while he strikes a feminine pose and begins modeling the gown. Prancing around in the wedding gown while maintaining his trademark frozen face, he milks the scene for all it's worth and the effect is hilarious.[38]

Still in the wedding dress, Al and his henchman arrive on the scene and kidnap the person they think is Alice, but, because they throw a bag over 'her' head, no one realizes it's Buster. They make their way to the justice of the peace, where Al will force her to marry him. Roscoe gets wind of the kidnapping and goes to save her, which he does, then pays the parson to marry the two, without knowing yet that 'the bride' is still Buster. In other words, the two men almost get married, which is humorous enough, but when Alice arrives and uncovers the kidnapped Buster, the reveal is even better. To make sure the audience is paying attention, Buster smiles and winks at Roscoe, an action that reflects back to when he initially entered the drugstore with the wedding dress and a bum eye, which he was winking to set it straight, but an act that Roscoe had interpreted otherwise.

The next Comique was *Oh Doctor!* No one has really discussed this, but Buster's role as Roscoe's recalcitrant son *has to* be based on the role he played in the Three Keatons' act for more than 15 years. In this film, he is dressed in more of a Buster Brown-type outfit – a sort of sailor suit with a straw hat with ribbons on it. His expressions and behaviors had to have been familiar, as would have been the moments when Roscoe throws his son around, à la Joe Keaton. The first act of the film occurs at a racecourse, where Dr I. O. Dine (Roscoe) gets into trouble, first by flirting with 'vampire' Alice Lake, who plays Al's wife, while Roscoe's wife, played by Josephine Stevens, and child Buster sit nearby. In dealing with Alice, he gets caught up in some illegal horse betting that Al is engaging in, bets his entire fortune on a horse named Lightning, and loses it all. The next scene features a street seller of medicines, a mountebank, who gives Arbuckle an idea. Needing new patients immediately, he pushes his car into a crowd, wounding and hurting people, calls it back with a whistle, then works the crowd handing out business cards. In the second act, Al and Alice decide to touch Roscoe for some money, so Alice lures the doctor over to her place while Al robs Mrs. Iodine of her necklace. This second half is fairly complicated, but Buster's recalcitrant boy character becomes a sort of hero, first when he sees Al take his mother's necklace and chases him back to his home, then when he calls his mother and informs her, and finally, when he rounds up the police, who arrest the criminals. Mrs. Iodine (Josephine) busies herself with getting her necklace back from Alice Lake but gets locked in the closet before succeeding. Roscoe first is informed about a 500-to-1 bet opportunity from Alice, goes to the private gambling club to make his bet, then returns to Al and Alice's residence, finds a chubby cop coat in the kitchen, dons it, and begins to chase Al. Buster arrives with the police. Josephine breaks out of the closet and reclaims her necklace but is 'arrested' by Roscoe. The cops take down Alice and Al. Finally, Roscoe returns to the private gambling club, which has been vacated, so it initially looks like he won't get his money, even though he won this time, but the gamblers and bookies have left their money behind, which Roscoe gathers up in basket loads. The film was released on 30 September. One reviewer noted that 'many of the situations are time-worn, but portrayed by the inimitable fat man, they should bring laughs wherever the film is shown.'[39]

Roscoe had decided to move the studio back to the west coast, but wanted to sneak in one more film beforehand, at a locale that gave itself over to fun of one kind or other on a daily basis, Coney Island. The amusement park that Roscoe used for his fifth film entitled *Fatty at Coney Island* was named Luna Park. Buster plays a down-in-the-mouth boyfriend in the film, who's trying to get himself and his girlfriend, Alice Mann, into the amusement park. She decides to go in with Al, who has money, and Buster then is relegated to entering inside a garbage can. Meanwhile, Roscoe has just ingeniously ditched his wife, played by Agnes Neilson, by burying himself in the sand, after watching Luke dig a hole. Agnes spends the rest of the film trying to locate him, often with the assistance of the cops. Buster's gal stays with Al a bit and they go to ride the Witching Waves, an actual Coney Island ride. Buster follows them. As James Neibaur notes, it is a ride in which a wicker cart 'is propelled across a rippling floor that simulates the waves of the sea.'[40] With that in mind, of course, the gag writers had Alice become seasick and run off the ride to rest on a bench. Al follows and goes off to get them a couple of ice cream cones. By the time he returns, Roscoe has moved in, grabs the two cones, spits ice cream out at Al, engages in an ice cream fight with him, then a policeman finally grabs and takes Al away. Roscoe grabs Alice and runs off.

Their next ride is like a water flume, but with a cart instead of a log. Both fall out after they hit a big bump and neither seems to be able to swim. Buster enters here, saving first Alice, then Roscoe, but still loses the girl for his efforts. Buster then takes a job as a lifeguard, seeing the two enter the swimming plunge, where Roscoe steals a fat lady's bathing suit and dons it (not having his own), and Alice joins Roscoe inside, after he spends a bit of time in the ladies' lounge. At the police department, Al and Agnes recognize each other. Agnes shows him a photo of Roscoe, who he exclaims has stolen his girl, so Agnes posts his bail and the two go off looking for him. Roscoe and Alice go from the bathhouse out to the beach, where Agnes and Al happen to be. Agnes asks Buster if he knows who Roscoe is and he indicates the 'she' is a 'he,' by lifting Roscoe's hat and hair. Al recognizes him, too, and a fight begins. Buster grabs Alice and they go off. Al and Roscoe are hauled off to the pokey and continue fighting in the cell, with no policemen able to break it up. Agnes comes into the police station to bail out her husband, but he locks her in the cell, and both he and Al escape. Both men vow to give up women, but at the threshold of the police station, Al spots a skirt and runs off with her. Roscoe soon does the same, except in an ending removed within a couple of years after the film's release, he approaches a woman from behind, discovers she's black and takes off running. This is changed to his approaching a white woman and going off with her. Joe Bordeaux mans the sledgehammer contest, famous for featuring one of Buster's smiling and laughing scenes. The film was released 29 October.

By the end of September, Roscoe had persuaded Joe Schenck to move his studio back to the west coast.[41] He had some history with the Long Beach area, and in fact, the local papers were announcing his return as early as 3 October. It reported that Arbuckle had leased a space at the Balboa Studios in Long Beach but would be working separately from the Balboa companies themselves. As of the same date, Al St. John was already established in Long Beach and giving interviews for Roscoe about the transition.[42] Buster signed a new contract with Roscoe before the move,[43] likely for $250 a week, and stopped in Muskegon on the cross-country journey for a week-long visit. He had ordered his natural gas turned on by 5 October, for a residence at 421 East Third Street in Long Beach,[44] so was most likely in residence there at that time or shortly thereafter. Everybody was in town by 17 October, however, because they were due to appear in person at the Liberty Theatre in Long Beach that night.[45] While most of his company came along to Long Beach, Alice Mann made the decision to stay in the east.[46] It was believed that Roscoe's company would be paying Balboa approximately $300,00 a year for five years, the term of the contract.

H. M. and Elwood Horkheimer were the owners and executives of the Balboa Amusement Producing Company located at the southeast corner of Alamitos and 6th Street in Long Beach. Fred Mace, former Keystone comedian, was the first comedy actor to work at Balboa, and he probably had something to do with Roscoe's eventual interest in moving here.[47] The studio seemed to be doing very well in the mid-1910s, but by 'March 25, 1918, the Horkheimers declared voluntary bankruptcy. By April 1918, with heavy hearts, H. M. and Elwood assigned their studio to the Los Angeles Wholesalers Board of Trade for liquidation, while they secretly prayed for the Wheel of Fortune to bring them another chance in the volatile market.'[48] Regardless of the financial situation of the Horkheimers, however, Roscoe was able to use the studio buildings and equipment until he eventually moved to the Diando Studios in 1918, where he filmed only *The Sheriff.*

The first film in the new studio would be titled *The Country Hero*, written by Lou Anger. A set was being built on the Balboa lot 17 October, which included a blacksmith shop, 'placarded with "Uncle Tom's Cabin" lithographs.' Roscoe announced his new company would include Valerie Bergere, recently married to scenario writer Herbert Warren, Al St. John and Buster Keaton, of course, Luke the dog, Alice Lake, Wilfred Lucas, and Sophye Barnard, prima donna late of the Hippodrome New York and Anger's wife. Lou Anger continued as studio manager, Herbert Warren as scenario writer and George Peters as cameraman.[49] Roscoe also promised to hire some local help, with the result that an ad to that effect was answered by 250 people of all ages and types. The ad called for only 150 people, of which 50 were put to work immediately on *The Country Hero* set as 'country village inhabitants.'[50] Jean Jacques Jura and Rodney Norman Barden related that 'in December 1917, Balboa Studios built a separate glass studio, the world's biggest, for the Comique Film Corporation. The new structure measured 100 feet x 200 feet and was used for producing Roscoe's *The Country Hero*.[51]

Unfortunately, as of this writing, *The Country Hero* is the only Comique that is lost. This is unfortunate for many reasons, but perhaps the biggest is that the film was reputed to be the film debut of Joe Keaton. Joe was supposedly hired to play Cy Klone, one of the two largest parts in the story, with Roscoe having the other one. However, this is not borne out by the press and publicity materials that exist. In fact, Al St. John played the character of Cy Klone, making it a more predictable casting. A couple of oblique mentions of Joe playing one role or another in the film appeared – in a brief snippet in *Variety* dated 7 December: 'Joe Keaton is with the Fatty Arbuckle motion picture company at Long Beach, Cal. [. . .] Joe is the storekeeper in the latest Arbuckle release, "The Country Hero,"'[52] and in a news article dated 11 January 1918:

'Joe Keaton gives an amusing caricature of the rube hotel proprietor.'[53] So, which was it? It's also unfortunate, because it was the first Comique film produced at Balboa, and probably worked hard to demonstrate the benefits of filming out west again, in a larger and more technologically advanced studio. Even though it is lost, there's a lot of information available about the film. One interesting item is that Arbuckle built an entire town, dubbed Jazzville, on the studio grounds, to act as the setting: 'it is said Arbuckle spent much time immediately after reaching California [. . .] motoring around in search of a site for Jazzville, but no luck attended the trips and it was decided to build the town in the rear of the Arbuckle Long Beach Studio.'[54] Reporter Paul Hubert Conlon visited the set and devoted an entire page of the *Los Angeles Times* to the visit. Three-quarters of the page was taken up with cartoons by noted illustrator Gale, of the actors and their particular comedic situations, except for Joe, who wasn't included, more evidence that he did not play a large part in the film. Even Natalie Talmadge, Herbert Warren, and Lou Anger were caricatured.

Conlon described Jazzville as sparing no expense in recreating a western town, some even said Arbuckle's birthplace, Smith Center, Kansas.[55] At the corner of one street stood Hotel Jazz, Hoke M. Jazz, proprietor. Down the right side of the village square was the school, No. 93, its yard filled with urchins. Next to that was the corner store and general emporium, with quaint villagers hanging around on the steps and sitting on a bench outside, such as the old Civil War soldier telling yarns, the local gossip and the village sheriff with his big shiny badge and the store proprietor and a commercial traveler haggling over the prices of merchandise.[56] Hound dogs hung about. Next door to the general store was Oh Yoy's laundry and at the far end of the square was I. Cutem's Barbershop. Also present was a livery stable, the Neptune fire department, and the village smithy. Buildings were made more authentic by their being adorned with old-time theatre posters, such as 'The Black Hand' and 'The Queen of the Opium Ring.' Cy Klone's Garage was across the square, the center of much of the film's comedy. Conlon and Gale witnessed a flivver fly out of the roof of the garage, as if in flight, landing next to the general store:

> Hotly pursued by a wild-eyed individual, who was evidently
> Cy Klone, the garage owner, played by the acrobatic Al St.
> John, came Roscoe 'Fatty' Arbuckle down the square, his
> blacksmith's apron flying in the wind. Behind the hating
> rivals came the village pest, Buster Keaton, who was hugely

enjoying the trouble he had created, and a frightened and very pretty country maiden, Alice Lake.[57]

Roscoe's 'Country Hero' had just attempted to fix the flivver, but failed due to Buster's machinations and was ultimately being chased by Cy Klone, Al's character. Margaret I. MacDonald noted that 'the water trough at the door of the blacksmith shop figures largely as a source for a dip at various critical points in the comedy.'[58] The old cop directing traffic in the square held up a sign that said 'Advance' as Roscoe approached, then changed to 'Halt' as Al did. Roscoe sped away laughing and the traffic cop then decided to change the sign to 'Use Your Own Judgment.' An exciting car race followed, ending in a crash with a locomotive.[59] Surprisingly, this rivalry is calmed when Roscoe and Al join together to get Alice back from the city slicker who appears on the scene. Their reconciliation is expressed in the final scene – amateur night at the local village ball. Besides the turns each of the company's actors undertakes in this scene – a Spanish dance for Roscoe and Buster in his Salome dance – it was reported that Roscoe threw a piano in the chaos created.[60] Alice Lake was also thrown around a bit, to remove her from the arms of the city slicker and to bring her and Roscoe's character back together.

Roscoe employed four cameramen and two Graflex machines to capture the flivver explosion.[61] He expressed to Conlon that he hoped to leave pies behind and present more creative jokes to his audience:

> There is much more enjoyment to be derived from laughable situations in which clever gags are presented naturally and with some semblance of truth enhancing the worth of the comedy. [. . .] It's the most interesting part of a hard day's work to study the plot and the set from every angle to discover some possible stunt or gag, which will awaken responsive laughter in the comedy lovers.[62]

Herbert Warren, by 25 November, was already writing the scenario for the next film *Out West*, and Conlon claimed the company was already shooting scenes for that film. *The Country Hero* would be released on 10 December.

Out West also required a town to be built as its setting, which was achieved through the location of a particular gravel pit:

> dug deep into the sand hills of the ocean shore, it stands after fifteen years of gravel dredging, a perfect small replica of the

Grand Canyon. Three hundred feet above its floor its ragged skyline cuts sharp against the blue. There are cliffs of packed gravel, which appear sheer precipices of granite. There are slopes of shifting sand, which need only the dislodging of a rock to become tremendous landslides.[63]

The first part of the film was set on location in the Mojave desert[64] – in other words, an actual Western setting, which an oceanside gravel pit didn't actually bring to mind. Jim Kline labels this film 'extremely nightmarish, like a film dream.' It's 'totally illogical, chaotic, and amoral.'[65] *Out West* can also be considered a parody of the Westerns William Hart, Douglas Fairbanks, and others were making. The first scene places Roscoe on a train, upon which he is attempting to take a free ride, complete with a dinner plan – provided by the three railroad workers attempting to have their lunch, one of which is Joe Keaton. After a chase atop the train and an unfortunate confrontation with three armed Native Americans, Roscoe lands in Mad Dog Gulch and enters the Last Chance Saloon, owned by Buster, aka Bull Bullhorn. In this film he sports a top hat and a very large revolver. The saloon is equipped with a trap door, through which dead men are dropped. It had just been visited by the crazy Wild Bill Hiccup played by Al, of course. He and his henchmen engage in a shootout, killing the bartender, who is dumped through the trap door. Buster immediately puts up a 'Bartender Wanted' sign and Roscoe gets the job. An unfortunate scene ensues in which the cowboys in the bar shoot at the feet of a black boy to make him dance, Roscoe joining in. Alice Lake arrives, in character as a Salvation Army volunteer, and stops the humiliation. She immediately becomes a figure of interest to the men. Al returns and decides to have her, even if it takes violence, and begins to harass her. Roscoe and Buster do their best to free her; Roscoe hits him over the head with bottle after bottle with no effect and even tries to shoot him, but these methods don't work. He then gets the idea of tickling him with a feather, and this works; Al is subdued and kicked out and Alice is freed, but Al soon lassoes her and takes her away to his hideout. His henchmen keep Roscoe and Buster at bay for a while, but Roscoe eventually gets to the hideout, while Buster keeps the henchmen busy. One long scene involves Buster in a weirdly staged battle with a Mexican at what looks like an actual historical adobe building. Roscoe subdues Al with tickling once again, rescues Alice and then shoves Al's house over the cliff, with Al inside. Buster experienced the first of what would be many accidents on this set, falling about 20 feet off one of the highest cliffs, hitting some slippery sand and rolling and tumbling to the bottom, hitting a rock on the way down, which created a few bad bruises.[66] The film was released on 20 January 1918. Having participated in two Comique films now, Joe Keaton was finally advertised as part of the company in a quarter-page ad in the *Los Angeles Times* dated 18 January 1918, where he is described as 'Joe Keaton – Characters.'

Another article-plus-cartoons endeavor was published in the Long Beach papers on Sunday 23 January. Paul Conlon, now Roscoe's publicity director, was probably the writer, although his name isn't printed this time. The illustrator is Wick, not Gale. The subject of this article and its accompanying caricatures was *Out West*. Peter Milne submitted a review of the film in *Motion Picture News* that wasn't particularly positive: 'The long shots of furious fighting possess no comedy value and are quite out of place, while Arbuckle as director has shown a marked tendency to cater directly to Arbuckle the star, sometimes to the detriment of the incidental action of the scene.'[67] Margaret I. MacDonald, however, found a few more positive things to write about, suggesting that the premise of the film was 'new' and she actually found the shootouts the funniest bits.[68] Walter Finnigan Reed joined the Comique scenario department at the end of January,[69] perhaps because Roscoe was feeling the need for another comedy perspective. In any event, *Out West* did the poorest at the box office of the Comiques so far.

Filming on *The Bell Boy* commenced in early February, if not a bit before, with Roscoe playing the head bell boy, barber, and elevator operator, Al the desk clerk, Alice a manicurist 'Cutie Cuticle,' and Buster Roscoe's 'nimble assistant, [. . .] the inimitable Buster Keaton, whose pantomime and amazing falls in the last three Arbuckle comedies have made him famous.'[70] Joe Keaton takes part in one short scene near the end of Act I and Buster's girlfriend, Natalie Talmadge, was also hired on for the film.[71] For this film, another town, Ouchgosh, Pennsyltucky, was built to provide the setting, this time on the Balboa lot. It was essentially a u-shaped village set, with the building nearest the camera (on the right) labeled the Last National Bank, which would be the location of focus for the second act. At the Elk's Head Hotel, everyone has several jobs, and the team of Roscoe, Buster, and Al work together to wait on customers, but more importantly, to make their jobs satisfying. After Alice Lake arrives, their focus is always on her and while the three vie for her somewhat, there's no real conflict between them, for a change. Al does not play the villain here but works well and in tandem with the other two. This is a refreshing change. Also, the film contains several very inventive gags that make it a standout, and for those who know and understand Buster's way of working, there is a lot in the film that can be identified as distinctly his.

The Bell Boy is full of elaborate gags. The first is a familiar one – Buster's cleaning the glass in the telephone box, when there is no actual glass in the thing. Roscoe is busying himself mopping the floor by sitting down and applying soap and water to a small space, then scooching on the floor to the next bit. A hairy scary-looking fellow arrives, who Buster is sure is the devil. The fellow minces up to the front desk, thereby deflating that evil image. Eventually they figure out he wants a haircut and a shave, which is Roscoe's department. What follows is an incredibly complex and well-considered gag. As Roscoe cuts and shaves the gentleman (played by Charles Dudley), he makes him into different characters from history – first General Ulysses S. Grant, (complete with stogie), Abraham Lincoln, complete with mole and top hat, and then the Kaiser, who, in one of the two apparent anti-German comments the film makes, Roscoe tries to smother with shaving cream. When the customer gets down to his real hair and face, he's quite boyish looking, and takes a seat at Alice's manicure station. As Kline describes, the next gag involves Joe Keaton, who's playing a hotel guest:

> While Buster mops the floor, Joe's top hat is knocked off by an overhead conveyor belt carrying hot towels from the kitchen to the barbershop. Suspecting that Buster has insulted him, Joe kicks him in the rear then upends his pail of water onto his head. When the conveyor belt again knocks off Joe's hat, he turns, spots Al walking by with a tray of food, and kicks him across the floor through several rooms. Joe then pulls out a close-fitting cap, slaps it on his head, and skulks out of the hotel.[72]

Al, in one of his many duties, leads his patrons into the dining room and begins to prepare a meal for them (French cooking being the specialty, with German cooking crossed out – the second anti-German note). He also operates the horse-drawn elevator. The guests plus Buster or Roscoe get in the elevator and pull a rope, which activates a bell, that communicates to Al that someone needs to be hoisted up in the elevator. Then, he coaxes a rather recalcitrant horse to move forward and pull up the box. A long gag comes from this procedure, when the elevator box only gets halfway up and Buster's head gets stuck in the crack, because the horse will no longer pull the thing. The old veterans on the hotel porch suggest lighting a fire under the animal, which Al does. The horse moves, but it just makes Buster's situation more dire, until the fire burns through the rope and releases the elevator box altogether, shooting him out of the elevator and Alice up onto the horns of the elk head above. Of course, there's some problem getting her down, which Buster finally does, but he ends up caught on the antlers by his suspenders, where Roscoe and Alice leave him. He eventually pulls himself off by ripping his pants, but lands on a board that Roscoe was using to release him, that has now become a sort of see-saw, which keeps throwing Buster up in the air. Al comes along and, after some monkey business with a phone, saws the board in two. The boys celebrate by sharing a sandwich.

Act II begins with the boys and Alice attending the hotel dance and Roscoe coming up with a plan to impress her: Al and Buster should pretend to rob the bank and Roscoe will come in at the end and play the hero. This goes awry when four other men have already planned to hit the bank at the same time and are on site when Al and Buster arrive (having just walked down the village street with their robbing implements and with goofy black masks on). This scene, in which several rooms of the bank can be seen in one shot, with either Buster or Al sailing through them, demonstrating their acrobatic agility, seems purely Buster, and similar scenes will be filmed in Buster's shorts and features to come, such as in *The High Sign* (1921). So, after several minutes of fighting between the two parties, the actual robbers and the fake ones, Roscoe arrives and contributes to the mêlée. The robbers eventually escape the bank and commandeer the trolley for their escape, but the thing can't get up the hill properly, so it rolls back down, into the hands of Roscoe, Buster, Al, and the local lawman. Somehow, of all the 'heroes' here, only Roscoe gets rewarded, with both money and the girl. The film was released 18 March 1918.

Even Peter Milne of *Motion Picture News* was pleased this time, praising everyone in the company, even Joe Keaton: 'The two reeler [. . .] reaches the very heights in the type of comedy which gave [Arbuckle] his reputation. The utter ease with which they go about their ridiculous work is a rare treat in the comedy line. [. . .] A better comedy than "The Bell Boy" would be hard to find and this statement may be taken to include the Chaplins and the Sennetts.'[73] Chaplin and his studio manager Alf Reeves, coincidently, had made a visit to the Balboa Studios the last week of February, ostensibly to visit Roscoe, who wasn't in attendance. What resulted was a nice photo op that included Buster, Lou Anger, H. M. Horkheimer, and Chaplin (Myra and Joe were also in attendance).[74] One wonders what other knowledge Chaplin took away with him.

By March, Roscoe and company were in desperate need of a studio site, due to Balboa's compounding financial problems. The company filed bankruptcy 25 March and turned the studio over to its creditors, but the idea was at that time that Comique would remain, at least for the time being.[75] At the end of March, Joe Keaton presented the press with a couple of old stories about Buster's genesis, which was then disseminated in the papers. Also in March, the entrance of the States into World War I on 6 April 1917 finally began to affect the Comique Film Company. On 30 March, it was reported that Roscoe was considered exempt from service due to being overweight, but Buster, having transferred from New York State, was accepted for service, and waiting for the call. Paul Conlon, the publicity director, had been exempted twice by this point, but was soon to be examined again.[76] By 28 April, Conlon had been accepted A-C (special service) and Buster A-1.[77] Roscoe had 'adopted' Company C, 159th Infantry, stationed at Camp Kearny mid-March and was honored at an event 18 March, somehow knowing that this would be the group that Buster would serve in just a few months later.[78]

Meanwhile, Roscoe began what would be another groundbreaking film, for both himself and history, *Moonshine*. Most of this was filmed on location in the Angeles Forest, specifically in San Gabriel Canyon, a setting perhaps a little too desert-like to mimic the Appalachian Mountains exactly, but the effect was the same. Roscoe and Buster play revenuers and Al is back in his old guise of the evil villain, in this case a moonshiner. Alice Lake plays the pure but aggressive hillbilly gal who is Al's desire and Charles Dudley the patriarch of the moonshining clan. The company (including scenario writers Warren and Reed and manager Anger) camped out during the shoot, so as not to waste time and money commuting.[79] Costumes for the moonshiners consisted of 'black slouch hats, butternut pants, hickory shirts, boots, long beards, and scraggly moustaches.'[80]

The innovativeness this film displays lay in its use of title cards to break the fourth wall, which is when a character stops, looks in the camera and addresses the audience directly. In the case of this film, however, it is the work of the scene cards that makes this happen. The director immediately provides the mountain setting to the viewer in a quick iris-in and iris-out, labeling this the hideout of the bootleggers in a scene card. The next card reads: 'Rehearsal of the first scene with the two bootleggers,' text which *reveals* the filmmaking process almost immediately. The next card includes the actors' dialogue about the bootleggers' secret entrance to their hideout and the password needed to enter. And then, the card reads: 'One press on the pedal lifts a contraption – the director's idea,' again revealing the artifice involved. This speaking directly to the moviegoer about the technology involved in the making of this film is new and can be considered one aspect of the satire employed: the satirizing of the cinematic process. The other is more traditional and straightforward: the satirizing of a genre, in this case the melodrama of both theatre and film. This may be the most ambitious method of comedy making that Roscoe had attempted as yet, except perhaps for his Keystone comedy *He Did and He Didn't* (1916), the idea for which was rumored to be stolen from Syd Chaplin.

The melodrama at the core of the film is basically about two revenuers trying to find the bootleggers' hideout and take them into custody. Unlike other films, Alice Lake's pretty lass character is not the center of the film or the conflict; it's simply the government versus the hillbillies. Al again plays an evil villain, but although he tries to manhandle Alice's character, in this film, she gives as good as she gets. The big joke that starts the film – after the revenuers arrive in a car, of all things, is the old clown-car joke, although it may not have been that old at the time. After Roscoe and Buster alight, Roscoe asks Buster to assemble the troops, so he opens the back door and a long stream of armed revenuers emerges, totaling about 40 men, who line up in formation. Roscoe tells them to hide until they're needed, and we never see them again. Roscoe and Buster then climb atop a tall steeple-shaped cliff, which provides a nice view of the valley below (San Gabriel Canyon) and engage in some acrobatics involving falling off, Roscoe losing his pants, and the cliff not really being as steep as first suggested. Meanwhile, Alice is trying to read a *Vogue* magazine (an odd choice for a mountain girl) in a hammock and Al, entering the shot in a stark closeup moving toward the camera, begins to harass her by tickling her feet, but she turns the tables on him, until she's reprimanded by her father, played by Charles Dudley, who tells her to wait until they're married to treat him that way. She says she will never marry him. Roscoe enters the scene then and chastises Alice for hitting her father, even throwing her in the river, to which she responds, 'I love you.' Dudley complains that the story seems to be moving too fast, and Roscoe breaks the frame again, with the card reading, 'This is only a two-reeler, we have no time to build up to love scenes.' Al and Roscoe take pot shots at each other for a few minutes, then Buster and Al meet and start behaving like monkeys – even climbing high in a tree and continuing the behavior.

Roscoe is now taken captive by Alice's four brothers (and father) and thrown down in the cabin's basement, which is laid out like an art nouveau palace, with comfy chairs, a fireplace and Alice, now dressed smartly, serving him food on a serving cart. Roscoe then gets inspiration from Alexandre Dumas's *The Count of Monte Cristo* (a book laying nearby) about how to escape – as a dead man – so he uses the catsup to make a wound, then shoots the revolver Alice had provided away from him, thereby being drug off to the river, where he is thrown in and escapes, at least for a while. Buster is sitting right there beside the stream and yells 'Bravo' at Roscoe's performance, in a continuation of the satire. The brothers realize the revenuer isn't dead and take him captive again, this time deciding to blow him up along with their cabin. Roscoe is tied to a chair and a barrel of dynamite in the center of the house and the next scene is it blowing to smithereens, but, of course, this can't be the end. The film is reversed, the house comes back together, and Roscoe walks out – saved – in another innovative reversal of the expected. Finally, thinking Roscoe will now walk off with the gal, he claims that he forgot to mention he was married and hands Alice over to Buster, for the first time in their films together. The shoot took a lot longer than expected (more than four weeks), because they were marooned in the canyon for an extra 10 days by torrential rain, which kept the crew from completing much of the exterior scenes.[81] One writer noted that 'flood waters caused by the recent rains raged through the canyon, carrying trees before them and causing many cave-ins of land where the embankment was steep.'[82] The film was finally released 12 May 1918.

The reviews were overall very good, with Peter Milne writing that 'it has originality, a plentiful supply of gags which bespeak the inventive genius of Arbuckle and his partners-in-fun, and is so obviously a burlesque of the old moonshine picture that it registers with every scene.'[83] *The Billboard* stated that the film was 'running over with nonsensical action and is properly labeled a burlesque on the making of pictures.'[84] Edward Weitzel noted that 'aside from being a complete departure from the usual style of story used for the Arbuckle ribticklers, the picture has many mirth-provoking moments.[85] A satire of movie-making, the melodrama and old moonshine pictures – all in a two-reel Arbuckle comedy. The film was a triple threat to its competitors and a strong harbinger of things to come – at least for Buster.

At the beginning of May, Joe and Myra had made Patsy Smith's column, 'Among the Women,' in *Variety*, for she covered their recent visit into Los Angeles proper, due, she said, to the fact that Long Beach was a dry town and Joe needed to stock up. Asked if he liked working for Roscoe, he said '"Oh, it's alright if Arbuckle wouldn't try and tell me how to kick my boy. Shucks [or its equivalent] ain't I been kicking him all his life?"[86] Indeed, Joe would not work for Roscoe again. By mid-May, the next film, *Good-night Nurse*, was about to wrap up, when the company took off for Arrowhead Hot Springs, a sanatorium, north of San Bernadino, California to shoot exteriors: 'With the hundreds of health-seekers as "extras," the sanatorium and the mud baths for atmosphere, and the mountain scenery for the beauty eye of George Peters, the cameraman, Fatty Arbuckle promises to get much fun out of a sanatorium.'[87] Again a two-act film in which the acts occurred in very different settings, *Good Night Nurse* begins with an inebriated Roscoe standing on a street corner in front of a drugstore in a teeming rainstorm. In the next few minutes, he and his street companions perform a hilarious ballet, with Roscoe's focus always on trying to light his cigarette. An out-of-control woman with a broken umbrella (Buster in drag) flies down the street and engages with Roscoe, tumbling and sliding, with Roscoe trying to get a fire on his cigarette under her broken umbrella, to no avail. Another inebriated gentleman comes by (Snitz Edwards), trying to find his way home, and asks for help, receiving postage stamps on his face, his address written on his shirt and placed atop a mailbox. Meanwhile, the druggist refuses to let Roscoe inside his store every time he tries to get in out of the rain. Finally, a dancer and an organ grinder with a monkey come by and Roscoe takes to them right away, inviting them back to his house. As Kline remarks, 'This hilarious, wonderfully acted opening segment is filled with a loopy, freewheeling exuberance, a tone that dominates the entire film.'[88] At home his wife waits, wringing her hands, but soon finds that her husband has come home with an organ grinder and a dancer, when the monkey finds her in her bedroom. She realizes drastic measures must be taken to get Roscoe on the right path and talks him into checking into a sanitorium the next morning.

Act II begins outside the No Hope sanitorium, where Roscoe and his wife meet a patient coming out of the building all wrapped in bandages (Al). He's yelling that he's cured, which Roscoe, about to be admitted, takes as a bad omen, and tries to escape. The patient gives Roscoe one of his high kicks in the chin and gets him back on course. In the next few moments, Roscoe and his wife meet Buster, straight from surgery in a smock covered in blood, carrying a bloody cleaver. A scantily clad Alice Lake, a patient, walks into the room and jumps into Roscoe's arms and is then removed by Al. The wife departs and Roscoe is made to change into a hospital gown, eats a thermometer during the exam and then is immediately moved to the surgery theatre in an attempt to remove it. Roscoe is put under, and the dream plot begins. First, Alice reappears and together with Roscoe, they plan an escape. They enter a large ward of patients, and a pillow fight ensues. Escaping from that, Roscoe spots the matronly nurse's uniform hanging in a closet and puts it on. Out in the hallway, female Roscoe meets Buster and the two engage in a prolonged bit of flirting, until the matron returns from lunch, sees Roscoe in her uniform and simply rips it off him. He escapes with Buster and Al in pursuit and ends up, through some clever serendipity, as an entrant in a foot race, which he wins. The two sanitarium workers finally catch him up and the audience then sees the two waking Roscoe up from the operation. It has all been a dream! During the course of filming this second act, Roscoe ended up in the hospital. In the scene in which he and Buster spoof a fencing match with a knife on Buster's part and a cane on Roscoe's: 'Springing to position with his walking stick posed for a thrust, Fatty was disarmed by one stroke of his fellow comedian's knife with nearly fatal results.'[89] The film was released 8 July 1918. Peter Milne also enjoyed the opening scenes in the rainstorm, calling them 'some of the funniest he has ever given the screen. [. . .] His constant attempts to light a cigarette in a downpour are uproarious and the gags that the wind and the wet provided are surprisingly natural as well as funny.'[90]

Roscoe was determined to get one more film made before Buster left the studio for service. His continued use of the Balboa studios, despite their bankruptcy, too, was on borrowed time, so all things being equal, the production of *The Cook* was expedited. Filming had begun on a beach café set the second week of June.[91] At this time Buster and Natalie Talmadge were actually living together at the Gibbs Apartments in Long Beach,[92] but just two weeks later, Buster was noted as being a guest at the Schuyler Hotel,[93] also in Long Beach, creating a question as to why. Of course, this could have had something to do with going into the service, appearances, etc. The first act of the film takes place in the Bull Pup café set, focusing on Roscoe as the cook, who is incredibly dexterous with the kitchen utensils, all performed while facing the camera. He has a nice, syncopated fulfilling of orders thing going with Buster, the waiter, in which he serves up the food, throws it at Buster, who grabs it without spilling anything and then serves the customers. John Rand, a familiar face in the Charlie Chaplin company, plays the head waiter/maître'd. He tries to keep Buster and Roscoe in line, to no avail. At one point, an Arabian-type dancer takes the floor and Buster joins her, mimicking her movements, then moving into the kitchen, where Roscoe likes the idea and begins to adorn himself with various pots and pans, becoming a version of Salomé, then morphing into Cleopatra who is bitten by several sausages standing in for the asp. Alice Lake plays Buster's girlfriend this time and, of course, Al is her harasser. He grabs Alice and makes her dance violently on the dance floor, with John Rand, Buster, and Roscoe all trying to save her without luck. Luke the dog is in this film and spends quite a bit of time chasing Al all over the place, even up steep ladders. Al and Luke eventually fall through the restaurant roof, where everyone is engaged in eating spaghetti in his own original manner: Roscoe loops it around his finger, Buster piles a bunch in a coffee cup, trims off the access and eats it like a beverage, and at one point, the two drape their napkins over a strand of spaghetti as if it were a clothesline.

In Act II, the restaurant is closed, and the staff decides to spend their free time at the nearby beach. Roscoe packs up inside the kitchen, grabs his dog and his very long fishing pole and goes to the beach. The setting then moves to an amusement park, specifically the Pike in Long Beach, that includes the Jack Rabbit racer, a roller coaster, which features in the film. The restaurant workers start out at the goat-cart ride, with Buster and Alice in one and Roscoe, still with the huge fishing pole, and Luke in another. Roscoe leaves the park and goes to the beach to fish. Most of this is shot in chiaroscuro. Roscoe battles the big pole and an equally big fish while Luke looks on from his position on a post, barking and helping out where he can. Alice and Buster get separated and, of course, Al takes advantage and starts to harass Alice. They end up on the Jack Rabbit in different cars, the cars stop atop the big hill and Alice decides her only way out is to dive what looks like several hundred feet into the ocean. Roscoe and Buster race around trying to find a lifesaver or a rope to rescue her. Because only two prints of the film were found recently – one in 1998 and the other in 2002 – and both were incomplete, the ending does not exist. However, the text of a press book provides some information about that unknown ending: 'While the pest waiter is rescuing his girl with the aid of the cook, the courageous Luke dives into the ocean after the tough guy, chasing him so far out into the ocean that he can't swim back to shore. It is fitting that after all this action, everything ends happily.'[94] Also missing from the restored film, which is mentioned in the publicity, is Buster and Roscoe's competition for Alice, culminating in Buster crashing a bass fiddle over his rival's head.[95]

The film was released on 15 September 1918. One reviewer compared the film to Roscoe's previous *The Waiter's Ball* (1916), remarking on the similarities between the two.[96] Edward Weitzel argued that 'the principal and favorite food served in "The Cook" by Roscoe Arbuckle is food for laughter. [. . .] [The cast] turns a respectable and orderly restaurant into a mirth factory, with efficiency experts holding on to all the jobs.'[97]

Buster received a huge sendoff at the Jewel Café in Seal Beach, California. Many well-known Hollywood folk came by to wish him well. An impromptu minstrel and vaudeville show was given, with Roscoe as master of ceremonies and Lou Anger, Eddie Cline, Al St. John, and Buster himself providing the entertainment.[98] At the end of the night, Buster was gifted a handsome leather wallet with a crisp $100 bill inside. He reported to Camp Kearney, Company C of the 40th Division, 159th Infantry, commanded by First Lieutenant Harry Spain, with his ukulele on 8 July and landed in quarantine. Somehow Roscoe, Al, and Lou Anger were able to visit him there and entertain him with their own minstrel show of sorts. Roscoe also informed Buster that he would be receiving a portion of his paycheck every week ($25) while he was gone. Roscoe asked Buster where he wanted the money sent. He replied, '"Why ask?" And that is why the "little mother" received her boy's first war check at her home in Muskegon, Michigan this week.'[99] His company received orders before his quarantine was up, but he was able to go along anyway when they shipped out 28 July, reaching Camp Mills, Long Island on 5 August.[100] Buster provides lots of information about his war service in his autobiography, including that Natalie moved home to New York during this time and that he supposedly impersonated an officer to get off base at Camp Mills in order to spend the day with her before he sailed. From Long Island, Buster boarded a troop ship, the HMS *Otranto*, on 8 August, which landed in Liverpool, before being sent to France. On the trip over, it was reported that Buster 'staged a burlesque boxing bout which the soldiers said was worth five dollars a ticket for admission.'[101]

In Amiens, France, where his company landed several days later, conditions were difficult to say the least. Buster recalled,

> We slept in circular tents ... our feet in the center and our
> heads close to the drafts from the great outdoors. This was the
> beginning of an experience I have never forgotten. During my
> seven months as a soldier in France, I slept every night but one
> on the ground or on the floor of mills. barns and stables. There
> is always a draft close to the floor of such farm buildings, and
> I soon developed a cold which imperiled my hearing.[102]

Buster was trained as a cryptographer, which meant he could read Morse code and semaphore communications. He volunteered to be part of a 22-person entertainment group within the company, named 'The Sunshine Players,' that worked wonders in terms of boosting troop morale. One of Buster's favorite turns was as 'Princess Rajah,' performing her snake dance with sausages. He never saw fighting on the front lines, but even though armistice was achieved 11 November, he had to remain in France until the following March, when his company was moved to the Bordeaux Embarkation station. Taking the USS *Luckenback* home on what was a 'rough voyage of fourteen days from Bordeaux,'[103] he arrived, along with 2,280 soldiers and officers at Debarkation Hospital No. 3 in Brooklyn New York on 5 April 1919. Continuing hearing problems caused Buster to be moved to General Hospital No. 2 at Fort McHenry on 15 April. He was eventually examined by doctors at Johns Hopkins as well. The doctors believed that his hearing would eventually return, however, he would remain deaf in one ear for the rest of his life. As Buster told it, "'I was deaf as a post, not from the racket of bursting shells, as you might suppose, but due solely to the climate. The army doctors said they had never seen a case like mine, and I guess they were telling the truth, for none of them were able to do anything for me.'"[104] Buster left for Camp Custer, Michigan on 21 April and was finally discharged 29 April. Of course, he visited his parents in Muskegon for three days and then made his way back to Hollywood, arriving on 6 May. Buster was ecstatic to be back in the entertainment business he loved so much. Reinstated at his $250 a week salary, he was to make three more films with Roscoe by the end of 1919.[105]

Chapter 8

Final Comiques and First Buster Shorts

Back Stage, The Hayseed, The Garage, One Week, The Saphead, and The High Sign

■■■■■■■■■■■■■■■■■■■■■■■■■■■■■

While Buster had been overseas, Roscoe was mandated to find a new studio to move into, because the Balboa studios situation was not resolved successfully. He moved to the Diando Studio in Glendale, California temporarily, very near Keystone, 20 July. Roscoe and his associates, Lou Anger and, of course, Joe Schenck, were concerned about 'the uncertainty of not being able to make definite arrangements for a permanent stay. [. . .] The comedian could not go ahead with his plans, such as the erection of two large permanent street sets absolutely necessary for the production of his next comedies and other propositions which meant a large outlay of money.'[1] The first film he would make in Buster's absence was *The Sheriff* (1918) and he would complete six more before Buster's return to Hollywood: *A Scrap of Paper* (1918), a World War I propaganda short, *Camping Out* (1919), *The Pullman Porter* (1919), *Love* (1919), *The Bank Clerk*, and *A Desert Hero* (1919). Oddly and seemingly out of the blue, a three-line piece appeared in the *Wichita [Kansas] Beacon* 28 September that may have signaled what would be a 'Who's Better?' rivalry that continues to this day: 'Buster Keaton will step into Charlie Chaplin's shoes some day. He is as droll and comical as the little Englishman.'[2]

By December 1918, supposed Buster letters to Roscoe were being received and printed in the papers. One particular letter, obviously post-armistice, expressed Buster's strong desire to rejoin the company and get back to work: 'Please have my dressing room and wardrobe in shape as I will be rarin' to go when I get there. Incidentally, I'm chock full of ideas about discipline since they made me Corporal, and I'll be ready for work every morning at eight o'clock.'[3] Something else had changed, too. Roscoe had renegotiated his contract in August and was now bound to make 10 films a year instead of eight, supposedly giving up his vacation time between films in order to do so.[4] By the time he began production on *Love*, just into the new year, his fifth film without Buster, Roscoe had leased a part of his old stomping grounds at the Keystone Studios, a portion located on the opposite side of Allesandro Street in Glendale.[5]

Mid-February, another Buster letter 'arrived' and was printed in the papers. This one complained about the fact that Bordeaux, where he was at that moment, waiting to embark, was experiencing teeming rain, but there didn't seem to be a drop to drink in the city. Continuing the Frank Cutler tradition once again, he wrote a poem about it.[6] Then on 23 February, Roscoe signed another new contract, this one for approximately $3 million in three years and for Famous Players-Lasky. He was to be paid $125,000 upon submitting each film, with 24 films expected.[7] In March, Jean Havez arrived at the Comique Studios to begin work as a scenario writer,[8] this time as a contracted part of the company. Havez had had an incredible vaudeville career, working with Bert Williams on his Ziegfeld shows and writing Joe Keaton's favorite song, *Everybody Works but Father*.[9] In early April, having lost Alice Lake to her own film ambitions elsewhere, Roscoe borrowed Molly Malone from the Al Christie Studios.[10] She would star as the leading lady in Roscoe's last three films with Buster. As Steve Massa writes, Mollie started her career at 19 in dramas, especially Westerns, in which she was often paired with Harry Carey. When she moved over to Universal, she started making a few comedies, which turned into her forte by the time she started working at the Christie Studios, so she came to Comique with more than adequate comedy experience.[11] Roscoe also hired a new cameraman, Elgin Lessley, who would shoot the last three Comiques, then become Buster's own cameraman for some time.

Buster's rejoining his Comique colleagues didn't really hit the trade papers until mid-May. With his return, the subject matter of *Back Stage* became a no-brainer. Who better to advise on such a project than Buster Keaton and Jean Havez? Roscoe was working in the Astra Studios, located at Verdugo Road above E. Lexington Drive[12] in Glendale, while trying to arrange a deal for a new studio to be built in Culver City. Besides a few new players in this film, it would be Al St. John's last with the company and his role was a small one.[13] Except for one short scene on the street outside the theatre, the entire film was shot on a theatre stage set, the Hickville Bijou, complete with dressing rooms, curtains, backdrops and other props.[14]

The film opens on Buster and another stagehand, played by Rube Miller, organizing the stage for newly arriving acts. Roscoe is the poster hanger, so goes outside to get this job done. He's bothered by a young boy, so much so that Roscoe eventually pastes him right into the poster. Having finished, he agrees to take the boy down, but when he does so, he leaves the back of the kid's pants behind, so he wraps him in another poster and sends him off. The poster originally says, 'You Must Not Miss/ Gertrude McSkinny/Famous Star Who Will Play/The Little Laundress/First Time Here/Tomorrow at 2.00 pm,' but when he folds the theatre door to go back inside, it reads 'Miss Skinny Will Undress Here,' interesting a passerby to the extent that he runs to buy a ticket. Back inside the acts are arriving, first an old dramatic monologuist, Julius Hamlet Omlette, played by Monty Collins, Sr. late of the vaudeville stage. He demands the star dressing room, but the star is on a pulley, and as soon as he enters his room, Buster pulls the lever and moves it to another room. Next, an eccentric dancer, Clarence Marmalade, arrives, played by John Coogan, Sr., the father of Jackie Coogan, soon to begin filming the Chaplin masterpiece *The Kid* (1921). Coogan does some high kicks, knocking everyone's hat off and more, and all try to mimic him, which they do badly. Finally, the humongous strong man, Professor Onion, played by Charles 'Buddy' Post, arrives with leading lady Molly Malone, his put-upon assistant. She is carrying his five pieces of luggage by herself, and Onion won't let Roscoe or the stagehands help her. Roscoe, Buster, and the other stagehands decide to try to subdue the bully, but an axe and several other implements fail to have an effect. They then decide to wire his set of barbells with electricity, and this does the trick. Afterwards, they throw the unconscious body into his dressing room.

About when the show is supposed to start, all the performers decide to walk out, including the strong man, who has since recovered. Molly stays behind and suggests that they all put on a show themselves. She starts with an exotic dance and is soon followed by Roscoe playing a king in leopard skins and Buster, with a very long blond wig, playing his consort, whom he throws around the stage rather mercilessly. The camera shoots to Coogan's character, sitting in a box and heckling the performance a time or two. Tired of this irritation, Roscoe throws Buster into Coogan's lap in desperation. Now the onstage setting changes to a snow scene (Al hangs in the rafters throwing the confetti/snow down on the actors). There is a large façade of a building on the left and Roscoe arrives in a cart driven by Buster on the right. Molly appears at an upstairs window and Roscoe looks up at her, ready to recite some dramatic dialogue, when Buster, backstage, gets his cart caught in the works and causes the building façade to drop, with one window opening allowing the thing to just miss Roscoe standing under it, the first of several times Buster will use this bit in his films – the most famous, of course, being in *Steamboat Bill* (1927). At this point, the strong man, sitting in the balcony, makes his presence known, objecting in every way to what's occurring onstage. He draws a gun and shoots Molly. It's not a comedy shot, for she goes down and stays down. Buster rigs up a swing and swings it out over the balcony, grabbing the strong man and pulling him onto the stage. Rube and Al are busy filling a trunk with all of the strong man's weights. Roscoe pulls this up over the stage with a pulley and drops it on the strong man's head, knocking him out. Buster and Al are knocked out, too. The final scene is Roscoe visiting Molly in the hospital as she recovers, in a very tender and out of the ordinary ending for a Comique short. The film was released 7 September 1919. Tom Hamlin noted the many merits of the film in a lengthy and descriptive review: 'It is full of laughs and rapid action. [. . .] In the Romeo and Juliet episode the scenery falls and shows the girl standing on the top step of a ladder. Innumerable situations of this kind are responsible for the almost continuous laughter.'[15]

Meanwhile, Roscoe was in negotiations with his old nemesis Henry Lehrman about leasing a studio at Lehrman's new Culver City studios. There seemed to be some confusion about the deal on Lehrman's part, as Roscoe had it reported in print that he was not amenable to any financial partnership with Lehrman in the deal, but just wanted to be his tenant when the facility was completed.[16] The Lehrman studios (once the Thomas Ince studios) were supposed to be completed by the end of August,[17] and indeed, it was reported that Roscoe had moved in by 26 July. His stage was 70 by 220 feet, and he was equipped with all the modern amenities, such as dressing rooms, cutting and assembly rooms, etc.[18] *The Hayseed*, Comique's next effort, was the first film to be produced at this studio.

The Hayseed was completed already by the end of August. The set was dominated by a huge general store, that was 'sixty feet deep, with a stock of everything from needles to baled hay.'[19] Grimes General Store seems to be constructed of brick and features some decorative architectural elements; in other words, it looks expensive. The absence of Al St. John as Roscoe's rival in this film makes a huge difference in terms of speed, style, and focus. While many recent critics have panned the film, James Neibaur lauds it for being 'a more relaxed comedy of situations that offered greater depth to the character he [Roscoe] played. It was simply a decision by Arbuckle for *The Hayseed* to be a relaxed situation comedy with a rural setting and he created clever gags that stem from this setting and these situations.'[20] He believes that the film signals a sort of evolution for Roscoe that would naturally lead to his success in the feature films he would soon begin to make and star in.

Roscoe plays a rural post office delivery person in the film. Early on, he is portrayed driving the RFD (Rural Free Delivery) horse cart down a country lane, throwing letters into mailboxes with ease, until he gets to a big piece of mail that doesn't fit and has to tear it in pieces to get it in the box. His girlfriend Molly receives a love letter and Roscoe tries to find out who sent it, but she won't tell. Her mother, played by Chaplin studios regular Kitty Bradbury, gives Roscoe a registered letter with $300 in it for her mortgage (interestingly, there's a bit about Kitty and her mortgage money in Chaplin's *The Pilgrim* just four years later), and this sum becomes the source of the main conflict. Jack Coogan plays the rival for Molly's hand in the film. He wears a badge and so is a sort of corrupt lawman. This works to compound the goodness and sweetness of Roscoe's character, as well as the childlike relationship he has with Molly. Back at the general store, Buster does a few bits with a broom again, an implement with which he has a lot of experience and familiarity. He sits the broom upside down, with the handle sitting on the floor, then turns the head this way and that, as if directing traffic. This happens outside the store on the street, as well as inside, after Roscoe returns. Roscoe gives the registered letter to the store owner, played by Rube Miller. When Rube places it in the back of the store, Jack takes his chance, steams the envelope open, steals the money, then seals it back up. Buster has witnessed the whole thing and immediately confronts Jack with the information, but is beat down, Jack telling him that if he informs on him, he will kill him. Next comes the engagement ring plot. Molly asks Roscoe for a ring, so he arbitrarily sizes her finger by jamming it through a block of cheese, then sends information about her size to the synthetic diamond company by choosing an appropriately sized pickle to send along. Jack has bought Molly an authentic diamond ring with the $300, which he gives to her first. She accepts it, but it has a small stone, and she isn't that impressed. Roscoe's order arrives and he presents it to Molly. Because it has a much bigger stone, she rejects Jack's ring and eagerly replaces it with Roscoe's, which she loves.

Later, the village is celebrating 'English Week,' by holding a dance and entertainments in the general store, which has been cleared of its contents for the occasion. Buster performs a magic trick for his contribution and Roscoe is supposed to sing some sentimental songs, but his throat is too dry.

Buster suggests to him that eating onions will solve the problem, so he eats a dozen and a half of green onions, then begins singing. There's not a dry eye in the house, except for Jack's. Once again, he becomes jealous, this time of Roscoe's singing gifts, and suddenly announces to everyone that Roscoe has stolen the money out of the registered letter. Roscoe goes from person to person and tries to get support for the fact that his character doesn't allow such behavior, since Jack has no real evidence, but unfortunately, he has onion breath and scares every one of them away, even Luke the dog. Finally, Buster pipes up and tells what he knows about the robbery, Luke chases Jack out of the store and out into the country and Roscoe tells Molly to eat some onions, so he can kiss her. Buster has less to do in this film than he did in his first, *The Butcher Boy*, which may have something to do with just getting back to work and wanting to be deferential towards the boss who graciously took him back. He gets in a few nice pratfalls, but little else. The film was released on 26 October 1919. The reviewer for *Wid's Daily* argued that the film would credit any bill: 'He gets in a lot of original business and his supporting company headed by Buster Keaton and Molly Malone works like a smooth machine in helping along the comedy tricks.'[21] Several diversions from the existing film, described in the publicity material include that the general store is Judson's store, with Judson (Rube Miller) being Jack's father. Also, Roscoe is exonerated at the end, not by Buster, but by Jack's returning the diamond and sneaking the $300 into Kitty's handbag.[22] This bit of narrative would have answered some questions, surely, but wouldn't necessarily make the film better.

Roscoe began the final collaboration with Buster under the Comique banner right away. It promised to include some tricks 'involving automobiles and the like that will make some of the daredevils of the screen look to their laurels.'[23] Entitled *The Garage*, the mostly plotless film consisted of a string of creative gags that worked to end the Arbuckle–Keaton collaboration on a high note. The film begins with Buster and Roscoe working the garage of the title. Roscoe is finishing up washing and polishing a car, when Buster manages to blow a bunch of large pieces of dust on it, ruining the job. The owner arrives facing away from the camera and Roscoe tells Buster to stall him while he re-cleans the car. Roscoe does this by placing the car on a huge revolving platform, then hosing it off as it whirls around and drying it with a nearby fan on a pole. Buster and the owner of the garage, Rube, played by Dan Crimmons, take turns dancing and doing flips to keep the customer occupied, until Roscoe drives the clean car up and achieves a satisfied customer. Comedian Charles Dorety now enters the garage and asks to rent a car for half a day – not a good one, because he's a nervous driver. He drives the car Roscoe gives him out of the garage and it immediately falls into a million pieces. He walks back in the garage and asks to rent another one, this time giving Roscoe a tip, which he forgot before. This time he is able to drive away. Molly, Rube's daughter and a tomboy, comes downstairs to greet her boyfriend, played by Harry McCoy. The couple stands too close to Buster and Roscoe, who are making a mess with grease, and the flowers Harry has brought for Molly get covered with the stuff, so that when he hands them to her, she gets covered with grease, as does Harry. Molly gets angry and storms off. Buster and Roscoe subject Harry to the same treatment as the car, on the rotating platform, and somehow, they all get clean.

Molly comes downstairs again, clean, and meets Harry who tries to get her to forgive him, but she is adamant that she won't, so he seeks revenge of one type or another in the rest of the film. First, outside the garage, he consults three men and gets one of them, played by Monty Banks, to start running so that Luke will chase him, and he can yell 'Mad Dog,' in hopes of getting the animal taken away from Roscoe. Luke does chase Monty for a while and then Buster, who has gone out to find him. Luke bites off Buster's pants while he is stuck between the boards of a fence. Buster then starts walking in only his underwear below the waist, when he runs into a young lady, played by Polly Moran, who is horrified by the sight of him. Buster suddenly gets the great idea of cutting a kilt out of a Harry Lauder poster – his tam as well – and wraps them around himself, while Polly runs for the police. The policeman arrives, sees what he thinks is Buster in a kilt and chastises Polly for making a big deal out of nothing. As he turns away, so does Buster, revealing the backside that shows his underwear, causing Polly to faint. He meets up with Roscoe, makes his predicament known and they begin a synchronized walking that is familiar to Keaton viewers from his later *Sherlock, Jr.* (1924). Then they stop at a men's store, and Buster steals some pants from a mannikin sitting outside and puts them on. Back at the garage, they tuck in bed, tying ropes on themselves, in case of a fire (they are the firemen). Harry, meanwhile, has not achieved enough revenge yet, so now he rings the fire bell to get Roscoe and Buster out of the garage, so he can set it on fire. While they're on a wild goose chase, Harry sets the fire, but then realizes that Rube has locked the garage door with a padlock, so he's trapped inside as well. Molly is upstairs taking a bath, when she hears Harry banging on her door and starts to smell smoke. Rube has rounded up Buster and Roscoe and brought them back to the garage with the firehose, which is hooked up to a hydrant quite a distance from the fire itself, so it pops one leak, which Roscoe closes by sitting on it and then two more when a trolley runs over it. The 'fire department' then resorts to holding a life net (also known as a jumping sheet) below the window that Harry is hanging out of, but then sees Molly and moves it over to her, with the result that Harry falls to the ground. Then the city clock chimes noon and everyone but Rube, Roscoe, and Buster leave for their regular two-hour lunch, with Molly still in the burning building. They can't lift the life net but get her to jump anyway; she lands on the power lines outside the building and can't get down. Roscoe and Buster in a crazy, messy but somewhat acrobatic sequence, climb up to her and hang from the wires upside down in order to deliver her into a car, which sits up high enough to break the fall. Buster and Roscoe then fall into the car as well, Roscoe grabbing Molly into the back seat with him and Buster driving them off 'into the sunset.' The film was released 26 October 1919. Laurence Reid, in a review for *Motion Picture News* panned the film, arguing that Roscoe was 'capable of offering us better achievements.'[24] Edward Weitzel, however, felt otherwise: 'for refreshing novelty of theme and all-around entertaining qualities the picture is among the best directed by the heavyweight comedian, with the expansive smile and quick sense of humour.'[25]

By 21 December, it was being hinted that Buster was to leave the Arbuckle fold in the manner of his predecessor, Al St. John,[26] but it wasn't until the end of March 1920 that the contract and plans for Buster were announced. Roscoe had already been signed to do features, which would require him to act in diverse roles and not necessarily rely on his comedic gifts. By the end of 1919, he was beginning his first such venture, *The Roundup* (1921) a Western. Buster's apprenticeship in filming slapstick comedy was officially over. He would credit Roscoe with giving him the opportunity and expertise he would use the rest of his life. The two remained stalwart friends, even through the crisis to come in Roscoe's life, the death of starlet Virginia Rappé at his Labor Day party in 1921, believed initially to be a murder he committed. 'The Day the Laughter Stopped,' as Buster termed it, was to ruin Roscoe's film career, even though he was eventually acquitted of the crime.

Three films and their productions rounded out 1920: *One Week*, *The Saphead*, and *The High Sign*. These films were released completely out of production order, but together demonstrate Buster's development as a solo performer. The first Buster Keaton Production was *The High Sign*, but Buster had some reservations about it and shelved it until 18 April 1921. The second film produced was *The Saphead*, not a slapstick comedy at all, but an acting part for Buster in a feature film outside his own studio. This one was not released until October 1920. So, the first film moviegoers were to see him in would be the second Buster Keaton Productions film, *One Week*, which proved to be key to his rising success in 1920 and beyond. The films will be discussed here in their order of production rather than release.

The specifics of Buster's new contract with Metro were not disclosed until March, with the suggestion that it had been signed earlier: 'Buster Keaton will make two-reel comedies for Metro when he completes his work in Winchell Smith's production of *The New Henrietta*. This became known yesterday when the existence of a contract signed in New York between Joseph M. Schenck and Metro Pictures[27] was disclosed.' The contract called for eight films a year and, at this point, were to be made at Metro studios and also released by Metro. Lou Anger was to be his production manager.[28] Eddie Cline, former Keystone cop, would join his company as director. Cline had worked his way up from actor, to assistant director, then director at the Sennett studio and even is said to have come up with the idea for the Sennett Bathing Beauties.[29] *The High Sign* is hinted at having started in late January, when several companies were trying to use the Lehrman studio at the same time:[30] 'The first release was started at the Arbuckle studio in Culver City.'[31] Beyond this hint, there is no mention of it in the press until it was released more than a year later: Roscoe was filming *The Round Up* at the same time, so it became a priority to find new studio space for Buster. Kline suggests that this film was shelved due to one small scene in which Buster fails to slide on a banana peel, as the audience expects, turns to the camera, flips the 'high sign' instead and moves on his way. Buster, in viewing the scene later, felt this might be taken offensively by the audience and so, that was it. He shelved it. Yet, the film contains some brilliant gags and is a sort of omnibus of Keaton creativity. The first scene alone is enough to confirm that. It begins with Buster falling unceremoniously off a passing train, suggesting that he had hitched a ride. He lands at an amusement promenade, the actual Ocean Walk near Venice, California. No rides are shown, nor is the beach or ocean. What the audience sees are the games and restaurants. Buster sits down on the first of several rows of benches in the middle of all this, having grabbed a newspaper from someone riding the nearby carousel. He unfolds the paper and unfolds and unfolds it, until it is about the size of a sheet, which causes him to fall backwards, taking several benches with him. His eye falls upon the perfect job ad, which reads: 'Wanted – Boy in shooting gallery. Must be expert shot to attract a crowd. Ask for TINY TIM, 233 Spring Street.' And so begins Buster's enigmatic odyssey. He starts off by stealing a gun from a cop and replacing it with a banana, then finding Al St. John in the sand, who has been emptying wine bottles in the usual way. Buster sets three up and starts practicing with the gun, but whichever bottle he aims at, the one next to it gets shot, including Al, who then runs off out of scene and out of the film. With this practice, Buster shows up for the job prospect, finding Tiny Tim, played by Ingram B. Pickett, to be huge (of course). Tim leaves him and suggests that when he returns, he wants to hear the bell ring every time Buster shoots. The apparatus Buster comes up with to guarantee this for himself is pure Keaton: he hooks a boxer up to the bell and hangs its bone just out of reach, which Buster is then able to entice the dog with each time he shoots, by means of another rope, thereby causing the dog to ring the bell. When Tim returns, the exhibition goes well until Buster mistakenly shoots the ceiling (Tim leaves with an idea) and then must shoot off in rapid succession multiple shots, because the dog has been threatened by a cat and rings the bells repeatedly, trying to get loose – and eventually does. At this point, Mr. August Nickelnurse and his daughter, played by Bartine Burkett, enter the shooting gallery. They've been threatened by the Blinking Buzzards gang, a group Tim heads, and Mr. Nickelnurse needs a bodyguard. Buster refuses at first, until the daughter entices him into it, presenting her father's card. After they depart, Tim returns and takes Buster to the Blinking Buzzards meeting place, showing him the 'high sign.' The bright idea Tim had was to force Buster to kill August Nickelnurse. They make him swear on a skull ('Do you know what an oath is?' 'Yes, I play golf.'). Back at the shooting gallery, Buster has three male customers, a drunk man, who shoots a clay pipe out of Buster's mouth and discovers the cigar prizes are explosive, played by Charles Dorety, a man who takes the gun Buster offers, then holds him up for the cash drawer, and a third man (Charles Bennett?) who brings his own powerful rifle and destroys the place with one shot. Buster then tries to make his way to the Nickelnurse home, but tussles with a cop on the way, the same one who he swapped a banana for his gun. Meanwhile the Nickelnurses have been fitting their house with trapdoors and secret passages. Buster arrives and is soon informed that the butler is a Buzzard. He tells Buster to 'do your duty.' Buster convinces Mr Nickelnurse to play dead after he 'shoots' him, which he does. The Buzzards are outside and think they have succeeded, until Nickelnurse gets up and blows the charade. What transpires next is an extremely well-choreographed 'dance' through the rooms of the house, using the trapdoors and passages. Some frames show two rooms at a time and some four, so the viewer can see the intricacy of this unusual chase. It ends when Buster is able to pull the cord of a trapdoor and Tiny Tim falls through it. Buster then receives his reward from the Nickelnurse daughter. The film was shelved until 18 April 1921. Reviews were weak, with one writer mentioning that it did not come up to the standard of his last one, which would have been *Hard Luck*: 'Your crowd will say he is not as good in this as the others, but, on the other hand, the standard maintained has been so high that Keaton may be entitled to slip once in a while.'[32] One wonders what the effect would have been if *The High Sign* was Keaton's first released film.

By the end of March, when the papers were announcing Buster's new contract, he was given the role of Bertie Van Alstyne in what would be the film version of the stage play *The New Henrietta* written by Victor Mapes.[33] This feature would not be a slapstick comedy. It would feature stars such as William H. Crane, who had played the role of Nicholas Van Alstyne on Broadway. June Mathis wrote the screenplay, and its production would be overseen by two men: producer Winchell Smith and director Herbert Blaché (husband of Alice Guy Blaché). Douglas Fairbanks, who had played the role of Bertie on stage in 1913, recommended Buster for the part and he was basically hired on that recommendation. Filming began the week of 29 March.[34] By 24 April, the project had been retitled *The Saphead*,[35] which certainly put the focus more on Bertie's character than on the Henrietta mine – the original focus – which may suggest the overall feeling about his particular performance in the film. Kline sums up this performance well, writing,

> Buster is totally convincing both as a sheltered Milquetoast and as a spirited dynamo. His vaudeville experience, where he was not only exposed to an endless variety of acting styles but also played several assorted parts himself, gave him the resources to adapt to the role. Seeing Keaton create a fully developed screen character, knowing that for the previous three years he had been indulging in roughhouse slapstick with Arbuckle, is a revelation, proving that Buster was a gifted actor as well as a superb comedian. Like Fairbanks, he was fond of the Bertie character and based many – arguably all – of his feature film portrayals on this type, one who appears weak and dimwitted at first but becomes the strongest, most resourceful and dynamic figure of all.[36]

Grace Kingsley devoted her column to interviewing Buster on 16 May, about the same time filming wrapped, starting it with what she calls Buster's bleating about the Bertie role:

> 'I gotta do some sad scenes. Why, I never tried to make anybody cry in my life! And I go 'round all the time dolled up in kippie clothes – wear everything but a corset! Can't stub my toe in this picture nor anything! Just imagine having to play-act all the time without ever getting hit with anything!'[37]

The story, as it exists in this film, is about a wealthy businessman, Nicholas Van Alstyne, played by William H. Crane, known as 'Old Nick of "The Street,"' whose ownership of the Henrietta silver mine is the basis of his fortune. He has a daughter, Rose (Carol Holloway), who has married a scoundrel named Mark Turner, played by Irving Cummings, an adopted daughter named Agnes (Beulah Booker) and a son who is a wastrel named Bertie (Buster). The old man gets angry at Bertie on several occasions, culminating in him being written off with a million-dollar check and told to leave. Agnes and Bertie find out early on that they love each other and then plan to get married, but Bertie has been spending time trying to create a wild man persona while Agnes is away at school, thinking that she will love him more for it. He even places an autographed picture of someone named 'Henrietta' on the mantel in his bedroom to create this image. The name 'Henrietta' becomes important in the story for several reasons: the photo in Bertie's room, the name of the actress Mark Turner ruins and leaves destitute, who still has his love letters, and the name of the silver mine. The Bertie character seems more than just naïve in the story, although he does understand how to get up late, dawdle at a luxurious breakfast and enjoy a lengthy shave. He doesn't understand what is going on in a gambling casino, though, or what happens in a stock exchange and what even 'buying a seat in a stock exchange' means, but somehow this 'not knowing' ends up saving the day. Mark Turner encourages his father-in-law to go on a voyage in the second half of the film, so that he can manhandle his finances. His idea is to devalue the shares on the Henrietta mine to such an extent that they become worthless, and Nick will be ruined. One of the problems is that Mark has degraded a young woman, who still has his letters in her possession and threatens to give them to Rose unless he takes care of her. She dies and his letters arrive at the Van Alstyne home just as Agnes and Bertie are about to get married. Somehow, as naïve as he

173

is, Bertie understands that he must take the fall for this discretion in order to save the feelings of his sister, and so Mark gets away with it for a short time. He decides to steal from his father-in-law at this point, because he's sure the scandal will eventually be found out. Later, as the stock plummets and Mark looks on, Bertie is trying out his first day on the stock exchange, thinking it involves knocking gentlemen's hats off and other such things. He goes out and buys a bunch of hats and when he gets back, he hears the word 'Henrietta' everywhere, thinking it has to do with his disgrace, and yells to Nick's stockbroker that he wants it to stop. The stockbroker gets an idea at that moment that if Bertie buys up all the stock, its price will rise, and his father's fortunes will be saved. He tells Bertie that every time someone says 'Henrietta' that he should yell 'I'll take it.' Having saved the fortune and returning home in tatters from the mêlée on the exchange floor, he doesn't even realize what he's done until his father explains it to him. In the meantime, with the police on the way, Mark has conveniently dropped dead. Bertie's marriage to Agnes now happens off-screen, but the film ends a year later when she is delivering him twins and everyone is reconciled.

While this plot is, at its essence, a melodrama of the nineteenth-century variety, and Buster certainly didn't play his part for laughs, he is given a few entertaining moments: sliding down a staircase on his backside and being thrown around the stock exchange in the final scene there. Some more subtle moments are also amusing, like when he comes to his first wedding attempt with Agnes armed with five wedding rings, just in case, then forgets them all in another room when the time comes, or when he thinks he has succeeded in achieving his rake image at the casino, because the place is about to be raided, even tendering a brief grin at the prospect (the only one in the film), and is foiled when the police refuse to include him in the raid. In addition to these glimmers, though, perhaps the most important aspect of this part for Buster was the experience it gave him in creating a persona that he would then occupy in every film going forward. As Eileen Whitfield remarks,

> Keaton's reserve, the way he gives a little to imply a great deal, is not just effective as technique. It is part of what made him a movie star. His face is never 'dead' (as in 'pan'), or blank. There's always a trace, a suggestion of something, in those famously huge, heavy-lidded eyes. [. . .] The bare-bones nature of Keaton's acting makes anything he does do highly suggestive. And it works like a tease; he's unknowable, so, of course, we want to get to know him more.[38]

Buster had been using his face in this way ever since he discovered its magic in vaudeville, but the role of Bertie allowed him to try it out in 360 degrees. It's no wonder he was the only actor in the film to receive rave reviews: 'The latter [Buster Keaton], however, has the title role and provides all of the interest that the picturized version of the play holds.'[39] *Variety* noted that Buster's Bertie was 'just as much the vacuum who doesn't know what it's all about, but reads and dresses him as a present-day Fifth Avenue goldfish. [. . .] Buster, [although] a cyclone when called upon, his quiet work in this picture is a revelation. He is the personification of a mental minus sign in facial expression.'[40] Filming was complete shortly after the time Metro bought Buster the old Lone Star studio at the corner of Eleanor and Lillian (the press locates it on the other corner, Romaine Street and N. Cahuenga Blvd.) in early April.[41] The film's release was held over, though, until 18 October 1920 from its initial release date of 1 September.[42]

By early May, Buster had acquired Eddie Cline as a director and Jean Havez to write scenarios.[43] By 16 May, it was being reported that Buster's first story at the new studio would be: 'about a portable house and a young married couple.'[44] Filming started about a week later, and the week after that, one writer noted, 'Buster Keaton was the only Metro star who broiled under the blistering sun yesterday in pursuit of his art. He seemed as full of pep as ever and expects to have his first starring comedy vehicle ready by the middle of June.'[45] By 4 June, Buster had chosen Sybil Sealy, former Mack Sennett Bathing Beauty, and member of a vaudeville swimming act before that,[46] as his leading lady for the new project. Then, by 19 June, 'Big Joe' Roberts, of the vaudeville team Roberts & Shaw, was completing his last vaudeville engagements and planned to join Buster at Metro.[47] 'Big Joe' would soon become one of Buster's most stalwart character actors and a great foil for his timid film persona, although his role in this first project was a small one. The new production, entitled *One Week*, was reportedly completed by 20 June, when Buster took his first vacation since beginning *The Saphead*.[48]

One Week was a sophisticated riff off a nine-minute short made by Ford Motor Company in 1919 entitled *Home Made*. It contains a dramatization of a young couple deciding to ameliorate their financial woes in buying a house by choosing a kit house, for which every element could be chosen to the buyer's specifications. As they wait for the kit to arrive, the young couple then chose a plot of land to build it on. The making of the kit parts is shown in detail as they move through the factory, with a tearing-off-of-a-calendar page designating the passage of time – here 28 June to 4 July, or exactly one week. The film ends with a shot of the completed house, then of the young couple coming down the church steps after their wedding service (much like the first scene of Buster's short), entering their car and taking off for their new house. What the Ford film leaves out is the construction of the kit *in situ*, and this is the gap Buster fills up with fun. Buster's film, or at least his title, was also touted as being a play on the name of a 1907 Elinor Glyn novel, *Three Weeks*, an erotic romance novel concerning a relationship between an English nobleman and a parson's daughter.

Buster's film begins by emphasizing the pull-off calendar, which has a date of Monday the 9th (no month) and also the fact that he and Sybil have just married. The calendar days will effectively divide the film into seven parts. Immediately after the service, Handy Hank, the villain, is introduced. This unidentified actor (recently discovered to be one of the taunters in the first stock exchange scene in which Buster appears in *The Saphead*) is fairly tall, but what height he does have is emphasized by the fact that all of his clothes are too small. He has been rejected by Sybil who favors Buster, so is determined to create as much conflict as possible. He's driving the 'Just Married' vehicle and tries to separate the newlyweds as best he can in the car, but he is foiled and there are a few great gags in the meantime. At lot number 99, their plot of land, what seems to be a box of lumber arrives in a truck unceremoniously, a wedding present from Uncle Mike. It's a 'HOME' from the Portable House Company, with the following directions: 'To give this house a snappy appearance, put it up according to the numbers on the boxes.' Naturally, this is where Hank is provided another opportunity; he changes the numbers on the boxes with paint. The result is a cockeyed house; the bathroom door leads to the outside (and it's on the second floor), the roof only covers half of the house and doors and windows are all askew, among other things. Big Joe Roberts makes his debut when he appears carrying an upright piano on one shoulder. He drops it toward Buster for him to catch and it pins him underneath instead. Joe is loath to help out, but finally does, then leaves. The couple are left to try to get the piano in the house. Buster creates a pulley by tying a rope to a chandelier downstairs. For some reason, Hank is upstairs plotting something and so he gets shot through the roof when Buster sees the ceiling failing and releases the pulley. Hank's face is now sticking through the roof and Buster accidentally knocks his head back down through it. Also in this film is another iteration of the building falling with Buster just fitting through the window hole, a gag that originated in *Back Stage* and will become a spectacle in *Steamboat Bill*.

On Friday the thirteenth, or day five of the week, the couple gives a housewarming party, unbelievably with Hank in attendance, but he is soon done away with when Buster entices him through the upstairs bathroom door. A storm kicks up; it begins raining inside the house and then the simple rainstorm becomes a cyclone. The house responds by rotating round and round. In the first ever use of a 360-degree revolving camera, Buster is thrown around the periphery of the inside of the house. But he keeps getting thrown outside and eventually so does Sybil and the rest of the guests. One old man nonchalantly looks at his watch, notes the time, and makes his excuses. After the storm, the house is a shambles. This is when the couple find out that they have built on lot 66 instead of 99 and need to move the house across the railroad tracks to the correct plot. They work together to get it on 'wheels' (beer barrels really) and begin to pull it successfully with the car, but then the chain breaks, leaving the house squarely on the tracks. Buster tries to nail his back car seat to the house and pull it that way, but the whole chassis comes loose from the wheels and engine. The house is stuck where it is, and it finally dawns on them that a train is coming (this scene was shot at Inglewood train station), and the house can't be moved. Surprisingly, the first train misses the house completely, but Buster and Sybil breathe easy too soon, because another train coming from the other direction plows right through the house, leaving it a pile of broken boards. Buster sticks a 'For Sale' sign near the pile, attaches the directions, and the two walk off, hand in hand.

Besides the humor, Buster and Sybil's young married couple is very endearing, sneaking kisses here and there, holding hands and drawing hearts on the outside of the house. This is in keeping with the lighter, more gentle style of comedy that the critics adored in Roscoe's portrayal of the Hayseed, in the film of the same title. It was a great place for Buster to start with his comedy and his film persona. The film was previewed at Hoyt's Theatre in Long Beach Thursday 1 July and received a great response.[49] It wasn't released to the theatres, however, until 1 September.[50] The critics *and* the public went wild for the film, causing it to be held over several weeks. Robert C. McElravy noted that the film 'contains one funny situation after another, piling up the risibilities until it is likely to create "the laugh heard round the world." [. . .] It is hard to apportion the credit, though the comedian, of course, gets the lion's share. Intelligent direction, excellent planning and mounting of the sets and general business and skillful editing of the film count for much.'[51] Joseph L. Kelley wrote that 'not only is the comedy of the real hilarious brand but without an exception, every incident, every situation is original and presents a front new to the comedy-loving public. [. . .] Buster is a show in himself and is one of the few eccentric comedians working before the camera who appreciates that the day of the pie-throwing comedy has passed.'[52]

Buster enticed his parents and siblings to come to California in July and three of them would take part in his second short, *Convict 13*: Joe, Louise, and Harry. He married long-time girlfriend Natalie Talmadge on 31 May 1921 (the same day and month his parents had married) and soon had two sons, his namesake Joseph (called James) born 2 June 1922 and Robert born 3 February 1924. His collaboration with Eddie Cline and later Clyde Bruckman would result in continued success in the months and years to come, until the silents ended and the film business changed for good. But for now, Buster was entering his salad days, and he deserved to enjoy them.

Epilogue

Highs and Lows of the Film Business

■■■■■■■■■■■■■■■■■■■■■■■■■■■■

Beyond the successes of his first year, Buster continued to make and perfect the comedy short with the help of Eddie Cline, releasing such small masterpieces as *Cops* (1922), *The Blacksmith* (1922), and *The Baloonatic* (1923). Then with the film *The Three Ages* (1923), he attempted to move into comedy features quite successfully. Among these were *Our Hospitality* (1923), which featured members of his own family in the cast, including wife Natalie and son Joseph, Jr., *Sherlock, Jr.* (1924), *The Navigator* (1924), *The General* (1926), which included one of the most expensive scenes in silent film history – the wrecking of a steam locomotive on a trestle over a river – and *Steamboat Bill, Jr.* (1928). After producing one successful film after another for several years, allowing Buster to rise to the levels of his nearest competitors Charlie Chaplin and Harold Lloyd, he made a terrible business decision that would essentially end his creative filmmaking career; Joe Schenck informed him that he was leaving film production and that Buster should sign with Metro-Goldwyn-Mayer, a deal engineered by Schenck's brother Nicholas, a family member by marriage, thereby transferring all decision-making to people who knew nothing and cared nothing about Buster or his films. Both Chaplin and Lloyd had argued fiercely against Buster's accepting this deal, one that he later related as the worst of his life.

While his first film for Metro has many fans to this day – *The Cameraman* (1928) – his next, *Spite Marriage* (1929) would be his final silent film and was demonstrably inferior to his others. Then things became even worse. The new studio began to pair Buster with other comics, Ukelele player Cliff Edwards first and then 'the Schnozzola' Jimmy Durante. Meanwhile, Buster's marriage to Natalie began to decline perceptibly after the birth of their second child, Robert, in 1924. At the same time, she spent his earnings, demanding he build her a big house, which he did in 1926 – an estate they referred to as the Italian Villa and which he lost in their divorce in 1932. With the loss of his creative agency, Buster turned to alcohol as the marriage came to an end. With the divorce, he not only lost the house, but his sons were renamed 'Talmadge,' a surname which eventually became permanent. Buster actually ended up in an institution – a sort of rehab – and married one of the nurses there, a woman by the name of Mae Scriven, in 1933, but they divorced only three short years later. Finally, on May 29, 1940, Buster married dancer Eleanor Norris, 20 years his junior. Eleanor was credited for saving Buster; she gave him back his desire for creative output and success.

Betwixt and between these personal events, Buster's film career had gone off the rails. After three fairly successful films with Durante, his last one being *What No Beer?* (1933), Louis B. Mayer fired him. Irving Thalberg, Metro's reigning wunderkind producer at the time, tried to argue with Mayer on Buster's behalf, to no avail, because Buster refused to ever return to the studio. In 1934, he went to Paris to make *Le Roi des Champs-Élysées*. Upon his return to the States the same year, Buster began to make two-reel shorts again, this time for Educational Pictures and had some success in that effort, such as the film *Grand Slam Opera* (1936). However, Educational downsized in 1937, cutting its operations in Hollywood altogether and, therefore, its ties with Buster Keaton. This turn of events resulted in Buster returning again to MGM, this time to write gags for the Marx Brothers' final three films, including *At the Circus* (1939). That same year, Buster was hired by Columbia Pictures to make 10 two-reelers, with *Pest from the West* (1939) being his personal favorite.

With his marriage to Eleanor in 1940, Buster left the world of two reelers behind and returned to writing gags, this time for Red Skelton. By 1949, he began to be hired in prime supporting roles in big films, such as *In the Good Old Summertime* (1949) with Judy Garland, *Sunset Boulevard* (1950) with Gloria Swanson and William Holden, and *Around the World in 80 Days* with David Niven and Shirley MacLaine. In 1952, he was even hired by the other great comedian, Charlie Chaplin, to take a small part in his film *Limelight*.

In 1949, Buster also tried the new medium of television. He was offered his own live show in 1951, entitled *Life with Buster Keaton*, but it was short-lived, with Buster himself canceling the show due to the stress of coming up with new material every week. Instead, he found some success guest-starring on the shows of others, such as *The Ken Murray Show*,

The Garry Moore Show, and *The Ed Sullivan Show*. He also had some success appearing in television advertisements, such as ones for Colgate Toothpaste, Alka-Seltzer, and RCA Victor. Buster even appeared on the show *You Bet Your Life* on 3 April 1957. Then, by 1954, Buster and Eleanor met the infamous Raymond Rohauer, who arranged to have Buster's silent films moved over to cellulose acetate film from the dangerous nitrate and began a huge resurgence of interest in Buster's silent film work, as well as silent film comedy in general. He received a lifetime achievement award at the 32nd Academy Awards in Hollywood in 1959 and began to be invited round the world to attend various retrospectives of his films.

Beginning in 1964, Buster played small roles in five films for American International Films, including *Pajama Party* (1964) and *Beach Blanket Bingo* (1965). In 1965, he made two other noteworthy films, *The Railrodder* with Gerald Potterton and *Film* with Samuel Beckett. His final feature film performance was a fairly substantial part in *A Funny Thing Happened on the Way to the Forum* (1966) with Zero Mostel, which taxed his, by this time, very fragile health. Then, after suffering with lung cancer, which was not officially diagnosed until January 1966, Buster succumbed and died on 1 February that year, leaving behind his wife Eleanor, the two sons he had reconciled with, and several grandchildren. He had lost his father in 1946 and his mother in 1955. Sister Louise and brother Harry would live until 1981 and 1984 respectively. Buster Keaton's legacy continues strong today, with a vibrant organization of fans congregating each 4 October (or thereabouts) as part of the International Buster Keaton Society, formed in 1992 and with the continuation of the age-old debate: Who's better, Buster Keaton or Charlie Chaplin? Most of his silent films have been restored and restored again and are available for home screening or public screening with orchestral accompaniment, and everything in between. Two great film critics should have the final words then on the great man:

James Agee:

Keaton's face ranked almost with Lincoln's as an early American archetype; it was haunting, handsome, almost beautiful, yet it was irreducibly funny; he improved matters by topping it off with a deadly horizontal hat, as flat and thin as a phonograph record. One can never forget Keaton wearing it, standing erect at the prow as his little boat is being launched. The boat goes grandly down the skids and, just as grandly, straight on to the bottom. Keaton never budges. The last you see of him, the water lifts the hat off the stoic head and it floats away.[1]

Walter Kerr:

It's no accident that what is probably our most familiar image of Keaton is of him scanning the horizon, hand at his brow to keep the sun from his eyes, body arched forward, feet hooked perilously onto the rigging of a ship. He doesn't have to be at sea or have rigging available, to adopt the posture. He does it all the time – on the backs of horses, on the tops of balloons. It is in fact his essential posture: he is an explorer. He explores the universe exactly as he explores film: with a view to measuring the immeasurable before he enters it, so that he will know how to behave when he is there. No matter that there is nothing at all to be seen on the horizon. The boundaries of the world are invisible, anyway. The rigging beneath his feet will give way. He understands that. The horse will move. He expects that too. He will be propelled into the indeterminate, the mockingly inscrutable. But he will be prepared to cooperate with it the moment he arrives.[2]

Notes

■■■■■■■■■■■■■■■■■■■■■■■■■■■■■■■■

Chapter 1: Preamble, or Setting the Groundwork for a Life in Entertainment

1. Meade, Marion, *Buster Keaton: Cut to the Chase*, London, UK: Bloomsbury, 1995: p. 8.
2. Cutler, Nahum S., *Cutler Memorial and Genealogical History*, Greenwood, MA: Press of E. A. Hall & Co., 1889: p. 225.
3. Cutler, Nahum S., *Cutler Memorial,* p. 226.
4. Cutler, Nahum S., *Cutler Memorial*, pp. 296–297.
5. Linda Airgood Neil, who is the living grandniece of Buster's maternal grandmother Elizabeth Shaffer Cutler, Frank's first wife, who died from consumption in 1887, has spent much of her adult life teasing out the small details of the Keaton/Cutler family legacy. She has worked out much of Frank Cutler's employment history, while this author has found and transcribed his twenty-two plays and sketches.
6. lindagoodair, *Why are the Cutlers in Berrien Center, Berrien County, MI in the 1870 Census?* posted on ancestry.com on 21 February 2015.
7. Cowles, B., Niles, MI: B. Cowles, 1871, p. 196.
8. Noble, Vergil, 'Separate Ways: The Cutlers after Keaton,' *The Keaton Chronicle,* Vol. 18. No. 1 (2010): pp. 2–5.
9. He became so enamored with writing in general that he made the *Sioux City, Iowa Journal* with the claim that he would start a newspaper in Modale in the near future (2 May 1882).
10. As Frank Cullen argues in *Vaudeville Old & New: An Encyclopedia of Variety Performers in America*, dialect comedy was popular in America for at least seventy years, beginning in about 1820 with the rise in German and Irish immigration. Some would argue that it continued in popularity even after World War 1, but diminished when these groups began to think of themselves more as American than as members of their original ethnic groups (Vol. 1, New York, NY: Routledge: 2007, p. 310).
11. The Cutler plays will be made available at a later date.

12. Keaton, Buster and Charles Samuels, *My Wonderful World of Slapstick*, Cambridge, MA: Da Capo Press: 1960, pp. 17–18.
13. '[Lincoln. – The People's Theatre],'*The New York Clipper*, 27 August 1887, p. 3.
14. According to ads in the *New York Clipper*, Delorme was performing on her own by 1890, so had either split from Neal or he had died.
15. Agnew, Jeremy, *Entertainment in the Old West: Theatre, Music, Circuses, Medicine Shows, Prizefighting and Other Popular Amusements,* Jefferson, NC: McFarland & Co., Inc., Publishers, 2011, p. 161.
16. 'patented' merely meant proprietary.
17. 15 May 1890, p. 5.
18. Armstrong, David and Elizabeth Metzger Armstrong, *The Great American Medicine Show,* New York, NY: Prentice Hall, 1991, p. 177.
19. *The Aurora [New York] Republican-Register*, p. 8.
20. 20 August 1892, p. 374.
21. A quick scan of a newspaper database retrieved twenty-seven hits for well-received performances of the play by local community theatre companies in the last decade of the nineteenth century.
22. 'Pleasant Ridge,' *Nance County Fullerton [Nebraska] Journal*, 2 April 1897, n. p.
23. p. 3.
24. p. 5.
25. Curtis, James, *Buster Keaton: A Filmmaker's Life*, NY, Alfred A. Knopf, 2022: p. 13.
26. 'Wonderland Musée' ad, *Lincoln [Nebraska] Evening Call,* 18 April 1894, p. 8.
27. Nobel, Vergil, p. 3.
28. Mohawk Indian Medicine Company ad, *DeWitt [Nebraska] Times*, 24 May 1894, p. 3.
29. Marriage certificate provided by Linda Neal, supported additionally by a notice in *Friend [Nebraska] Telegraph*, titled 'Marriage Record,' delineated for May 1894, although no more specific dates are given, 15 June 1894, p. 1. Both Joe and Myra are listed as being from Lincoln, Nebraska. See also n. 64.
30. Nobel, Vergil, p. 3.
31. Nobel, Vergil, p. 3.
32. 21 February 1901, p. 3.
33. p. 5.
34. Further research just makes the story more confusing. Ida May was calling herself 'Cutler' at least until 1897 and had had two boys by then, Max Weston (1893) and Ralph Earlton (1896). They were eventually surnamed Rae, when she took up with actor John George Rae shortly after the turn of the century and had two more children, another boy in 1900 and then her final child, a girl in 1903. All of these children bear the last name of Rae, but Ida May and John did not officially marry until 31 July 1915. And, when

she became very ill in 1916 (so ill, she was pronounced dead at one point) Rae left her and married someone else in 1917, so that she was forced to declare herself a widow on a 1920 census report, when John Rae actually lived until 1959! Divorce records don't exist for any of these couples, so it appears that it must have been common practice to simply abandon one's spouse, take up with someone else and legally marry them, despite being married to someone else. Maybe this was simply a common practice in the entertainment business.

35. 'Cutler's Theatre Company,' *St. Paul [Nebraska] Press*, 7 June 1901, p. 4.
36. '[The Cutler Theatre Company is here],' *Texmo [OK] Times,* 4 June 1909, p. 1.
37. 4 July 1914, p. 4.
38. 13 February 1924, p. 6.
39. 'Mother of Buster Keaton, Famous Movie Comedian, Visits Aged Father at Rockdale; Says Hollywood O.K.,' *The Waco [Texas] News-Tribune*, 4 May 1924, n. p.
40. "In the case of Robert P. Conner vs. Frank Cole," *Edmond [Oklahoma] Sun-Democrat*, 1 December 1893, p. 4. Date of the sale provided by the *Oklahoma Land Runs Roll,* Roll 01, Vol. 1–4, Washington, D. C., United States Department of the Interior, Bureau of Land Management. LAN
41. Cutting in the Myra Keaton scrapbook, Margaret Herrick Library, AMPAS, probably published after August 1904, because it mentions Jingles Keaton in the final lines.
42. In vaudeville parlance, back flips.
43. Slout, William Lawrence, *Theatre in a Tent: The Development of a Provincial Entertainment*, Bowling Green, OH: Bowling Green University Press, 1972, p. 99.
44. *Lincoln [Nebraska] Evening Call*, 11 December 1893, p. 8.
45. *Lincoln [Nebraska] Evening Call*, 21 December 1893, p. 3.
46. 'Corse Payton Answers Questions,' *Lincoln Nebraska State Journal*, 18 June 1911, p. 25.
47. 'Wonderland Musée' ad, *Lincoln [Nebraska] Evening Call*, 11 January 1894, p. 8.
48. *Lincoln [Nebraska] Evening Call*, 25 January 1894, p. 8.
49. 'Wonderland Musée' ad, *Lincoln [Nebraska] Evening Call*, 17 Feb 1894, p. 8.
50. Babiak, Paul, *Knockabout and Slapstick: Violence and Laughter in Nineteenth-Century Popular Theatre and Early Film,* Doctoral Thesis, Centre for Drama, Theatre and Performance Studies, University of Toronto, Canada: 2015, p. 66.
51. Babiak, Paul, pp. 186–187. The UK's version of Fred McNish was Alf West, who received this commentary following one of his 'Silence and Fun' acts: 'Mr. West's "Quiescent fun," a sketch in which he does some knockabout business with an air of genuine enjoyment and consummate slyness is not only funny but prodigiously clever. The final caper, with which, as if by accident, he came to grief on the floor, was so startling and so courageous as

to evoke a spontaneous cheer' (*Birmingham [UK] Post*, 30 November 1880, n. p.

52. Clearly, this act, as described, works smoothly into the acrobatic knockabout act that Joe Keaton became famous for, entitled at one point 'Man with a Table,' a point which then places significant importance on this initial performance at the Wonderland Musée in Lincoln Nebraska in February 1894.

53. 'Wonderland Musée' ad, *Lincoln [Nebraska] Call,* 18 April 1894, p. 8.

54. Joe's tenure with this group was probably a month at most. One traceable date for the group was in Hooper, Nebraska the week of 21 May 1894, including 'a select company of specialty artists and good music' (*Hooper [Nebraska] Sentinel*, 17 May 1894, p. 5.)

55. Mohawk Indian Medicine Company ad, *DeWitt [Nebraska] Times*, 24 May 1894, p. 3.

56. 'The Mohawk Medicine Co. are "right in line,"' *New York Clipper*, p. 227. Joe and Myra's marriage on 31 May was also announced in this piece, verifying the date yet again.

57. McNamara, Brooks, *Step Right Up.* Rev. ed., Jackson, MS: University of Mississippi Press, 1995, p. 16.

58. McNamara, Brooks, *Step Right Up*, p. 44.

59. McNamara, Brooks, *Step Right Up*, p. 47.

60. "The Umatilla Medicine Co.," *Independence [Kansas] Daily Reporter*, 17 May 1896, p. 2.

61. "The Umatilla Medicine Co., No. 90," *New York Clipper*, 8 June 1895, p. 211. LAN.

62. Others in the company included Mrs. St. George, Frank Howard and wife, and Tommie Chase, with Burt and Frank listed as managers ('Notes and roster of the Cutler Comedy Company,' *New York Clipper*, 12 October 1894, p. 505).

63. Curtis, James, *Buster Keaton: A Filmmaker's Life*, p. 15.

64. The parish itself was founded in 1884. An Italianate cathedral now marks the spot, built in 1922, which ceased operations in 1998, but still presents mass on Christmas Eve. It continues to be lovingly maintained. The area's current population is 72.

65. The question is whom did he marry? Burt's only marriage record is for 1901 to Carrie M. Schleckman in Columbus, Ohio.

66. 'Notes and roster of the Cutler Comedy Company,' *New York Clipper*, 12 October 1894, p. 505.

67. A probable route supported by the papers is Galesburg, Kansas 7 to 21 October, Leavenworth, Kansas 16 to 23 October, Brenner, Kansas 27 October to 3 November, Earlton, Kansas 4 to 17 November, and Neodesha, Kansas 29 November to 5 December. Hopefully, they took part in the Wellsville Kansas Benefit performance 9 December, for all proceeds went to the local poor fund.

68. 'Joe Keaton an old time boy,' *Edmond [Oklahoma] News*, 9 November 1894, p. 3.

69. George A. Pardey was at various times misnamed George W. Pardey, John Pardey, Dr. Perlee, and in the *New York Clipper*, George A. Lindsay. With just his initials, G. A. Pardey or Geo. A. Pardey, he created the perfect stage name, essentially "Jeopardy," made even more impactful with a "Dr." placed in front of it. As Curtis works out, he was a British entertainer, son of the famous H. O. Pardey, who had emigrated to Providence, Rhode Island and became an actor and playwright (*Buster Keaton: A Filmmaker's Life*, p. 706, n. 16). H. O. Pardey's day job was in tin plate and iron working.
70. Curtis, James, *Buster Keaton: A Filmmaker's Life*, p. 16.
71. 'Umatilla Indian Medicine Co.' ad, *New York Clipper*, 4 April 1896, p. 76.
72. "Roster and notes from No. 27," *New York Clipper*, 4 January 1896, p. 697. LAN
73. 'Montpelier Clippings,' *Muscatine [Iowa] Journal*, 14 February 1896, p. 5.
74. 'Roster of the Umatilla Indian Medicine Co., No. 45,' *New York Clipper*, 4 April 1896, p. 66. It's not clear how the company numbers were assigned, as essentially the same company may be designated with a different number here and there throughout a performance year.
75. 'Roster of the Umatilla Indian Medicine Co., Party No. 27,' *New York Clipper*, 25 April 1896, p. 121.
76. 'Umatilla Concert Co., No. 101,' *The New York Clipper*, 12 September 1896, p. 441.
77. 'The Umatilla Medicine Co.,' *Scammon [Kansas] Miner*, 9 October 1896, p. 4.
78. 'The Umatilla Indian Medicine Co's,' *Weir [Kansas] Weekly Tribune*, 17 November 1896, p. 4.
79. 'Umatilla Indian Medicine & Concert Company Program,' *Weir City [Kansas] Daily Sun*, 18 November 1896, p. 3.
80. 'Program. Umatilla Indian Medicine Co.,' *Weir City [Kansas] Daily Sun*, 20 November 1896, p. 3.
81. One particularly substantive write-up of the P. P. P. after a surprise performance 21 December 1896 in Galena, Kansas, offered that 'Mr. Joe Keaton is among the best comedians in the Irish role that has been seen here for some time. Mrs. Keaton is very clever; W. B. York is one of the best in his line; [and] Arthur Long in his unique performance is pleasing' (*Galena {Kansas} Evening News*, 22 December 1896, p. 3). The exact same review appeared in the *Pittsburg [Kansas] Daily Headlight* 9 January 1897, but is labeled from the *Galena Times*, making it uncertain as to whether any performance actually occurred in Pittsburg.
82. See 'Dr. G. W. Pardey managing,' *Columbus [Kansas] Weekly Advocate*, 17 December 1896, p. 7 and 'A Good Company,' *The Columbus Weekly Advocate*, 17 December 1896, p. 5.
83. 'Minden Items,' *The Pittsburg [Kansas] Headlight*, 4 February 1897, p. 2.
84. 'The Keaton and York Comedy,' *Liberal [Missouri] Enterprise*, 5 February 1897, p. 5.

85. 'The Keaton and York Comedy Co.,' *Pleasanton [Kansas] Observer-Enterprise*, 13 February 1897, p. 1.
86. 'The Keaton and York Pantomime troupe,' *Paola [Kansas] Times*, 25 February 1897, p. 3.
87. "During the week," *Warrensburg [Missouri] Daily Star*, 8 April 1897, p. 4.
88. An ad in the *Kansas City [Missouri] Star* 7 March 1897 indicates that Keaton and York were seeking a trombone player, as well as other musicians, possibly indicating a musical mutiny that could have brought the company to a grinding halt ("Wanted Trombone Player for Pantomime Co.," p. 14).
89. 'Joe and Myra Keaton,' *New York Clipper*, 7 August 1897, p. 368.
90. The Keatons are first mentioned as performing at the Newmarket Theatre in the 3 July 1897 issue of the *New York Clipper*, then not again until 13 November, 20 November 1897, then 27 November, 4 December and for three issues of *The Clipper* in 1898, 8 January, 22 January and 29 January. Curtis (*Buster Keaton: A Filmmaker's Life*) surmised that Joe had taken a job as stage manager of the place, but the probable source for this actually states 'Jas. Keaton' – James, not Joe or Joseph (*New York Clipper*, 13 November 1897, p. 606). Tommie Chase and the Howards, both old Umatilla medicine show friends, appeared with them at the Newmarket the week of 22 January, but mostly the other acts on the bill were strangers.
91. p. 3.
92. 'An "actress" on the rampage,' *Kansas City [Missouri] Journal*, 27 November 1897, p. 3.
93. p. 615.

Chapter 2: Practically Born on Stage: A Career at Age Three

1. 'Thomas B Hill and Dr Perry Pratt' ad, *New York Clipper*, 30 October 1897, p. 585.
2. Don Creekmore, of 'Wild about Harry' blog announced 18 May 2023 that the owner of the first Harry Houdini diary, dated 1897–1899 will be published in 2024 by its current owner, Mike Caveney. This should provide definitive information as to whether the Keatons were part of the California Concert Company and met the Houdinis at this time or not (wildabouthoudini.com). LAN
3. Blesh, Rudy, *Keaton*. New York, NY: The Macmillan Company, 1966. The photo in question appears on page 17. If the man on Myra's right with the derby (labeled 'the Doctor' by Blesh) or the couple on Joe's left could be properly identified, the mystery would be solved. Joe Notaro, in his blog harryhoudinicircumstantialevidence.com, wrote about this photo and provided some strong evidence against it containing the Houdinis. Also, he noted that Dr. Thomas Hill and Dr. Perry Pratt, the two lecturers and owners of the California Concert Company do not fit the description of the 'Doctor'

in the photo. Hill was in his twenties, wore his hair long and had a full beard. Pratt was a white-haired old man ('Mystery of the Medicine Show Photo and Its Performers,' 22 January 2017). The photo is dated 1894 and is certainly the Keatons as part of a medicine show troupe, either the Mohawk with J. T. Kerrigan or the Umatilla with George A. Pardey.

4. 'At Liberty: Keaton, Long, Keaton,' *New York Clipper*, 16 April 1898, p. 115.
5. 'Hear Joe Keaton,' *Miami [Paola, Kansas] Republican*, 10 June 1898, p. 3.
6. 'One Night Only,' *Pittsburg [Kansas] Daily Tribune*, 18 June 1898, p. 4.
7. 'The funny negro,' *Cherokee [Kansas] Sentinel*, 17 June 1898, p. 3.
8. 'Opera House, July 5,' *Burlington [Kansas] News*, 24 June 1898, p. 1.
9. Joe claimed this occurred during the Spanish-American war, which was waged April to August 1898.
10. 'Another "Three Keatons" on the Job,' *Camera!* 14 April 1923, p. 10.
11. 'Forest Park Stock Company,' *Pittsburg [Kansas] Daily Tribune*, 29 July 1898, p. 1.
12. 'Down in Old Kentucky,' *Pittsburg [Kansas] Daily Tribune*, 16 July 1898, p. 2.
13. 'Last Night's Show at the Park,' *Pittsburg [Kansas] Daily Tribune*, 22 July 1898, p. 4.
14. 'Wanted, a Good Black Face Comedian,' *New York Clipper*, 13 August 1898, p. 393.
15. Fritts dabbled in entertainment there in Pittsburg for some time, but finally made the plunge into vaudeville in 1901, meeting with some success.
16. Letter published in the *Pittsburg [Kansas] Leader*, 14 July 1907, p. 7. Robinson Locke collection. NYPL-PA
17. 'Manager Bert Christy's Vaudevilles,' *New York Clipper*, 5 November 1898, p. 608.
18. Clarke's home office was Rooms 24–27 Ridge Building, 912 Walnut Street, Kansas City, Missouri. At the end of the many testimonials he published in the 18 November 1898 edition of the *Sterling [Kansas] Bulletin*, Clark provided references from businessmen and creditors, such as W. H. Donaldson of the Donaldson Lithograph Co. of Cincinnati, Ohio: 'This is to certify that our dealings with Prof. J. T. R. Clark have extended over a period of eight years. In all that time, we have found him perfectly upright, exceptionally prompt and entirely straight. [. . .] We do not hesitate to extend him a credit running into five figures' (p. 5).
19. 'Sterling to Be Favored with a Visit by the German-American Staff of Physicians and Surgeons,' *Lyons [Kansas] Daily News*, 19 November 1898, p. 8.
20. 'Are You Sick?' *Sterling [Kansas] Bulletin*, 18 November 1898, p. 2.
21. 'Sterling to Be Favored,' p. 8.
22. 'The German-American Vaudevilles,' *Lyons [Kansas] Daily News*, 26 November 1898, p. 8.

23. The *Ellinwood [Kansas] Leader* reported that Brooks is 'a clever fellow both on and off the stage, and gained the personal friendship of all with whom he came in contact' (22 December 1898, p. 2).

24. 'Wanted: A Good Specialty Company,' *Claflin [Kansas]Clarion*, 8 December 1898, p. 2.

25. 'Lyons,' *Sterling [Kansas] Bulletin*, 2 December 1898, p. 5.

26. 'During the blizzard,' *Claflin [Kansas]Clarion*, 8 December 1898, p. 1.

27. 'J. T. R. Clark's German American Vaudevilles,' *New York Clipper*, 18 March 1899, p. 53.

28. 'The little Keaton boy,' *Kinsley [Kansas] Graphic*, 28 April 1899, p. 5.

29. Frank Colby's piece appeared in the *Montgomery [Alabama] Advertiser*, 31 May 1942, p. 30. He claims the episode took place in Larned Kansas. Given the length of time between 1942 and 1899, it's very possible he simply got a few facts wrong. Colby garnered some acclaim for several things in his life: 1) making the word 'quintuplet' part of general American parlance, 2) his well-loved wordsmith newspaper column 'Take My Word for It,' and 3) being the first to use a product advertisement accompanied by music, on the radio (Obituary, *Arizona Republic [Tucson, Arizona]*, 25 February 1951, p. 5). LAN

30. 'The medicine show which spent,' *Kinsley [Kansas] Graphic*, 19 May 1899, p. 4.

31. 'Occupation Tax,' *Stafford [Kansas] County Leader*, 12 May 1899, p. 1.

32. 'The German-American Staff,' *Stafford [Kansas] County Leader*, 5 May 1899, p. 4.

33. 'The Oliver-Colby co.,' *NYDM*, 10 June 1899, p. 18.

34. 'The Vagaries of a Cyclone,' *St. John's [Kansas] Weekly News*, 9 June 1899, p. 5.

35. 'Cyclone Baby,' May 1927, pp. 98, 125–126.

36. Keaton, Buster and Dwight MacDonald, *My Wonderful World of Slapstick*, Cambridge, Massachusetts: Da Capo Press, 1969, p. 21.

37. 'The Oliver-Colby Co.,' *New York Dramatic Mirror*, 10 June 1899, p. 18. LAN

38. 'The Opening Night,' *Daily North Topeka [Kansas] Newsletter*, 24 May 1899, p. 2.

39. 'Next Monday evening,' *Junction City [Kansas] Weekly Union*, 3 June 1899, p. 1. LAN

40. 'A rare treat,' *Evansville [Indiana] Courier and Express*, 11 August 1899, p. 4.

41. 'Hickman Park Show,' *Owensboro [Kentucky] Messenger*, 26 August 1899, p. 1.

42. 'There were many people,' *Virginian [Norfolk, Virginia] Pilot*, 12 September 1899, p. 3.

43. 'Ocean View,' *Virginia-Pilot [Norfolk]*, 27 August 1899, p. 3.

44. 'Diana Continues a Fad,' *Daily Press [Newport News, Virginia]*, 7 September 1899, p. 8.

45. 'Auditorium' ad, *Richmond [Virginia] Times-Dispatch*, 13 September 1899, p. 7.

Notes

46. Blesh, Rudy, pp. 41–42.

47. Marion Meade in her biography *Buster Keaton: Cut to the Chase* (1995) insists that the Keatons' first New York engagement was at Huber's Dime Museum but offers no proof of this (pp. 23–24).

48. Cullen, Frank, *Vaudeville Old and New: An Encyclopedia of Variety Performers in America,* Vol. 1, New York, NY: Routledge, 2007, p. 312.

49. Dennett, Andrea Stulman, *Weird & Wonderful: The Dime Museum in America,* New York: NYU Press, 1997, p. 5.

50. 'Law Stops Fight Pictures,' *The World [New York, New York]*, 29 November 1899, p. 10.

51. 'Huber's 14th Street Museum' ad, *New York Clipper*, 14 October 1899, p. 681.

52. 'Huber's Museum,' *New York Times*, 1 October 1899, p. 16.

53. 'Enoch, the Man Fish,' *The Journal [Meriden, Connecticut]*, 26 January 1912, p. 7.

54. 'Keaton, Mr. and Mrs. Joe – Pastor's N. Y., 18-22, *NYDM*, 23 December 1899, p. 86.

55. 'Mr. and Mrs. Joe Keaton are at the Casto Theatre, Fall River, Mass., this week, with Pastor's and Proctor's to follow,' *New York Clipper*, 28 October 1899, p. 716.

56. 'The Casto-Dewey Pictures,' *Fall River [Massachusetts] Daily Herald*, 21 October 1899, p. 1. See also 'Dewey Pictures at Casto,' *Fall River Globe*, 21 October 1899, p. 2.

57. The Atlantic Garden watched its well-to-do German and Irish patrons gradually leave the neighborhood and decided to become a Yiddish theatre in 1910.

58. Blesh, pp. 22–23.

59. 'Keatons, The,' *New York Dramatic Mirror*, 25 November 1899, p. 21.

60. 'Ninth and Arch Dime Museum,' ad *Philadelphia [Pennsylvania] Inquirer*, 3 December 1899, p.31.

61. Slide, Anthony, *The Encyclopedia of Vaudeville.* Westport, CT: Greenwood Press, 1994, p. 390.

62. Cullen, Frank. *Vaudeville Old and New: An Encyclopedia of Variety Performers in America,* Vol. 2, New York, NY: Routledge, 2007, pp. 866–869.

63. B. F. Keith, the inventor of the continuous performance, offered his method and rationale: 'It is designed to run twelve hours, during which period performers appear two or three times, as it would be manifestly impossible to secure enough different acts to fill out the dozen hours. The best class of artists appear twice, just as at matinee and evening performances in a dramatic theatre, and the balance do three "turns."' ('The Vogue of Vaudeville,' *National Magazine*, 9 November 1898, p. 146–153).

64. 'For next week's attractions,' *New York [New York] Tribune*, 17 December 1899, p. 30. Also, 'Tony Pastor's,' *New York Dramatic Mirror*, 30 December 1899, p. 16.

65. 'Mr. and Mrs. Joe Keaton' ad, *NYDM*, 11 November 1900, p. 19.

191

66. Only Rudy Blesh in his biography *Keaton* interprets the poem and its accompanying experiences correctly, that Pastor's was the site of success for the Keaton act, p. 26.
67. Cullen, Frank. *Vaudeville Old and New: An Encyclopedia of Variety Performers in America,* Vol. 2, New York, NY: Routledge, 2007, p. 900.
68. 'Proctor's,' *NYDM*, 6 January 1900, p. 18. See also 'Proctor's,' *NYDM*, 30 December 1899, p. 16, 'Proctor Group' ad, *The Sun [New York, New York]*, 24 December 1899, p. 12 and 31 December 1899, p. 9. William C. Paley was a British born X-ray exhibitor who emigrated to the United States and gave up the X-ray business in favor of inventing a cinematagraph projector, which he named the kalactechnoscope ('good technical viewer') and sold for $100. His first customer was New York's Eden Musée.
69. The Pleasure Palace was located on Third Avenue at 48th Street. It was a hybrid of a 2,500-seat vaudeville house, billiard hall, roof garden, palm court and beer garden before Proctor's renovations, which brought the disparate spaces into greater harmony (Cullen, p. 900).
70. Phelps, Charles N., 'Albany, N.Y.,' *NYDM*, 20 January 1900, p. 22.
71. 'Mr. Dockstadter,' *The Evening Journal [Wilmington, Delaware]*, 17 January 1900, p. 4.
72. 'Howard Atheneum,' *The Boston Globe*, 28 January 1900, p. 18.
73. 'Austin and Stone's' ad, *The Boston Globe*, 4 February 1900, p. 19.
74. 'Austin and Stone's' ad, *The Boston Globe*, 4 February 1900, p. 19.
75. 'Poli's Wonderland Theatre,' *The Morning Journal-Courier [New Haven, Connecticut]*, 16 February 1900, p. 6.
76. 'Paragraphs of Interest Concerning the Stage Lives and Doings of Vaudeville People,' *The Police Gazette*, 10 March 1900, p. 2.
77. 'Cast for Tony Pastor's,' *The Cast*, 2 April 1900, n. p.
78. 'Athletic Women at the Museum,' *Philadelphia [Pennsylvania] Inquirer*, 10 April 1900, p. 5.
79. 'Vaudeville Jottings,' *NYDM*, 26 May 1900, p. 18.
80. 'Howard Atheneum,' *New York Clipper*, 2 June 1900, p. 308.
81. 'Mr and Mrs J. Keaton,' *New York Clipper*, 16 June 1900, p. 351.
82. 'Atlantic Garden,' *New York Clipper*, 7 July 1900, p. 416.
83. 'The program at Tony Pastor's,' *New York Tribune*, 10 July 1900, p. 14.
84. 'Keith's Union Square,' *New York Clipper*, 28 July 1900, p. 478.
85. 'Mr and Mrs Joe Keaton,' *NYDM*, 18 August 1900, p. 18.
86. In addition to the Keatons' next three engagements which were return dates at Proctor's 23rd Street, Proctor's Pleasure Palace and Tony Pastor's, the ad listed the following engagements for the remainder of 1900: Dockstadter's Wilmington Delaware, Empire Theatre, Toledo Ohio, Columbia Theatre, Cincinnati Ohio, Olympic Haymarket, Chicago Illinois, Columbia, St. Louis Missouri, Opera House, Chicago, and G. O. H., Memphis Tennessee. The reality shows a quite different schedule, however.

87. 'Mr and Mrs Joe Keaton' ad, *NYDM*, 22 September 1900, p. 19. See also 'Bijou Theatre,' *The News [Paterson, New Jersey]*, 4 June 1900, p. 7.
88. McNamara, Brooks, *Step Right Up*, pp. 142–143.
89. 'Joe Keaton,' *NYDM*, 26 January 1901, p. 18.
90. 'Proctor's Palace' ad, *New York Tribune*, 23 September 1900, p. 16.
91. 'An Excellent Bill,' *The Sun [Wilmington, Delaware]*, 19 October 1900, p. 3.
92. 'A Diminutive Comedian,' *NYDM*, 13 July 1901, p. 16.
93. 'Clever Vaudeville,' *Allentown [Pennsylvania] Leader*, 25 October 1900, p. 6.
94. 'Grand Opera House' ad, *The Evening Journal [Wilmington, Delaware]*, 27 October 1900, p. 4.
95. 'Opera House,' *The Morning News [Wilmington, Delaware]*, 29 October 1900, p. 3.
96. p. 19.
97. 'Steubenville, Ohio,' 10 November 1900, p. 815.
98. 'At the Columbia,' *Cincinnati [Ohio] Enquirer*, 12 November 1900, p. 6.
99. 'Columbia Theatre' ad, *St. Louis Post-Dispatch*, 2 December 1900, p. 21.
100. 'They call it a women's dilemma,' *St. Louis Post-Dispatch*, 4 December 1900, p. 4.
101. 'Chicago Opera House' ad, *The Inter-Ocean [Chicago, Illinois]*, 9 December 1900, p. 29.
102. 'Hopkins Grand Opera House' ad *The Commercial Appeal [Memphis, Tennessee]*, 16 December 1900, p. 5.
103. '"Nell Gwynne" at the Grand,' *Nashville [Tennessee] Banner*, 22 December 1900, p. 10. See also 'Grand Opera House,' *The Tennessean [Nashville, Tennessee]*, 23 December 1900, p. 15.
104. Bourgeois, Maurice, *John Millington Synge and the Irish Theatre*, London: Constable & Co., Ltd., 1913, pp. 109–10.

Chapter 3: Life on the Road Becoming 'Buster'

1. 'Mr and Mrs Joe Keaton,' *Wichita [Kansas] Daily Eagle*, 4 January 1901, p. 4.
2. Again, this refers to the Cherokee Outlet land run, held in Edmond, Oklahoma on 16 September 1893. 'Mr. and Mrs. Joe Keaton,' *Daily Enterprise Times [Perry, Oklahoma]*, 11 January 1901, p. 1. This exact article was re-published on 14 and 17 January, the 17th in the *Noble County Sentinel [Perry, Oklahoma]*, p.1.
3. 'Mr and Mrs Joe Keaton,' ad, *Daily Enterprise-Times*, 18 January 1901, p. 3.
4. 'Mr and Mrs Joe Keaton,' ad *NYDM*, 19 January 1901, p. 20.
5. 'Joe, Myra and Buster Keaton,' ad *NYDM*, 16 February 1901, p. 19.
6. 'Joseph Keaton,' *The Perry [Oklahoma] Republican*, 22 February 1901, p. 5.
7. After Albany, it was 11 to 16 March Proctor's 125th Street, 17 to 21 March Proctor's 5th Avenue, 25 to 30 March Proctor's Palace, 29 April to 5 May Proctor's 23rd Street, and 5 to 11 May back at Proctor's 5th Avenue.

8. 'Albany, N. Y.,' *NYDM*, 9 March 1901, p. 22.
9. 'BUSTER,' ad, *NYDM*, 23 March 1901, p. 19.
10. Seven was the age demanded by the Gerry Society. Buster was only 5 years and 5 months old.
11. 'On Monday Montreal's,' *Montreal [Canada] Star*, 2 March 1901, p. 11.
12. 'Proctor's Palace,' *NYDM*, 6 April 1901, p. 18.
13. Joe Keaton was especially proud of this write-up and asked his friend Harry Houdini to look it up when he had a chance: 'If possible get The Mirror of wk of March 25 and read the Pleasure Palace notes which gives an accurate description of the act' (Letter Joe Keaton to Harry Houdini, 17 April 1901, Harry Houdini Collection, HRC, Austin Texas).
14. 'The Keatons,' *NYDM*, 6 April 1901, p. 18.
15. 'Keaton,' *NYDM*, 13 April 1901, p. 21. See also 'Pastor's,' *NYDM* 13 April 1901, p. 22.
16. 'Tony Pastor's Theatre,' *New York Clipper*, 13 April 1901, p.148.
17. 'BUSTER,' ad, *NYDM*, 25 May 1901, p. 19.
18. Elbridge T. Gerry (1837–1927) founded the Society for the Prevention of Cruelty to Children in 1875. An excerpt from his essay 'Children of the Stage,' published in *North American Review*, Vol. 151, July 1890, pp. 14–21, included the following statement: 'These child-slaves of the stage, but for the present humane provisions of the law, would be subjected to a bondage more terrible and oppressive than the children of Israel ever endured at the hands of Pharaoh or the descendants of Ham have ever experienced in the way of African slavery.'
19. 'Mayor Defends Coney Island,' 11 May 1901, p. 1
20. 'Myra, Joe and Buster Keaton,' *NYDM*, 15 June 1901, p. 19.
21. 'Keaton and Boom Part,' *New York Morning Telegraph*, 16 June 1901, p. 6.
22. Italics Joe Keaton's. p. 17.
23. 'Joe, Myra and Buster Keaton, *New York Clipper*, 6 July 1901, p. 402.
24. Anderson was simply Coley Anderson, the manager of the Lyceum.
25. 'Lyceum, Vaudeville,' *The Atlanta [Georgia] Journal*, 24 June 1901, p. 12.
26. 'Vaudeville at the Lyceum,' *Atlanta [Georgia] Journal*, 25 June 1901, p. 12.
27. 'Joe and Myra Keaton,' *New York Clipper*, 6 July 1901, p. 404.
28. Heelan, Will A. and J. Fred Helf, 'Tobie, I Kind 'o Likes You,' New York, NY: Jos. W. Stern & Co., 1900.
29. The exact same piece appeared in *The New York Clipper* a week later, on 20 July, with the title 'Buster Keaton,' p. 438.
30. 'A Diminutive Comedian,' *NYDM,* 13 July 1901, p. 16.
31. 'Keith's Theatre' ad, *Philadelphia Record*, 14 July 1901, p. 15B.
32. 'Electric Park,' *Baltimore [Maryland] American*, 23 July 1901, p. 10.
33. 'Toledo, O.,' *NYDM*, 31 August 1901, p. 19.
34. 'The Three Keatons,' *NYDM*, 21 September 1901, p. 20.
35. 'Ferris Wheel Park' ad, *Chicago Tribune*, 1 September 1901, p. 40.
36. 'The Three Keatons,' *NYDM*, 21 September 1901, p. 20.

37. 'How Martin Beck Became Vaudeville's Chief Mogul,' *Variety*, 23 October 1909, p. 27.
38. '3 Keatons' ad, *NYDM*, 31 August 1901, p. 17.
39. 'O'Meers Prove to Be Wonders,' *San Francisco [California] Call*, 7 October 1901, p. 7.
40. 'The Orpheum,' *San Francisco [California] Chronicle*, 7 October 1901, p. 12.
41. 'The Mother-in-law at the Orpheum is the Worst Ever,' *Los Angeles [California] Evening Post-Record*, 29 October 1901, p. 2.
42. 'At the Orpheum Theatre Los Angeles,' *New York Clipper*, 16 November 1901, p. 815.
43. Paraphrased from Blesh, Rudy, *Keaton*, p. 59.
44. A Corker,' *Youngstown [Ohio] Vindicator*, 26 November 1901 p. 8.
45. 'Presence of Mind,' *Bonner Springs-Edwardsville [Kansas] Chieftain*, 2 January 1901, p. 1.
46. 'The Plucky Keatons,' *Quad City Times [Davenport, Iowa]* 30 December 1901, p. 5.
47. 'Hopkins – Vaudeville,' n. d., Buster Keaton scrapbook, MHL-AMPAS.
48. Blesh, Rudy, *Keaton*, p. 38.
49. 'The Keatons,' Buster Keaton scrapbook, MHL-AMPAS
50. 'Miss Evie Bowcock Makes Her Debut in Vaudeville,' *Richmond [Virginia] Times-Dispatch*, 7 January 1902, p. 1.
51. 'Amusements,' *Richmond [Virginia] Times-Dispatch*, 11 January 1902, p. 6.
52. 'Dockstader's Theatre,' *The Morning News [Wilmington, Delaware]*, 21 January 1902, p. 2.
53. 'At Tony Pastor's Theatre,' *New York Tribune*, 26 January 1902, p. 28.
54. 'Polite Vaudeville,' *Evening Star [Washington, D. C.]* 29 January 1902, p. 10.
55. Rudy Blesh, in his book *Keaton*, describes an incident at Poli's in which the theatre is damaged by 500 college students after entertainer Gaby Deslys refused to go on due to the tumultuous crowd beyond the stage. The Keatons then dealt with the same group of students a week later, one of whom insulted Myra during the act, resulting in Joe throwing Buster directly at the offender (pp. 46–47). In fact, the 500 students were five Yale University Students, one Princeton University student and two New York businessmen. It happened in late November 1911 at the Hyperion Theatre in New Haven and the Keatons did not perform at that venue that year ('Hyperion Row Aired in Court Cowles' Views,' *The Journal [Meridien, Connecticut]*, 20 November 1911, p. 9).
56. 'Vaudeville at the Jacques,' *The Waterbury [Connecticut] Democrat*, 20 February 1902, p. 6.
57. 'Harcourt Comedy Company,' *The Day [New London, Connecticut]*, 6 March 1902, p. 6.
58. 'The Bastable,' *Syracuse Evening Telegram*, 18 March 1902, p. 4.
59. 'This afternoon,' *Democrat and Chronicle [Rochester, New York]*, 24 March 1902, p. 8.

60. 'Temple Theatre,' *Detroit [Michigan] Free Press*, 1 April 1902, p. 2.
61. 'Coming to the Columbia,' *St. Louis [Missouri] Republic*, 17 April 1902, p. 8.
62. 'Chicago Opera House' ad, *Chicago [Illinois] Tribune*, 1 May 1902, p. 5.
63. 'The Grand,' *The Tennessean [Nashville, Tennessee]*, 4 May 1902, p. 5.
64. 'Big Band Benefit,' *The Perry [Oklahoma] Republican*, 16 May 1902, p. 8.
65. 'Band Benefit Concert,' *Daily Enterprise-Times [Perry, Oklahoma]*, 20 May 1902, p. 1.
66. 'Park Opens Sunday,' *Pittsburg [Kansas] Headlight*, 22 May 1902, p. 1.
67. 'Forest Park Opening,' *Pittsburg Kansan*, 5 June 1902, p. 1.
68. 'New Bill at Casino Theatre is Popular,' 9 June 1902, p. 4.
69. 'Vaudeville Opening at Lakeside Theatre,' *Galena [Kansas] Evening Times*, 18 June 1902, p. 4.
70. 'Ferris Wheel park,' *Chicago [Illinois] Tribune*, 7 July 1902, p. 7.
71. 'West End Heights' ad, *St. Louis [Missouri] Post-Dispatch*, 13 July 1902, p. 14.
72. 'The new summer garden,' *St. Louis [Missouri] Post-Dispatch*, 14 July 1902, p. 7.
73. 'There is a good performance,' *St. Louis [Missouri] Post-Dispatch*, 17 July 1902, p. 11. See also, 'The Three Keatons,' *The Jewish Voice*, 18 July 1902, p. 7.
74. 'Koerner's Garten,' *Mississippi Blätter [St. Louis, Missouri]*, 13 July 1902, p. 30.
75. 'San Souci Park' ad, *The Inter Ocean [Chicago, Illinois]*, 27 July 1902, p. 4.
76. 'At Ramona,' *Grand Rapids [Michigan] Herald*, 4 August 1902, p. 3.
77. 'The Empire,' *Columbus Sunday Dispatch*, 24 August 1902, p. 15.
78. 'The Stage,' *Toledo [Ohio] Sunday Bee*, 18 August 1902, p. 6.
79. 'Celebration at Idlewilde Park,' *Newark [Ohio] Advocate*, 1 September 1902, p. 1.
80. 'Amusements,' *The Newark Advocate*, 2 September 1901, p. 3.
81. Hare, Jim, 'Elmira History: The Legend of Rorick's Glen,' *Elmira [New York] Star Gazette*, 9 September 1918, available at https://www.stargazette.com/story/news/local/twin-tiers-roots/2018/09/09/elmira-history-legend-roricks-glen/1224886002/.
82. 'Rorick's Last Week,' *Elmira [New York] Star-Gazette*, 9 September 1902, p. 6.
83. 'A Fire Dancer in Scranton,' *Carbondale [Pennsylvania] Daily News*, 9 September 1902, p. 5.
84. 'The usual variety performance,' *The New York Tribune*, 21 September 1902, p. 18.
85. 'Proctor's Twenty-Third Street Theatre,' *New York Clipper*, 11 October 1902, p. 7.
86. 'Keaton' ad, 11 October 1902, p. 734.
87. 'Bon Ton Theatre,' *Jersey City [New Jersey] News*, 13 October 1902, p. 4.

Notes

88. 'Grand Opera House,' *The New York Press*, 19 October 1902, p. 5.
89. 'Polite Vaudeville at Portland Theatre,' *Portland [Maine] Sunday Telegram*, 26 October 1902, p. 4.
90. 'Portland Theatre,' *Evening Express [Portland, Maine]*, 29 October 1902, p. 10.
91. 18 October 1902, n. p.
92. 'Harcourt Comedy Company,' *Nashua [New Hampshire] Daily Telegraph*, 8 November 1902 p. 8.
93. The word 'ginger' in this instance does not mean red-haired but 'piquant or animated.'
94. 'Joe, Myra and Buster Keaton,' ad, *NYDM*, 20 December 1902, p. 44.
95. 'Joe, Myra and "Buster" Keaton, *NYDM*, 20 December 1902, p. 32.
96. 'Keaton,' ad, *New York Clipper*, 20 December 1902, p. 939.
97. 'Keith's' ad, *Boston [Massachusetts] Globe*, 25 December 1902, p. 12.
98. 'Keith's Theatre: Vaudeville,' *Boston [Massachusetts] Evening Transcript*, 23 December 1902, p. 11.
99. 'Keith's Theatre,' *Evening Telegram [Providence, Rhode Island]*, 30 December 1902, p. 9.
100. 'New York Theatre' ad, *New York Tribune*, 4 January 1903, p. 7.
101. One piece from mid-week was still stating, 'The Three Keatons in their comedy grotesque act, scored a hit. Buster, the diminutive comedian [carried] off the honors and [gained] rounds of applause' ('Pastor's Theatre,' *New York Clipper*, 17 January 1903, p. 1042).
102. 'Buster On and Off the Stage,' circa 15 February 1904, Portland, Maine, Buster Keaton scrapbook, MHL-AMPAS.
103. 'Buster On and Off the Stage,' circa 15 February 1904, Portland, Maine, Buster Keaton scrapbook, MHL-AMPAS.
104. 'Katy Barry, another headliner,' n. d., Buster Keaton scrapbook, MHL-AMPAS. The 'mere tot' would have been Harry Keaton, born 25 August 1904.
105. 'Chase's – Martinettis and Vaudeville,' *The Washington [D. C.] Times*, 20 January 1903, p. 8.
106. 'Shea's Theatre,' *New York Clipper*, 14 February 1903, p. 1141.
107. 'Empire Theatre,' *Painesville [Ohio] Telegraph*, 12 February 1903, p. 1.
108. 'Cook Opera House,' *Post Express [Rochester, New York]*, 14 February 1903, p. 12.
109. 'The Three Keatons,' 28 February 1903, p. xvii.
110. 'Good Show,' *The Youngstown [Ohio] Vindicator*, 3 March 1903, p. 2.
111. Untitled Proctor's description, n. d., Buster Keaton scrapbook, MHL-AMPAS.
112. 'At Proctor's,' n. d., but probably 1904, Buster Keaton scrapbook, MHL-AMPAS. Another review dated 27 September 1904 for the Keith's Theatre also in the scrapbook mentioned the same imitations.

113. '"Buster" Keaton introduced,' clipping, sometime during 30 January to 5 February 1905, Buster Keaton scrapbook, MHL-AMPAS. This incident was also noted by Rudy Blesh in *Keaton*, p. 40.
114. 'Boston Theatre – A Yankee Circus on Mars,' *Cambridge [Massachusetts] Chronicle*, 5 May 1906, p. 16.
115. 'Avenue,' *The Pittsburg [Pennsylvania] Press*, 10 March 1903, p. 5.
116. 'Three Keatons,' *New York Clipper*, 21 March 1903, p. 95.
117. 'Countess at Head of Jockey Club,' *The New York Press*, 24 March 1903, p. 5.
118. 'Proctor's Twenty-third Street Theatre,' 28 March 1903, p. 120.
119. 'Proctor's Twenty-third Street,' 4 April 1903, p. 18.
120. This was possibly Marie M. Stone, who was supposed to perform in 'A Social Highwayman,' which disappeared from the bill ('Next Week's Offering,' *New York Tribune*, 5 April 1903, p. 22.
121. 'Harcourt Comedy Company,' *The Daily Item [Lynn, Massachusetts]*, 7 April 1903, p. 3.
122. 'Harcourt Comedy Company,' *The Daily Item [Lynn, Massachusetts]*, 11 April 1903, p. 7.
123. 'Amusements,' *Lewiston [Maine] Daily Sun*, 13 April 1903, p. 2.
124. 'Opera House Attractions,' *Bangor [Maine] Daily News*, 18 April 1903, p. 10.
125. 'St. Croix Valley,' *Bangor [Maine] Daily News*, 24 April 1903, p. 7.
126. 'Portland Theatre,' *Evening Express [Portland, Maine]* 5 May 1903, p. 3.
127. 'At Keith's,' *The Record [Hackensack, New Jersey]*, 12 May 1903, p. 5.
128. Galways are a type of facial hair for men that consists of a beard and sideburns that run along the chin, without the accompaniment of a moustache.
129. 'In Vaudeville Houses,' 21 May 1903, p. 7. This article was printed in its entirety in *The Excelsior [Omaha, Nebraska]*, 13 June 1903, p. 5.
130. 'Keith's Theatre,' *Boston [Massachusetts] Globe*, 24 May 1903, p. 33.
131. 'Keith's Vaudeville,' *Philadelphia [Pennsylvania] Record*, 31 May 1903, p. 5.
132. 'Vaudeville – Keith's,' *Philadelphia [Pennsylvania] Record*, 2 June 1903, p. 8.
133. 'Joe, Myra and Buster Keaton' ad, *New York Clipper*, 3 June 1903, p. 406.
134. 'McBeth Park,' ad, *The Lima [Ohio] News*, 19 June 1903, p. 4.
135. 'Fine Pavilion to Be Built Near Arcadia,' *Findlay [Ohio] Republican*, 21 June 1901, n. p.
136. In his ad for the *Clipper* dated 11 July 1903, Joe wrote that 'through a misunderstanding, was held over a second week. The audience didn't seem to like the act, but the manager did' (p. 475).
137. 'Reeves Park Attractions,' n. d., Buster Keaton scrapbook, MHL-AMPAS.
138. 'Attractions of the Week,' *Chicago [Illinois] Tribune*, 12 July 1903, p. 36.
139. 'Mannion's Park,' n.d., Buster Keaton scrapbook, MHL-AMPAS.
140. 'Mannion's Park,' 27 July 1903, p. 6.
141. 'Lake Contrary Park,' ad, *St. Joseph [Nebraska] Daily News*, 1 August 1903, p. 5.

142. Elsie Janis was six years older than Buster, so had had her experiences with the Child Protection Officers a bit earlier, and recounts some of those in her biography, *So Far, So Good* (New York, NY: E. P. Dutton & Co., 1933).
143. 'At the Standard,' *Guthrie [Oklahoma] Daily Leader*, 2 September 1903, p. 4. 'Humplutu' is untraceable as either a DeWolf Hopper sketch or any sketch.
144. 'Joe, Myra and Buster Keaton,' ad, 1 August 1903, p. 546.
145. 'Forest Park's Last Week,' *Kansas City [Missouri] Star*, 6 September 1903, p. 5.

Chapter 4: A Year of Solo Stardom and a Fourth Keaton

1. 'Mr. and Mrs. Keaton,' *Perry [Oklahoma] Republican*, 18 September 1903, p. 3.
2. 'A Night in Oklahoma,' *Perry [Oklahoma] Republican*, 25 September 1903, p. 1.
3. The definition of the word 'buster' here is different from the one that resulted in his nickname: 'a loud uproarious reveler.'
4. 'He's a Buster,' *Noble County Sentinel [Perry, Oklahoma]*, 2 October 1903, p. 2.
5. 'The Keatons,' *The Perry [Oklahoma] Republican*, 2 October 1903, p. 1.
6. *'Off for St. Louis,' The Perry [Oklahoma] Republican*, 9 October 1903, p. 7.
7. 'Crawford Theatre' ad, *New York Clipper*, 21 March 1903, n. p.
8. '"Across the Desert,"' *St. Louis [Missouri] Post-Dispatch*, 12 October 1903, p. 4.
9. 'Joe Keaton writes,' 31 October 1903, p. 849.
10. 'Hopkins,' *The Kentucky Irish American [Louisville, Kentucky]*, 17 October 1903, p. 4.
11. 'A Juvenile Comedian,' *Louisville [Kentucky] Courier-Journal*, 22 October 1903, p. 6.
12. 3 October 1903, p. 21.
13. 'Inquisitiveness Gives Lad a Severe Fright,' *Louisville [Kentucky] Courier-Journal*, 24 October 1903, p. 12.
14. '"Buster" Keaton Mixes with Boys and Has Fun,' *Indianapolis [Indiana] Star*, 13 October 1903, p. 10.
15. 'Headline,' *Youngstown [Ohio] Vindicator*, 16 November 1903, p. 8.
16. 'Avenue,' *Pittsburgh [Pennsylvania] Press*, 19 November 1903, p. 16.
17. 'Temple Theatre,' *Detroit [Michigan] Free Press*, 29 November 1903, p. 22.
18. 'Amusements,' n. d., Buster Keaton scrapbook, MHL-AMPAS.
19. 'Shea's Theatre,' *New York Clipper*, 26 December 1903, p. 1062.
20. 'Keith's Theatre, *Boston [Massachusetts] Post*, 3 January 1904, p. 20.
21. Joe had claimed the debut took place in Easton, Pennsylvania, a fact mentioned in Chapter 3.
22. 'Buster Keaton,' *Boston [Massachusetts] Post*, 3 January 1904, p. 21.

23. 'Keith's Theatre,' *News [Providence, Rhode Island]*, 12 January 1904, p. 5.
24. 'Keith's Theatre,' *News [Providence, Rhode Island]*, 12 January 1904, p. 5.
25. 'Little Buster Keaton,' *News [Providence, Rhode Island]*, 21 January 1904, p. 4.
26. 'B. F. Keith,' *The Sun [New York, New York]*, 17 January 1904, p. 30.
27. 'Edmund Day & Co.,' *New York Times*, 19 January 1904, p. 5.
28. 'Last Week's Bills: Keith's Union Square,'*NYDM*, 30 January 1904, p. 18.
29. 'Keith's New Theatre,' *New York Clipper*, 30 January 1904, p. 1178.
30. 'Portland Theatre,' *Evening Express [Portland, Maine]* 12 February 1904, p. 8.
31. 'The Portland Theatre,' *Evening Express [Portland, Maine]* 20 February 1904, p. 14.
32. 'Mechanic Hall, ad, n. d., Buster Keaton scrapbook, MHL-AMPAS.
33. 'At Mechanic Hall,' n. d., Buster Keaton scrapbook, MHL-AMPAS.
34. 'Vaudeville: Proctor's Twenty-third Street,' *New York Press*, 13 March 1904, p. 6.3
35. 'Proctor's Twenty-third Street Theatre,' *The New York Clipper*, 19 March 1904, p. 82.
36. 'Albany: Proctor's Theatre,' *New York Clipper*, 26 March 1904, p. 99.
37. 'Pastor's Theatre,' *New York Clipper*, 2 April 1904, p. 130.
38. 'The Stage,' *Herald Statesman [Yonkers, New York]*, 4 April 1904, p. 5.
39. 'Edna Wallace Hopper at Hyde & Behman's,' *Brooklyn [New York] Citizen*, 12 April 1904, p. 4.
40. 'Hyde & Behman's,' *Times-Union [Brooklyn, New York]*, 12 April 1904, p. 12.
41. 'Everybody Likes Buster Keaton,' n. d., Buster Keaton scrapbook, MHL-AMPAS.
42. 'Garrick' ad, *Evening Journal [Wilmington, Delaware]*, 27 April 1904, p. 8.
43. '"The Human Magnet,"' *Evening Star [Washington, D. C.]*, 23 April 1904, p. 24.
44. 'Chase's Theatre,' *Evening Star [Washington, D. C.]*, 3 May 1904, p. 16.
45. 'Roof Garden' ad, *Intelligence Journal [Lancaster, Pennsylvania]*, 7 May 1904, p. 4.
46. 'Roof Garden,' *Lititz [Pennsylvania] Express*, 13 May 1904, p. A1.
47. 'A few days,' *Waterbury [Connecticut] Democrat*, 14 May 1904, p. 7.
48. 'Does It Pay to Be an Actor?' *Evening Express [Portland, Maine]*, 12 May 1904, p. 10.
49. 'Temples of Thespis Where Bayonnese May Go for Diversion,' *Bayonne [New Jersey] Herald and Greenville Register*, 14 May 1904, p. 3.
50. Keaton, Buster, *My Wonderful World of Slapstick*, pp. 27–28.
51. 'Keatons' ad, 21 May 1904, p. 20.
52. 'Keatons' ad, *NYDM*, p.18.
53. 'Riverton Park Theatre,' *Portland [Maine] Sunday Telegram*, 26 June 1904, p. 4.

54. 'Joe Keaton Saved His Trunks,' n. d., Buster Keaton scrapbook, MHL-AMPAS.

55. 'During the fire,' n. d., Buster Keaton scrapbook, MHL-AMPAS.

56. 'Sheedy's' ad, *Newport [New Hampshire] Herald*, n. d., Buster Keaton scrapbook, MHL-AMPAS.

57. '"Buster" Has a Baby Brother,' n. d., Buster Keaton scrapbook, MHL-AMPAS.

58. 'The Four Keatons,' *Perry [Oklahoma] Republican*, 2 September 1904, p. 6.

59. Some believe that 'Jingles' refers to the sound Harry made with his toys.

60. 'Keatons' ad, 10 September 1904, p. 17.

61. 'Joe and "Buster" Keaton, *Boston Globe*, p. 34.

62. 'Keith's Theatre: Vaudeville,' *Boston Evening Transcript*, 27 September 1904, p. 11.

63. 'Chief among the musical numbers,' n. d. Buster Keaton scrapbook, MHL-AMPAS.

64. 'Vaudeville at Keith's,' *Philadelphia Inquirer*, 11 October 1904, p. 4.

65. 'Keith's Union Square,' *NYDM*, 29 October 1904, p. 18.

66. 'Vaudeville at the Maryland,' *Baltimore [Maryland] Sun*, 25 October 1904, p. 8.

67. 'Grand,' *Pittsburg [Pennsylvania] Press*, 30 October 1904, p. 33.

68. Blesh, Rudy, *Keaton*, p.40.

69. 'At the Arcade Theatre next week,' *Toledo [Ohio] News Bee*, 5 November 1904, p. 10.

70. 'Cleveland's Theatre,' *Chicago Livestock World*, 19 November 1904, p. 3.

71. 'Vaudeville at the Temple,' *Detroit [Michigan] Free Press*, 29 November 1904, p. 4.

72. 'Buffalo,' 4 December 1904, n. p.

73. 'Shea's,' *New York Clipper*, 17 December 1904, p. 1015.

74. 'Keith's,' *New York Clipper*, 24 December 1904, p. 1029.

75. 10 December 1904, p. 22.

76. 'Pastor's Theatre,' *New York Clipper*, 7 January 1905, p. 1086.

77. 'Pastor's Theatre,' *New York Clipper*, 7 January 1905, p. 1086.

78. 'For the coming week,' *Brooklyn Life*, 7 January 1905, p. 30.

79. 'Toozoonin Arabs at Hyde & Behman's,' *Brooklyn [New York] Citizen*, 10 January 1905, p. 3.

80. 'Trent,' *New York Clipper*, 21 January 1905, p. 1127.

81. 'An unusually attractive bill,' *Courier-News [Bridgewater, New Jersey]*, 21 January 1905, p. 6.

82. 'Proctor's Twenty-third Street,' *New York Press*, 29 January 1905, p. 9,

83. '"Pat" Rooney,' *Springfield [Massachusetts] Republican* 9 February 1905, p. 4.

84. 'Albany, N. Y.,' *NYDM*, 18 February 1905 p. 20.

85. 'Buster Keaton before Judge Brady,' n. d., Buster Keaton scrapbook, MHL-AMPAS.

86. 'Buster in Court,' n. d., Buster Keaton scrapbook, MHL-AMPAS.
87. 'Does "Buster" Do an Acrobatic Turn?' n. d., Buster Keaton scrapbook, MHL-AMPAS.
88. 'Poli's Theatre,' *Morning Journal-Courier [New Haven, Connecticut]* 20 February 1905, p. 3.
89. 29 April 1964. Reprinted in Sweeney, Kevin W., ed., *Buster Keaton Interviews*, Jackson, MS: U of MS Press, 2007, p. 156.
90. 'Next Week at Poli's,' *Hartford [Connecticut] Courant*, 25 February 1905, p. 7.
91. 'Two Star Stunts Are on at Poli's,' *Hartford [Connecticut] Courant*, 28 February 1905, p. 7.
92. 'Jacques,' *Waterbury [Connecticut] Democrat*, 4 March 1905, p. 6.
93. 'Jacques,' *Waterbury [Connecticut] Democrat*, 6 March 1905, p. 7.
94. 'Jacques,' *Waterbury [Connecticut] Democrat*, 7 March 1905, p. 7.
95. 'Poli's' ad, *Bridgeport [Connecticut] Herald*, 12 March 1905, p. 16.
96. 'Buster Is Coming,' *Bridgeport [Connecticut] Herald*, 12 March 1905, p. 12.
97. 'New Bedford, Mass.,' *NYDM*, 25 March 1905, p. 22.
98. 'Ten Features All Told,' *Brooklyn [New York] Daily Eagle*, 26 March 1905, p. 33.
99. 'Juvenile theatregoers,' 6 April 1905, p. 2.
100. 'Keith's' ad, *Boston Globe*, 6 April 1905, p. 11.
101. 'Buster Keaton,' 8 April 1905, p. 167.
102. 'Keith's Union Square Theatre: Week April 10th,' *The News [Paterson, New Jersey]*, 5 April 1905, p. 8.
103. 'Keith's Union Square,' 22 April 1905, p. 18.
104. 'Keith's' ad, *The Philadelphia [Pennsylvania] Inquirer*, 16 April 1905, p. 34.
105. 'Grand – Vaudeville,' *Pittsburgh [Pennsylvania] Weekly Gazette*, 23 April 1905, p. 23.
106. 'Buster Keaton,' 23 April 1905, p. 34.
107. *Pittsburgh [Pennsylvania] Daily Post*, 28 April 1905, p. 6.
108. 'Amusements,' *News Journal [Wilmington, Delaware]*, 3 May 1905, p. 6.
109. 'His Diamond Ring Attracted Footpads,' *Morning News [Wilmington, Delaware]*, 4 May 1905, p. 1.
110. 'Mr. and Mrs. Joe Keaton,' *Noble County [Perry, Oklahoma] News*, 11 May 1905, p. 5.
111. 'Charmion and her players,' *The Bayonne Herald and Greenville Register [Bayonne, New Jersey]*, 27 May 1905, p. 2.
112. 'Jersey City, N. J.,' *NYDM*, 10 June 1905, p. 20.
113. 'Jingles Makes His Mark,' *NYDM*, 8 July 1905, p. 12.
114. 'Lake Michigan Park Theatre,' ad, n.d., Buster Keaton scrapbook, MHL-AMPAS.
115. 'Joe, Myra and "Buster" Keaton,' 5 August 1905, p. 18.
116. 'Meyer's Lake Park Theatre,' ad, n. d., Buster Keaton scrapbook, MHL-AMPAS.

117. 'Toledo, O.,' *NYDM*, 19 August 1905, p. 20.
118. p. 20.
119. 10 August 1905, p. 4.
120. 'Joe Keaton,' 19 August 1905, p. 18.
121. 'Miniature Circus and a Good Vaudeville Bill,' *Detroit [Michigan] Free Press*, 13 August 1905, p. 25.
122. 'Vaudeville at the Temple,' *Detroit Free Press*, 15 August 1905, p. 4.
123. 'Shea's Theatre,' *Buffalo [New York] Commercial*, 19 August 1905, p. 5.
124. 'Shea's Vaudeville,' *Buffalo [New York] Enquirer*, 22 August 1905, p. 3.
125. 'Cleveland: Keith's, *New York Clipper*, 9 September 1905, p. 725.
126. 'Grand Opera House,' ad, *Youngstown [Ohio] Vindicator*, 10 September 1905, p. 7.
127. 'Maryland Theatre,' *Baltimore [Maryland] Sun*, 19 September 1905, p. 9.
128. 'Philadelphia: Keith's New Theatre,' *New York Clipper*, 30 September 1905, p. 804.
129. 'At Keith's,' *Passaic [New Jersey] Daily News*, 30 September 1905, p. 5.
130. 'Keith's Union Square,' 14 October 1905, p. 15.
131. 'The Keatons,' *NYDM*, 7 October 1905, p. 2.
132. 'The Keatons,' *NYDM*, 7 October 1905, p. 2.
133. 'The Theatres,' *News [Providence, Rhode Island]*, 9 October 1905, p. 4.
134. 'The Three Keatons,' *Boston [Massachusetts] Globe*, 1 October 1905, p. 35.
135. 'Vaudeville Jottings,' 28 October 1905, p. 21.
136. 'New Bedford, Mass.,' *NYDM*, 4 November 1905, p. 22.
137. 'Buster Keaton,' *NYDM*, 4 November 1905, p. 20.
138. 'There is a good show,' *Brooklyn [New York] Daily Eagle*, 31 October 1905, p. 17.
139. 'Troy, N. Y.,' *NYDM*, 18 November 1905, p. 22.
140. 'Howard's' ad, *Boston [Massachusetts] Globe*, 12 November 1905, p. 27.
141. 'Howard Atheneum,' *Boston Globe*, 14 November 1905, p. 7.
142. 'Empire Theatre,' *Paterson [New Jersey] Daily Press*, 17 November 1905, p. 10.
143. 'Hoboken, N. J.,' *NYDM*, 9 December 1905, p. 22.
144. 'This Week at Pastor's,' *The Billboard*, 9 December 1905, n. p.
145. '"Buster" Keaton introduced,' *NYDM*, 23 December 1905, p. 55.
146. 'Trenton, N. J.,' *NYDM*, 30 December 1905, p. 21.
147. 'Grand,' ad, *Pittsburg [Pennsylvania] Press*, 24 December 1905, p. 34.
148. 'Buster Keaton's Dad Tells about Rogers,' *Spokesman Review [Spokane, Washington]*, 22 August 1935, p. 2.
149. '"Buster" Keaton,' 23 December 1905, p. xxx.
150. 'Newark, N. J.,' 6 January 1906, n. p.
151. 'Albany, N. Y.,' *NYDM*, 20 January 1906, p. 21.
152. 'Keaton' ad, *NYDM*, 27 January 1906, p. 17.
153. 'Poli's,' *New York Clipper*, 20 January 1906, p. 1223.

154. 'Home and Well,' *Daily Enterprise-Times [Perry, Oklahoma]*, 18 January 1906, p. 1.
155. 'Springfield,' *New York Clipper*, 27 January 1906, p. 1247.
156. 'Poli's Theatre,' *Hartford [Connecticut] Courant*, 3 February 1906, p. 7.
157. 'Hartford, Conn.,' *NYDM*, 10 February 1906, p. 18.
158. 'Poli's New Theatre,' *Morning Journal-Courier [New Haven, Connecticut]*, 5 February 1906, p. 8.
159. 'Poli's New Theatre,' *Morning Journal-Courier [New Haven, Connecticut]*, 8 February 1906, p. 3.
160. 'Poli's,' *Bridgeport [Connecticut] Sunday Herald*, 11 February 1906, p. 12.
161. 'Poli's New Theatre,' *Morning Journal-Courier [New Haven, Connecticut]*, 5 February 1906, p. 8.
162. 'Jacques Vaudeville,' *Waterbury [Connecticut] Democrat*, 19 February 1906, p. 3.
163. 'Buster Keaton,' *North Adams [Massachusetts] Transcript*, 24 February 1906, p. 4.
164. 'The Theatres: Buster a Youthful Headliner,' *North Adams [Massachusetts] Transcript*, 27 February 1906, p. 4.
165. 'Proctor's Fifty-Eighth Street,' *New York Press*, 4 March 1906, p. 5.
166. Boxer and heavyweight champion James J. Corbett (1866–1933).
167. 'Proctor's Fifty-Eighth Street,' 17 March 1906, p. 17.
168. 'The Orpheum,' *Reading [Pennsylvania] Times*, 12 March 1906, p. 8.
169. 'Vaudeville at the Portland,' *Portland [Maine] Sunday Telegram*, 18 March 1906, p. 4.
170. Information about the Jingles kidnapping was compiled from the following sources: 'Kidnapped on Preble Street,' n. d., Buster Keaton Scrapbook, MHL-AMPAS, 'Gossip of the Stage,' *Hartford [Connecticut] Courant*, 23 March 1906, p. 7, 'Jingles Keaton Kidnapped,' *NYDM*, 31 March 1906, p. 18.
171. Meade, Marion, *Cut to the Chase*, p. 41 and Curtis, James, *Buster Keaton*, p. 54.
172. 'Howard' ad, *Boston [Massachusetts] Globe*, 29 March 1906, p. 13. Also, 'Howard' ad, *Boston [Massachusetts] Globe*, 25 March 1906, p. 27.
173. 'Amusement Notes,' *Boston [Massachusetts] Globe*, 31 March 1906, p. 3.
174. 'Grand Vaudeville,' *Syracuse [New York] Journal*, 31 March 1906, p. 3.
175. 'Harcourt Comedy,' *New York Clipper*, 14 April 1906, p. 232.
176. 'In 1879, Alphonse Bertillon invented a method that combined detailed measurement and classification of unique features with frontal and profile photographs of suspects – and which recorded the information on standardized cards in orderly files. Bertillon's system was later overtaken by fingerprinting, but the Bertillon "mug shot" endures' ('Visible Proofs: Forensic Views of the Body: Technologies,' National Library of Medicine, available at https://www.nlm.nih.gov/exhibition/visibleproofs/galleries/technologies/bertillon.html.
177. 'Bijou Crowded at Police Play,' *Jersey City [New Jersey] News*, 17 April 1906, p.1.

178. Cover caption, 21 April 1906.
179. 'Gertie Reynolds,' *News Journal [Wilmington, Delaware]*, 27 April 1906, p. 6.
180. 'The Theatres,' *Atlanta [Georgia] Journal*, 16 May 1906, p. 13.
181. 'First Bill at Casino,' *Montgomery [Alabama] Times*, 17 May 1906, p. 8.
182. 'At New Casino Theatre,' *Montgomery [Alabama] Advertiser*, 23 May 1906, p. 3.
183. 'Bijou Theatre Will Keep Open,' *Birmingham [Alabama] Post-Herald*, 19 May 1906, p. 5.
184. 'At the Bijou,' *Birmingham [Alabama] Post-Herald*, 29 May 1906, p. 7.
185. 'Drummer Girl to the Rescue,' *NYDM*, 9 June 1906, p. 16.
186. 'Good Vaudeville Bill,' *Roanoke [Virginia] Times*, 5 June 1906, p. 6.
187. 'Two Performances Today,' *Ledger-Star [Norfolk, Virginia]*, 20 June 1906, p. 2.
188. *NYDM*, 16 June 1906, p. 19.
189. 'Louise Dresser the Head Liner,' *Richmond [Virginia] Times-Dispatch*, 24 June 1906, p. 10.
190. 'Coliseum Theatre Vaudeville,' *Cleveland [Ohio] Plain Dealer*, 29 July 1906, p. 10.
191. 'Coliseum Theatre Vaudeville,' *Cleveland [Ohio] Plain Dealer*, 31 July 1906, p. 5.
192. 'Buster Laughs at his Bumps, *Cleveland [Ohio] Plain Dealer*, 1 August 1906, p. 10.

Chapter 5: The 'Three Keatons' Become Five and Enjoy Buster's Fame

1. 'Fenberg Stock Co. Making a Big Hit,' *Central New Jersey Home News [New Brunswick, New Jersey]*, 3 April 1907, p. 7.
2. 'Little of Everything,' *Star-Gazette [Elmira, New York]*, 15 February 1907, p. 6.
3. 'Fenberg Stock Company,' *Lewiston [Maine] Daily Sun*, 22 January 1904, p. 2.
4. 'World of Players,' *New York Clipper*, 18 August 1906, p. 682.
5. '"Buster" Keaton is now playing,' 18 August 1906 p. 19.
6. 'Peekskill,' 25 August 1906, p. 6.
7. 'The Fenberg Stock Co. All Next Week,' *New Rochelle [New York] Pioneer*, 11 August 1906, p. 3.
8. 'The Fenbergs,' n. d., Buster Keaton scrapbook, MHL-AMPAS.
9. 'Lyceum Theatre,' *The Day [New London, Connecticut]*, 11 September 1906, p. 12.
10. 'Amusements,' *The Day [New London, Connecticut]*, 15 September 1906, p. 7.
11. 'Buster Keaton with Fenberg,' *Morning Sentinel [Waterville, Maine]*, 29 September 1906, p. 6.
12. 'Precocious Buster,' *Bangor [Maine] Daily News*, 2 October 1906, p. 3. This story also appeared as '"Buster" Made His Father Lose,' *NYDM*, 27 October

1906, p. 20 and in the *Waterbury [Connecticut] Democrat*, 27 October 1906, p. 7.

13. 'News of the Local Stage,' *Bangor [Maine] Daily News*, 8 October 1906, p. 8.

14. 'The Fenberg Stock Co.,' *Kennebec Journal [Augusta, Maine]*, 13 October 1906, p. 11.

15. 'New Member of Troupe,' *Lewiston [Maine] Daily Sun*, 31 October 1906, p. 5.

16. 'The Keatons are back,' n. d., Buster Keaton scrapbook, MHL-AMPAS.

17. 'The Fenberg Stock Co.,' *Nashua [New Hampshire] Telegraph*, 10 December 1906, p. 7.

18. Mitchell, Sally, Introduction, *East Lynne*, 1861. Reprint edition. New Brunswick, New Jersey: Rutgers University Press, 1984, p. xiii.

19. Quoted in Blesh, Rudy, *Keaton*, p. 54.

20. 'Fenberg Stock Company,' n. p., Buster Keaton scrapbook, MHL-AMPAS.

21. 'Lynn Theatre,' ad, *The Daily Item [Lynn, Massachusetts]*, 20 December 1906, p. 2.

22. 'Vaudeville Jottings,' *NYDM*, 15 December 1906, p. 16.

23. 'It Is Keith and Proctor Now,' *NYDM*, 16 June 1906, p. 16.

24. 'No More "Continuous,"' *NYDM*, 8 December 1906, p. 16.

25. Curtis, James, p. 57.

26. 'Houdini made his return week,' *NYDM*, 23 February 1907, p. 19.

27. 'Keith's' ad, *Philadelphia [Pennsylvania] Inquirer*, 2 February 1907, p. 14.

28. 'Newark, N. J.,' *NYDM*, 16 February 1907, p. 17.

29. 'The Keatons were,' quoted in *New York Clipper*, 23 March 1907, p. 129, originally from the *Newark [New Jersey] Evening News*.

30. 'Union Square,' *Perth Amboy [New Jersey] Evening News*, 16 February 1907, p. 4.

31. 'Keith and Proctor's Union Square,' 2 March 1907, p. 17.

32. 'Howard Atheneum' ad, *Boston [Massachusetts] Globe*, 3 March 1907, p. 25.

33. 'Bowdoin Sq. Theatre' ad, *Boston [Massachusetts] Globe*, 10 March 1907, p. 27.

34. 'Binghamton, N. Y.,' *NYDM*, 23 Mar 1907, p. 22.

35. 'Keith & Proctor's Theatre' ad, *Bayonne [New Jersey] Herald and Greenville Register*, 16 March 1907, p. 1.

36. 'Julia Redmond and Company,' *Evening Journal [Wilmington, Delaware]*, 26 March 1907, p. 8.

37. 'Fast Fun at Maryland,' *Baltimore [Maryland] Sun*, 2 April 1907, p. 12.

38. 'The Grand Opera House, *Pittsburgh [Pennsylvania] Post*, 9 April 1907, p. 6.

39. 'The Theatres,' *Toledo [Ohio] News-Bee*, 16 April 1907, p. 4.

40. 'Keith's' ad, *Cleveland [Ohio] Plain Dealer*, 21 April 1907, p. 39.

41. 'Amusements: Keith Vaudeville, *Columbus [Ohio] Dispatch*, 6 May 1907, p. 4.

42. 'Amusements: Keith Vaudeville,' *Columbus [Ohio] Dispatch*, 7 May 1907, p. 4.

43. 'Joe, Myra and "Buster" Keaton,' *NYDM*, 11 May 1907, p. 18.
44. 'Toronto: Shea's,' *New York Clipper*, 25 May 1907, p. 389.
45. 'Six English Rockers,' *Buffalo [New York] Courier Express*, 26 May 1907, p. 31.
46. 'Shea's Vaudeville Show,' *Buffalo [New York] Courier*, 28 May 1907, p. 8.
47. 'The New Lakeside Park Casino' ad, *Akron [Ohio] Beacon Journal*, 1 June 1907, p. 5.
48. 'At the Casino,' *Akron [Ohio] Beacon Journal*, 4 June 1907, n. p.
49. 'Meyer's Lake Park Theatre' ad, *Massillon [Ohio] Evening Independent*, 8 June 1907, p. 7.
50. 'Creatore at Fairview Park,' *Dayton [Ohio] Herald*, 22 May 1907, p. 5.
51. 'Vaudeville at Fairview a Hit with the Children,' *Dayton [Ohio] Herald*, 19 June 1907, p. 10.
52. 'The Keatons Will Rest,' p. 16.
53. 'Books Big Act,' *Oklahoma Post [Oklahoma City, Oklahoma]*, 15 June 1907, p. 5.
54. 'Joe H. Keaton,' *Daily Enterprise-Times [Perry, Oklahoma]*, 25 June 1907, p. 4.
55. 'Matinee Girls Stay for Another Week,' *Oklahoma Post [Oklahoma City, Oklahoma]*, 9 July 1907, p. 3.
56. 'Keatons Kut Kute Komicalities,' *Perry [Oklahoma] Republican*, 16 August 1907, p. 5.
57. 'Keatons' ad, *NYDM*, 7 September 1907, p. 14.
58. 'First Week's Program,' *The Dispatch [Moline, Illinois]*, 17 August 1907, p. 7.
59. 'The Garrick,' *St. Louis [Missouri] Globe-Democrat*, 1 September 1907, p. 34.
60. 'Shubert Vaudeville,' *Kansas City [Missouri] Star*, 9 September 1907, p. 12.
61. 'Mary Anderson Theatre' ad, *Courier-Journal [Louisville, Kentucky]*, 15 September 1907, p. 11.
62. 'The Duquesne,' *Pittsburgh [Pennsylvania] Press*, 22 September 1907, p. 33.
63. 'Vaudeville at the Forrest,' *Philadelphia [Pennsylvania] Inquirer*, 1 October 1907, p. 4.
64. 'Advanced Vaudeville in Great Variety at Tremont,' *Boston [Massachusetts] Globe*, 6 October 1907, p. 37.
65. 'Philadelphia, PA: People's,' *NYDM*, 19 October 1907, p. 19.
66. 'Academy of Music,' *The Gazette [Montreal, Quebec, Canada]*, 29 October 1907, p. 5.
67. 'Springfield: Nelson,' *New York Clipper*, 9 November 1907, p. 1044.
68. 'Worcester: Franklin Square,' *New York Clipper*, 16 November 1907, p. 1077.
69. p. 14.
70. 'Gerry Takes in Keaton,' *Variety*, 24 November 1907, p. 6.
71. 'Springer and Keaton in Court,' *NYDM*, 30 November 1907, p. 13.

72. 'John H. Springer Fined,' *New York Times*, 28 November 1907, p. 5.
73. 'Vaudeville War Ended,' *NYDM*, 16 November 1907, p. 14.
74. 'Settling the Details,' *NYDM*, 23 November 1907, p. 14.
75. 'Majestic Vaudeville,' *Birmingham [Alabama] News*, 3 December 1907, p. 2.
76. 'At the Majestic,' *Birmingham [Alabama] Post-Herald*, 3 December 1907, p. 4.
77. N. B. Scotty Beckett, who plays Cary Grant's son in *My Favorite Wife* (1940) recites this poem at the behest of Irene Dunn's character, the mother he believed to be dead, to demonstrate his ability to memorize.
78. 'Majestic' ad, *Daily Arkansas Gazette [Little Rock, Arkansas]*, 14 December 1907, p. 4.
79. 'The Majestic Theatre,' *Houston [Texas] Post*, 29 December 1907, p. 27.
80. 'Orpheum's Good Bill,' *El Paso [Texas] Herald,* 9 January 1908, p. 8.
81. 'The current bill at the Orpheum,' *Los Angeles [California] Times*, 22 January 1908, p. 21.
82. 'Orpheum Theatre,' ad, *Los Angeles [California] Herald*, 27 January 1908, p. 2.
83. 'Will Distribute Precious Jewels,' *San Francisco [California] Examiner*, 2 February 1908, p. 43.
84. 'Rice and Cohen in New Sketch,' *San Francisco [California] Examiner*, 3 February 1908, p. 9.
85. 'Orpheum Theatre' ad, *San Francisco [California] Call*, 9 February 1908, p. 27.
86. 'Orpheum,' *Oakland [California] Tribune*, 16 February 1908, p. 19.
87. 'Musical Skit,' *Berkeley [California] Gazette*, 17 February 1908, p. 5.
88. 'Orpheum Theatre' ad, *Denver [Colorado] Post*, 23 February 1908, p. 19.
89. 'Orpheum Theatre,' ad, *Kansas City [Kansas] Star*, 8 March 1908, p. 25.
90. Blue Laws are any law prohibiting something – shopping, buying alcohol, attending performances, etc. – on a Sunday.
91. On 6 March it had been decided that managers would only have to pay $50 bond per performer caught in the suit, instead of the original $200 demanded by the initial judge, Judge Wallace. This suggested that the managers had a long way to go before their case was finally decided, and by virtue of that fact, the Keatons would be safely out of town and far away ('The Theatres Win a Point,' *Kansas City [Missouri] Star*, 6 March 1908, p. 15).
92. 'He's Busy Buster Keaton,' *Kansas City [Missouri] Times*, 12 March 1908, p. 3. Two other iterations of this interview appeared as 'Buster Is Almost Busted, *Sioux City [Iowa] Journal*, 21 March 1908, p. 6 and 'Little Buster Keaton Is in Town, *Virginian-Pilot [Norfolk, Virginia]*, 4 April 1908, p. 12.
93. 'Retailers Here in Force,' *Sioux City [Iowa] Journal*, 18 March 1908, p. 5.
94. Words and Music by Jeff T. Branen and Evans Lloyd, 1907.
95. 'This Week's Stars at the Colonial,' *Ledger-Star [Norfolk, Virginia]*, 6 April 1908, p. 3.

96. '"Somebody Lied" – Nothing Personal!' *Virginian-Pilot [Norfolk, Virginia]*, 15 April 1908, p. 3.
97. 'Amusements,' *Richmond [Virginia] Times-Dispatch*, 14 April 1908, p. 8.
98. 'Empire,' *Paterson [New Jersey] Morning Call*, 21 April 1908, p. 9.
99. 'Hoboken,' *NYDM*, 9 May 1908, p. 13.
100. 'The Three Keatons at the Poli, *Tribune [Scranton, Pennsylvania]*, 4 May 1908, p. 4.
101. 'Clever Comedy at the Poli,' *Tribune [Scranton, Pennsylvania]*, 4 May 1908, p. 4.
102. 'At the Poli,' *Tribune [Scranton, Pennsylvania]*, 5 May 1908, p. 4.
103. 'Poli's' ad, *Hartford [Connecticut] Courant*, 9 May 1908, p. 7.
104. 'At Poli's Next Week,' *Morning Journal-Courier [New Haven, Connecticut]*, 15 May 1908, p. 8.
105. 'Vaudeville Jottings,' *NYDM*, 30 May 1908, p. 18.
106. 'Keaton' ad, *NYDM*, 13 June 1908, p. 15.
107. 'Vaudeville Comedy Club,' *NYDM*, 30 May 1908, p. 16.
108. 'Vaudeville Jottings,' *NYDM,* 6 June 1908, p. 14.
109. 'Vesta Victoria and Nat M. Wills Among the Buyers of Plots,' *New York Tribune*, 19 January 1908, p. 12.
110. Muskegon information gleaned from *Muskegon, Michigan Actors' Colony at Bluffton*, Muskegon, MI: Dobb Printing, 2016, especially pages 2–6. A documentary will be released Fall 2023 on the same subject, which should provide even more information, entitled *Buster Keaton Home*, by Clear Vision Films.
111. 'Vaudeville Jottings,' *NYDM*, 26 September 1908, p. 19.
112. 'Nat Wills Talks of Love at Proctor's Theatre,' *Newark [New Jersey] Star-Eagle*, 15 September 1908, p. 3.
113. 'Trent' ad, *Daily True American [Trenton, New Jersey]*, 29 September 1908, p. 5.
114. 'Hudson, Union Hill,' *Jersey Journal [Jersey City, New Jersey]*, 6 October 1908, p. 4.
115. 'Great Bill at Orpheum,' *Morning Call [Allentown, Pennsylvania]*, 13 October 1908, p. 7.
116. Lyrics by Robert Burns.
117. 'Public Reception,' *Allentown [Pennsylvania] Democrat*, 15 October 1908, p. 1.
118. 'Johnstown,' *NYDM*, 31 October 1908, p. 16.
119. Soward, Lucien A., 'Dayton,' *NYDM*, 31 October 1908, p. 15.
120. Slocum, Palmer, 'In the Limelight,' *Dayton [Ohio] Herald*, 28 October 1908, p. 4.
121. 'The Richmond's Bill,' *North Adams [Massachusetts] Transcript*, 24 November 1908, p. 2.
122. 'Jacques Vaudeville,' *Waterbury [Connecticut] Democrat*, 28 November 1908, p. 10.

123. 'Poli's,' *Bridgeport [Connecticut] Sunday Herald*, 6 December 1908, p. 6.
124. 'Keaton' ad, *NYDM*, 19 December 1908, p. 18.
125. 'The Orpheum,' *Reading [Pennsylvania] Times*, 31 December 1908, p. 5.
126. 'Buster Keaton,' *NYDM*, 26 December 1908, p. 4.
127. 'Amusements,' *News Journal [Wilmington, Delaware]*, 2 January 1909, p. 6.
128. 'Buster Keaton,' *The Morning News [Wilmington, Delaware]*, 8 January 1909, p. 8.
129. 'Keatons,' *NYDM*, 9 January 1909, p. 20.
130. 'The Orpheum,' *Harrisburg [Pennsylvania] Daily Independent*, 21 January 1909, p. 5.
131. Quoted in 'Vaudeville Comedy Club,' *NYDM*, 30 January 1909, p. 13.
132. 'At the Majestic,' *Birmingham [Alabama] Post-Herald*, 2 February 1909, p. 2.
133. 'Good Bill at the Majestic,' *Birmingham [Alabama] News*, 2 February 1909, p. 2.
134. 'At the Majestic,' *Houston [Texas] Post*, 2 March 1909, p. 10.
135. 'News of the Theatres,' *The Atlanta [Georgia] Journal*, 16 March 1909, p. 13.
136. 'Orpheum Theatre' ad, *Easton [Pennsylvania] Sunday Call*, 21 March 1909, n. p.
137. 'Worcester,' *NYDM*, 10 April 1909, p. 19.
138. 'Broadway Theatre' ad, *The Morning Post [Camden, New Jersey]*, 10 April 1909, p. 3.
139. 'Easter Show at Broadway Composed of Stellar Acts,' *The Morning Post [Camden, New Jersey]*, 10 April 1909, p. 3.
140. Bridgman, E. A., 'Syracuse,' *NYDM*, 1 May 1909, p. 49.
141. 'Hoboken,' *NYDM*, 8 May 1909, p. 20.
142. 'Vaudeville Jottings,' p. 15.
143. p. 28.

Chapter 6: London Disappointments and Buster Becoming a Fake Sixteen

1. Alfred Butt,' *New York Clipper*, 25 May 1907, p. 37.
2. 'Shipping and Mails,' *New York Times*, 1 July 1909, p. 17.
3. Ship Manifest, S. S. *George Washington*, arrival 8 July 1909.
4. Most of this story is gleaned from Joe's exposé, '"London": "Mr. Butt and Company,"' *Variety*, 11 December 1909, p. 40, 106.
5. 'Palace,' *Daily Telegraph*, 12 July 1909, p. 10.
6. 'A Chat with Alfred Butt,' *NYDM*, 7 April 1906 p. 18.
7. 'Billy Gould in London Again,' 24 July 1909, p. 10.8
8. Keaton, Joe, '" London": "Mr. Butt and Co.,"' *Variety*, 11 December 1909, p. 40, 106.
9. 'Buster, 16, Oct. 4th,' *Variety*, 18 September 1909, p. 36.

10. Joseph Z. Keaton's obituary noted that he had been ill since 1904, and that all four of his children were scattered here and there, well away from Perry at the time of his death. Only his youngest child Bert, who had been vacationing in Joe and Myra's Bluffton Michigan home at the time of his father's death, was on his way back to Perry to arrange the funeral. He was the only child in attendance ('Joseph Keaton Dead,' *Perry [Oklahoma] Daily News*, 21 July 1909, p. 1).

11. Ship manifest, S. S. *Oceanic*, 21 July 1909 departure.

12. 'Bennett's Theatre,' *Ottawa [Ontario, Canada] Journal*, 14 September 1909, p. 10.

13. 'George Beban at Shea's,' *Buffalo [New York] Courier Express*, 28 September 1909, p. 8.

14. '3 Keatons' N Y Opening,' *Variety*, 15 May 1909, n. p.

15. p. 25.

16. 'Hammerstein's,' *Variety*, 23 October 1909, n. p.

17. 'Vaudeville and Minstrel,' 13 November 1909, p. 1007.

18. 'Peter, the Monkey, Remains,' *The Baltimore [Maryland] Sun*, 30 November 1909, p. 9.

19. 'The first rehearsal,' *Times Union [Brooklyn, New York]*, 6 December 1909, p. 6.

20. 'Note and Comment,' *Boston Evening Transcript*, 17 December 1909, p. 14.

21. 'The Three Keatons,' 18 December 1909, p. 21.

22. 'Bronx,' *Variety*, 18 December 1909, p. 20.

23. Keaton, Buster, *MWWOS*, p. 34.

24. 'Trying for Settlements,' *Variety*, 18 December 1909, p. 22.

25. 'Settling Titles,' n. p.

26. 'Vaudeville Jottings,' *NYDM*, 1 January 1910, p. 26. See also 'Albany, N. Y.,' *NYDM*, 1 January 1910, p. 28.

27. 'Buster Too Young for Acrobatics,' *Yonkers [New York] Statesman*, 6 January 1910, p. 4.

28. 'Vaudeville at the Warburton,' *Yonkers [New York] Statesman*, 4 January 1910, p. 4.

29. 'At the Colonial Theatre,' *Ledger-Star [Norfolk, Virginia]*, 10 January 1910, p. 10.

30. '"Buster" Keaton Hurt by Engine,' *Harrisburg [Pennsylvania] Daily Independent*, 14 February 1910, p. 8.

31. With several more verses and a chorus, written by J. Fred Helf and composed by Frederick W. Hager in about 1908.

32. '"Buster" Keaton Hurt by Engine,' *Harrisburg [Pennsylvania] Daily Independent*, 14 February 1910, p. 8.

33. 'The Orpheum,' *Harrisburg [Pennsylvania] Daily Independent*, 15 February 1910, p. 5.

34. 'Peerless Bill for Broadway,' *The Morning Post [Camden, New Jersey]*, 1 March 1910, p. 9.

35. 'Alhambra,' *Variety*, 12 March 1910, n. p.

36. 'Colonial Theatre,' 26 March 1910, p. 161.

37. 'Colonial,' 2 April 1910, p. 22.
38. 'Victoria Theatre,' 2 April 1910, p. 187.
39. 'Star – Dainty Duchess Company,' *Brooklyn [New York] Citizen*, 17 April 1910, p. 20.
40. 'Dinner to the Keatons,' *Brooklyn [New York] Daily Eagle*, 21 April 1910, p. 15.
41. 'Gayety – Dainty Duchess Company,' *Brooklyn [New York] Citizen*, 26 April 1910, p. 7.
42. 'Our Chicago Letter,' *New York Clipper*, 14 May 1910, p. 338.
43. *North Bay [Ontario, Canada] Nugget*, 13 June 1910, p. 5.
44. 'Victoria Theatre,' *New York Clipper*, 10 September 1910, p. 753.
45. 'At the Forsyth,' *Atlanta [Georgia] Constitution*, 4 October 1910, p. 9.
46. 'The Orpheum,' *The Tennessean [Nashville, Tennessee]*, 11 October 1910, p. 9.
47. 'The Gayety,' *Pittsburgh [Pennsylvania] Press*, 8 November 1910, p. 8.
48. 'Poli's Theatre,' *Hartford [Connecticut] Courant*, 22 November 1910, p. 6.
49. 'Hathaway Theatre,' *Lowell [Massachusetts] Sun*, 6 December 1910, p. 13.
50. 'Farmer Newsies to Have Jolly Time at Poli's, *Bridgeport [Connecticut] Times and Evening Farmer*, 19 December 1910, p. 3.
51. 'Poli's,' *Bridgeport [Connecticut] Times and Evening Farmer*, 22 December 1910, p. 5.
52. 'Cohan Sketch is at the Poli,' *Wilkes-Barre [Pennsylvania] Times Leader, the Evening News*, 3 January 1911, p. 7.
53. 'Dominion Theatre' ad, *The Ottawa [Ontario, Canada] Citizen*, 4 March 1911, p. 20.
54. 'Majestic, Paterson,' *Passaic [New Jersey] Daily Herald*, 14 March 1911, p. 9.
55. 'Majestic,' *Morning Call [Paterson, New Jersey]*, 15 March 1911, p. 13.
56. 'Philadelphia,' *Variety*, 1 April 1911, p. 27.
57. 'B. F. Keith's Theatre,' *Boston [Massachusetts] Globe*, 4 April 1911, p. 13.
58. 'Jimmy Pinkerton Wins His First Case,' *Morning Post [Camden, New Jersey]*, 18 April 1911, p. 5.
59. 'Mack and Orth,' *Variety*, 22 April 1911, p. 20.
60. 'A New Comedy at the Majestic; New Brighton Opens for Season,' *Brooklyn [New York] Daily Eagle*, 16 May 1911, p. 9.
61. 'Mr. and Mrs. Joe Keaton,' *Variety* 17 June 1911, n. p.
62. 'An All-Girl Farm,' *Variety*, 27 May 1911, p. 10.
63. 'Victoria Theatre,' *New York Clipper*, 10 June 1911, p. 6.
64. 'Temple Theatre – Vaudeville,' *Detroit [Michigan] Free Press*, 4 July 1911, p. 4.
65. 'Temple,' *Detroit [Michigan] Evening Times*, 4 July 1911, p. 4.
66. Buster Keaton's datebook, MHL-AMPAS.
67. 'Keith's Vaudeville,' *Boston [Massachusetts] Globe*, 26 September 1911, p. 8.
68. 'Pertinent Patter,' *Billboard*, 14 October 1911, n. p.

Notes

69. 'Poli's Theatre,' *Hartford [Connecticut] Courant*, 12 October 1911, p. 6.
70. Mark, 'Hammerstein's,' *New York Clipper*, 4 November 1911, p. 19.
71. 'Poli's Has Good Bill for Patrons,' *Bridgeport [Connecticut] Times and Evening Farmer*, 7 November 1911, p. 4.
72. 'Poli's,' *Bridgeport [Connecticut] Times and Evening Farmer*, 9 November 1911, p. 5.
73. 'Amusements,' *The Standard Union [Brooklyn, New York]*, 4 December 1911, p.13.
74. p. 57.
75. 'Poli's Bill Is Real Live One,' *Wilkes-Barre [Pennsylvania] Times Leader, the Evening News*, 2 January 1912, p. 11.
76. 'V. C. C. Election,' *New York Clipper*, 30 December 1911, p. 16.
77. 'Poli's Bill Is Real Live One,' *Wilkes-Barre Times Leader, The Evening News*, 2 January 1912, p. 11.
78. '"Maid Mary" To-night by Savoy Stock Theatre,' *Atlantic City [New Jersey] Gazette Review*, 1 March 1912, p. 2.7
79. 'Keaton-Hurley,' *Perry Republican*, 4 July 1912, p. 1.
80. 'Poli's Theatre,' *Hartford Courant*, 23 December 1912, p. 6.
81. 'Savoy Theatre,' *Atlantic City Sunday Express the Sunday Gazette*, 29 December 1912, p. 11.
82. 'Poli's Vaudeville,' *Bridgeport [Connecticut] Times and Evening Farmer*, 6 January 1913, p. 5.
83. 'Joe Keaton,' *Variety*, 21 February 1913, n. p.
84. Letters to the Editor, *Variety*, 28 February 1913, n. p.
85. Letters to the Editor, *Variety*, 7 March 1913, n. p.
86. '*Clipper* Registry ad,' *New York Clipper*, 8 March 1913, n. p.
87. 'Majestic,' *Variety*, 9 May 1913, p. 23.
88. Curtis, Jim, p. 78.
89. 'Statuary Poses Well Executed at the Orpheum,' *The Gazette [Montreal]*, 11 March 1913, p. 13.
90. '"The Dixie Pirate,"' *Variety*, 29 August 1913, p. 29.
91. See reviews 'B. F. Keith's,' *Evening Star [Washington, D. C.]*, 17 October 1913, p. 5 and 'Grand – Fritzi Scheff in Vaudeville,' *Pittsburgh [Pennsylvania] Post-Gazette*, 4 November 1913, p. 5.
92. 'Julia Murdock Sees Much of Merit on the Bill at B. F. Keith's Theatre,' *Washington [D. C.] Times*, 10 October 1913, p. 8.
93. 'The Keatons,' *The Billboard*, 21 February 1914, n. p.
94. 'Proctor's Fifth Avenue,' *New York Clipper*, 7 March 1914, n. p.
95. 'Bill of Unusual Variety Offered,' *Journal and Tribune [Knoxville, Tennessee]*, 14 April 1914, p. 7.
96. 'Among the Varieties,' *The Inter-Ocean [Chicago, Illinois]*, 28 April 1914, p. 6.
97. 'At the Varieties: Notes of the Stage,' *Chicago Tribune*, 29 April 1914, p. 12.
98. 'Colonial Company Issues Notice to the Public,' *The Bourbon News [Paris, Kentucky]*, 21 April 1914, p. 6.

Early Buster Keaton

99. 'Prospect,' *Variety*, 24 October 1914, n. p.
100. '"Sully's" Dramatized,' *Variety*, 25 December 1914, n. p.
101. 'New Winter Garden Artists,' *The Billboard*, 2 January 1915, n. p.
102. 'Flo Irwin, Celebrated Comedienne, at the Orpheum This Week,' *The Courier [Harrisburg, Pennsylvania]*, 17 January 1915, p. 7.
103. '"Buster Is a Big Boy Now," Mourns Daddy Keaton at New Palace,' *Fort Wayne [Indiana] Journal-Gazette*, 25 February 1915, p. 12.
104. 'The Three Keatons,' *Variety*, 26 March 1915, n. p.
105. Hammond, Percy, 'At the Palace: Other Theatre News,' *Chicago Tribune*, 11 May 1915, p. 15.
106. 'Rival of Durbar at Actors' Colony Celebrates Joe Keaton's Birthday,' *Muskegon Chronicle*, 6 July 1915, n. p.
107. 'Buster Keaton,' *Variety*, 22 October 1915, p. 27.
108. 'Good Bill at Forsyth,' *Atlanta [Georgia] Journal*, 23 November 1915, p. 8.
109. '"Bird Man" Goes Big This Week at Keith's,' *Dayton [Ohio] Daily News*, 29 February 1916, p. 7.
110. 'Palace,' *Variety*, 28 April 1916, p. 19.
111. 'Keatons Go with Loew,' *Variety*, 12 May 1916, p. 11.
112. 'American Roof,' *Variety*, 19 May 1916, p. 16.
113. 'Orpheum Vaudeville,' *Detroit [Michigan] Free Press*, 13 June 1916, p. 4.
114. 'Entertain at Shea's Theatre,' *Buffalo [New York] Inquirer*, 2 June 1916, p. 7.
115. 'The Keaton mansion,' *Press of Atlantic City [New Jersey]*, 23 December 1915, p. 12.
116. 'Muskegon's Clubhouse,' *Variety*, 11 August 1916, p. 13.
117. One particular review from Edmonton was pretty bad, however: 'The fun they provided would bore an audience in a hayloft theatre. [. . .] The atmosphere speedily became very chilly and by the time the curtain fell, there were many vacant seats' (Marmaduke, 'In The Footlight Glow,' *Edmonton Journal*, 10 October 1916, p. 11).

Chapter 7: Comique Films and Roscoe Arbuckle: Film's Initial Attractions

1. 'Pantages,' *Oakland [California] Enquirer*, 2 January 1917, p. 10.
2. 'Pantages,' *Los Angeles [California] Evening Express*, 6 January 1917, p. 7.
3. 'Pantages,' *Los Angeles [California] Evening Post-Record*, 9 January 1917, p. 3.
4. 'Keatons May Rejoin,' 21 February 1917, p. 6.
5. Buster's Datebook, MHL-AMPAS.
6. 'The Passing Show,' *New York Times*, 13 May 1894, n. p.
7. Charles Simic in his article 'Manhattan's Forgotten Film Studio (*New York Review of Books*, 7 December 2012) noted that the studio was located in a tough neighbourhood, 'west of the elevated subway tracks on First Avenue.' Available at https://www.nybooks.com/online/2012/12/07/manhattans-forgotten-film-studio/.

8. '$100,000 City Studio,' *Variety*, January 1917, p. 21.
9. 'Joseph M. Schenck in Los Angeles, *Moving Picture World*, 6 January 1917, p. 85.
10. Most of this information was taken from Keaton, Buster, *MWWOS*, pp. 88–92. Also, Buster's datebook, MHL-AMPAS.
11. Keaton, *MWWOS*, p. 94.
12. 'Arbuckle to Leave Keystone,' 7 October 1916, p. 832.
13. Kline, Jim, *The Complete Films of Buster Keaton*, New York, New York, Citadel Press, 1993, p. 34.
14. '"Writing" Comedy with Fatty Arbuckle,' April 1918, p. 49.
15. '"Fatty" Arbuckle Allied with Paramount,' *Moving Picture World*, 27 January 1917, p. 500.
16. '"Buster" Keaton,' *Deseret News [Salt Lake City, Utah]*, 14 April 1917, p. 19.
17. 'Initial Arbuckle Comedy Ready April 23,' *Motion Picture News*, 14 April 1917, p. 2330.
18. Josephine Stevens was the daughter of Benjamin D. Stevens, once a manager of the Klaw & Erlanger group of theatres. At this point just 19 years old, she had had some stage experience, appearing in *The Argyle Case*, *Daddy Long Legs*, and *Captain Kidd, Jr.* among others ('Josephine Stevens,' *Moving Picture World*, 21 April 1917, p. 433).
19. Kline, Jim, pp. 34–35.
20. It has been noted, however, that Buster doesn't smile in the final Comique film, *The Garage*.
21. The porkpie hat was one Buster used in vaudeville. When he went into films, he decided he would not wear a derby hat, like the other comedians and drug the old porkpie out of storage: 'It was easy to handle. [. . .] The first thing I learned when I got into pictures was: Never leave that scene without your hat.' (Markle, Fletcher, 'Telescope: Deadpan, CBC Television, 29 April, 1964, reprinted in Sweeney, Kevin W., p. 157).
22. '"The Butcher Boy,"' 28 April 1917, p. 634.
23. According to British comedian Lupino Lane, the neck roll is achieved by falling straight back on the head and when touching the floor, pushing with one shoulder to twist the body (*How to Become a Comedian*, London, F. Muller, 1945, p. 40.
24. '"The Butcher Boy,"' *Motography*, 28 April 1917, p. 915.
25. '"His Wedding Night,"' *Moving Picture World*, 28 April 1917, p. 586.
26. 'Second Arbuckle-Paramount Comedy May 21,' p. 991.
27. 'Arbuckle's Third Comedy "A Rough House,"' 16 June 1917, p. 1809.
28. 'Ziegfeld Sues Schenck,' *Variety*, September 1917, p. 26.
29. Arbuckle, Roscoe, 'The Cost of a Laugh,' *Motion Picture*, March 1918, p. 69.
30. '"The Rough House": The Story and Players,' 22 July 1917 clipping from the Motion Picture Copyright Descriptions Collection, Library of Congress (MPCDC-LOC).

31. 'The Rough House' ad, Motion Picture News, 7 July 1917, p. 3.
32. 'Arbuckle Now Cutting New Comedy "His Wedding Night" for Paramount,' Exhibitor's Herald, 4 August 1917, p. 38.
33. 'Movie Potatoes Serve in Comedy, Then Go to Poor,' Sacramento [California] Bee, 4 September 1917, p. 5.
34. 'Arbuckle Gives 'Em All a Chance,' Moving Picture World, 30 June 1917, p. 2127.
35. 'Newslets for Your Program,' Motography, 21 July 1917, p. 161.
36. 'Next Arbuckle Comedy,' NYDM, p. 25.
37. '"His Wedding Night,' New Comedy with "Fatty" Arbuckle Nearing Finish for Paramount Program,' Exhibitor's Herald, 28 July 1917, p. 30.
38. Kline, Jim, p. 37.
39. 'Roscoe Arbuckle in "Oh Doctor!,"' Exhibitor's Herald, 20 October 1917, p. 27.
40. Neibaur, James L., Arbuckle and Keaton, Jefferson, North Carolina, McFarland and Co., Publishers, 2007, p. 64.
41. 'Arbuckle Arranges to Return to the West,' Motion Picture News, 13 October 1917, p. 2544 and 'Arbuckle to Return to Pacific Coast, Moving Picture World, 13 October 1917, p. 220.
42. 'Famous Comedian Is Enroute to Old Home,' Long Beach Telegram and Long Beach Daily News, 3 October 1917, p. 12.
43. 'Buster Keaton,' Variety, September 1917, p. 26.
44. 'Gas Orders,' Press-Telegram [Long Beach, California], 5 October 1917, p. 5.
45. 'Roscoe (Fatty) Arbuckle in Person at the Liberty Theatre,' Long Beach Telegram and Long Beach Daily News, 16 October 1917, p. 12.
46. 'Alice Mann to Play Opposite King Baggott in Comedy,' Motion Picture News, 20 October 1917, p. 2729.
47. Jura, Jean Jacques and Rodney Norman Barden, Balboa Films: A History and Filmography of the Silent Film Studio, Jefferson, North Carolina, McFarland and Co., Publishers, 2007, p. 35.
48. Jura and Barden, Balboa Films, pp. 59–60.
49. 'Fatty Arbuckle Company Here Permanently,' Press-Telegram [Long Beach, California], 17 October 1917, p. 3.
50. 'Anxious to Star with Arbuckle,' Long Beach Telegram and Long Beach Daily News, 17 October 1917, p. 5.
51. Jacques and Barden, p. 57.
52. p. 11.
53. 'Arbuckle Revels in Country Life,' Los Angeles Times, 11 January 1918, p. 13.
54. 'Jazzville Built for New Arbuckle Comedy,' Motion Picture News, 24 November 1917, p. 3622.
55. Neibaur, Arbuckle and Keaton, p. 71.
56. Conlon, Paul Hubert, 'Visiting Roscoe Arbuckle in the Village of Jazzville, Los Angeles Times, 25 November 1917, p. III.1.
57. Conlon, p. III.25.

Notes

58. MacDonald, Margaret I. 'A Country Hero,' *Moving Picture World*, 8 December 1917, p. 1483.

59. It is believed that this car wreck scene cost more than $20,000 to film (Kline, Jim, p. 40).

60. It was reported that in this scene in which Roscoe is fighting five men by throwing various pieces of furniture, he received a nasty contusion on his head, despite the fact that the furniture was of the breakaway type. He refused to be treated, however, until the scene was in the can ('Roscoe's Breakaway Didn't Break,' *Moving Picture World*, 8 December 1917, p. 1474).

61. 'Arbuckle in "A Country Hero,"' *Moving Picture World*, 1 December 1917, p. 1359.

62. Conlon, p. III 25.

63. Lane, Rose Wilder, 'Fatty Arbuckle Earns Wealth in Gravel Pit,' *The Register [Santa Ana, California]*, 26 December 1917, p. 6.

64. 'Wild Canyon Found for Arbuckle's New Comedy,' Out West *Paramount Pictures Pressbook*, 1918, Motion Picture Copyright Descriptions Collection, Library of Congress (MPCDC-LOC).

65. Kline, Jim, p. 41.

66. 'Buster Keaton Hurt,' *Edmonton [Alberta, Canada] Journal*, 5 January 1918, p. 12.

67. '"Out West,"' *Motion Picture News*, 9 February 1918, p. 887.

68. '"Out West,"' *Moving Picture World*, 2 February 1918, p. 688.

69. 'Memories of the old musical comedy days,' *Long Beach Telegram* and *Long Beach Daily News*, 4 February 1918, p. 5.

70. 'Fatty Arbuckle in New Comedy,' *Motography*, 9 February 1918, p. 276.

71. 'Natalie Talmadge with Arbuckle,' *Moving Picture World*, 23 February 1918, p. 1117.

72. Kline, Jim, p. 42.

73. '"The Bell Boy,"' 30 March 1918, p. 1926.

74. Harleman, G. P., 'News of Los Angeles and Vicinity,' *Moving Picture World*, 2 March 1918, p. 1218. Also, 'Chaplin Visits Keatons,' *New Britain [Connecticut] Herald*, 1 March 1918, p. 6.

75. Harleman, G. P., 'News of Los Angeles and Vicinity,' *Moving Picture World*, 20 April 1918, p. 376.

76. 'Roscoe "Fatty" Arbuckle will report,' *Deseret News [Salt Lake City, Utah]* 30 March 1918, p. 21.

77. 'Buster Keaton and "Scoop" Conlon,' *Atlantic City [New Jersey] Sunday Press, the Sunday Gazette*, 28 April 1918, p. 14.

78. 'Comedian Adopts Company "C,"' *Los Angeles Times*, 10 March 1918, p. 40.

79. 'Arbuckle Moonshine,' *Los Angeles Times*, 8 March 1918, p. 13.

80. 'Fatty Arbuckle Plays New Role,' *Vancouver [British Columbia, Canada] Sun*, 17 March 1918, p. 6.

81. 'Arbuckle and Company Are Marooned on Location,' *Motion Picture News*, 27 April 1918, n. p.

217

82. 'Arbuckle Bring Home "Moonshine,"' *Moving Picture World*, 4 May 1918, p. 729.
83. '"Moonshine,"' *Motion Picture News*, 28 May 1918, p. 3141.
84. 'Moonshine,' 18 May 1918, p. 58.
85. '"Moonshine,"' *Moving Picture World*, 25 May 1918, p. 1185.
86. 3 May 1918, n. p.
87. 'Arbuckle's Idea of a Good Rest,' *Los Angeles Times*, 19 May 1918, p. 30.
88. Kline, Jim, p. 46.
89. 'Picture Perils, *Burlington [Vermont] Free Press*, 25 May 1918, p. 4.
90. '"Good Night Nurse,"' *Motion Picture News*, 6 July 1918, p. 116.
91. 'Comique Film Corporation,' *Press-Telegram [Long Beach, California]*, 24 June 1918, p. 5.
92. 'The Gibbs apartments,' *Long Beach Telegram* and *Long Beach Daily News*, 13 June 1918, p. 5.
93. 'Guests registering,' *Long Beach Telegram* and *Long Beach Daily News*, 1 July 1918, p. 5.
94. Qtd. in Neibaur, James L., p. 118.
95. This references an article entitled 'Arbuckle's New Comedy a Scream,' in the *Paramount Comedy Pressbook* for 1918.
96. '"The Cook,"' *Motion Picture News*, 28 September 1918, p. 1751.
97. '"The Cook,"' *Moving Picture World*, 14 September 1918, p. 1609.
98. '"Buster" Keaton on His Way,' *Moving Picture World*, 31 August 1918, p. 1255.
99. 'Buster Keaton Off to Show Huns How He and Fatty Fall,' *Pittsburgh [Pennsylvania] Post*, 18 August 1918, p. 34.
100. 'Buster Keaton,' *Dayton [Ohio] Daily News*, 11 August 1918, p. 38.
101. 'Two Transports Bring 4002 Men from France,' *New York Tribune*, 6 April 1919, p. 10.
102. Keaton, Buster, *MWWOS*, p. 100.
103. 'Two Transports Bring 4002 Men from France,' *New York Tribune*, 6 April 1919, p. 10.
104. 'Buster Keaton Back in Arbuckle's Company,' *Motion Picture News*, 5 July 1919, p. 325.
105. Dates and facts concerning Buster's World War I experience were gleaned from Jett, Martha, 'My Career at the Rear: Buster Keaton in World War I,' *Good Old Days Specials*, September 2000, n. p., available at http://www.worldwar1.com/dbc/buster.htm.

Chapter 8: Final Comiques and First Buster Shorts: *Back Stage, The Hayseed, The Garage, One Week, The Saphead,* and *The High Sign*

1. 'Famous Comedy Star Is Leaving Long Beach,' *Long Beach [California] Telegram and Long Beach Daily News*, 17 July 1918, p. 5.
2. p. 23.

3. 'Buster Keaton Asks for His Old Job Back,' *Wichita [Kansas] Eagle*, 29 December 1918, p. 9.

4. 'Ten Comedies a Year for Fatty,' *Moving Picture World*, 3 August 1918, n. p.

5. 'Comique Film Leases Part of Sennett Studio,' *Motion Picture News*, 11 January 1919, n. p.

6. 'Buster Can't Find Booze in Bordeaux,' *Oakland [California] Tribune*, 16 February 1919, p. 4.

7. 'Schenck's Record Contracts,' *Variety*, February 1919, n. p. Also, 'With Los Angeles Producers,' *Motion Picture News*, 5 March 1919, p. 4.

8. 'Jean Havez Writing Scenarios,' *Variety*, March 1919, p. 56.

9. Foote, Lisle, 'Jean Havez' in *Buster Keaton's Crew: The Team behind His Silent Films*, Jefferson, North Carolina, McFarland and Co., Publishers, 2014, pp. 159–164.

10. 'Roscoe Arbuckle,' *Motion Picture News*, 19 April 1919, p. 2537.

11. Massa, Steve, *Rediscovering Roscoe: The Films of 'Fatty' Arbuckle*, Orlando, Florida, BearManor Media, 2020, p. 252.

12. Address found in the Glendale, California City Directory, 1919. This section of Verdugo is now named S. Verdugo and, since the Ventura Freeway now crosses over top of it, the building's original property has likely been wiped out.

13. Al would go on to attempt a solo career at Fox and then Educational Pictures, with moderate success.

14. 'Flare and Flickers,' *Statesman Journal [Salem, Oregon]*, 27 July 1919, p. 5.

15. '"Back Stage,"' *Motion Picture News*, 11 October 1919, p. 2896.

16. 'Fatty Only a Tenant,' *Moving Picture World*, 19 July 1919, p. 364.

17. 'Lehrman Comedies to Be Produced,' *Motion Picture News*, 2 August 1919, p. 1099.

18. 'New Studio for Fatty Arbuckle,' *Moving Picture World*, 26 July 1919, p. 486.

19. 'The F. P. Lasky Studio,' *Motion Picture News*, 30 August 1919, p. 1851.

20. Neibaur, James L., *Arbuckle and Keaton*, p. 150.

21. '"The Hayseed," Arbuckle-Famous Players,' 16 December 1919, p. 4.

22. *Exhibitor's Pressbook:* The Hayseed, Paramount-Artcraft, 1919, MPCDC-LOC.

23. 'Fatty Arbuckle Busy,' *Los Angeles Times*, 8 October 1919, p. 32.

24. '"The Garage,"' 24 January 1920, p. 1125.

25. '"The Garage,"' *Moving Picture World*, 10 January 1920, p. 301.

26. 'Buster Keaton, Too,' *Anderson [Indiana] Herald*, 21 December 1919, p. 27.

27. Metro Pictures was owned by Marcus Loew.

28. 'Buster Keaton to Make Comedies for Metro,' *Camera!*, 27 March 1920, p. 6.

29. Foote, Lisle, 'Eddie Cline,' pp. 64–65.

30. 'Arrangements have been perfected for starring Buster Keaton in a three-reel comedy and the first release was started this week at the Arbuckle studio in Culver City' ('Jotting from the Coast,' *Motion Picture News*, 27 January 1920, p. 888).

31. 'Arrangements have been perfected,' *Motion Picture News*, 27 January 1920, p. 888.
32. '"The High Sign" – Buster Keaton – Metro,' *Wid's Daily*, 26 March 1922, n. p.
33. *The New Henrietta* was a re-envision of an older play, *The Henrietta*, written by Bronson Howard. 'Other late wire information,' *Motion Picture News*, 27 March 1920, n. p.
34. 'On Location,' *Camera!*, 3 April 1920, p. 6.
35. '"The Saphead," Co-stars Crane and Keaton,' *Motion Picture News*, 24 April 1920, p. 3677.
36. Kline, Jim, pp. 54–55.
37. 'Buster Busts into Stardom,' *Los Angeles Times*, 16 May 1920, p. 37.
38. '*The Saphead*: Small Is Beautiful,' *Masters of Cinema* #268, Eureka Entertainment Ltd., 2022, p. 24.
39. '"The Saphead,"' *Camera!*, 18 December 1920, p. 5.
40. '"The Saphead,"' 18 February 1921, p. 40.
41. 'Increases Holdings,' *Los Angeles Times*, 14 April 1920, p. 32.
42. '"The Saphead" Is Scheduled,' *Moving Picture World*, 11 September 1920, p. 191.
43. 'Jean Havez,' *Wid's Daily*, 8 May 1920, n. p.
44. Kingsley, Grace, 'Buster Busts into Stardom,' *Los Angeles Times*, 16 May 1920, p. 37.
45. Kingsley, Grace, 'Metro Is Rest Camp,' 28 May 1920, p. 21.
46. 'Buster Keaton's Lead,' *Los Angeles Times*, 4 June 1920, p. 30.
47. 'Change to Films,' *The Billboard*, 19 June 1920, p. 25.
48. 'Buster Keaton Vacations,' *Los Angeles Times*, 20 June 1920, p. 35.
49. 'People who attended,' *Long Beach [California] Telegram and the Long Beach Daily News*, 2 July 1920, p. 7.
50. '"One Week" Released September 1,"' *Motion Picture News*, 11 September 1920, p. 2059.
51. '"One Week,"' *Moving Picture World*, 21 August 1920, p. 1067.
52. '"One Week,"' *Motion Picture News*, 21 August 1920, p. 1575.

Epilogue: Highs and Lows of the Film Business

1. 'Comedy's Greatest Era,' *Life*, Vol. 27, No. 10, 5 September 1949, p. 82.
2. *The Silent Clowns*, New York: Alfred A. Knopf, 1975, p. 142.

Bibliography

■■■■■■■■■■■■■■■■■■■■■■■■■■■■■■■■■

Books

Agnew, Jeremy. *Entertainment in the Old West: Theater, Music, Circuses, Medicine Shows, Prizefighting and Other Popular Amusements.* Jefferson, NC: McFarland & Co., Inc., Publishers, 2011.

Anderson, Ann. *Snake Oil, Hustlers and Hambones: The American Medicine Show.* Jefferson, NC: McFarland & Co., Inc., Publishers, 2000.

Armstrong, David and Elizabeth Metzger Armstrong. *The Great Medicine Show: Being an Illustrated History of Hucksters, Healers, Health Evangelists, and Heroes from Plymouth Rock to the Present.* New York, NY: Prentice Hall, 1991.

Babiak, Paul, *Knockabout and Slapstick: Violence and Laughter in Nineteenth-Century Popular Theatre and Early Film,* Doctoral Thesis, Centre for Drama, Theatre and Performance Studies, University of Toronto, Canada: 2015.

Blesh, Rudi. *Keaton.* New York, NY: The Macmillan Company, 1966.

Bourgeois, Maurice. *John Millington Synge and the Irish Theatre.* London: Constable & Co., Ltd., 1913.

Bryant, Billy. *Children of 'Ol Man River: The Life and Times of a Showboat Trouper.* Chicago, IL: Lakeside Press, 1988.

Cullen, Frank. *Vaudeville Old & New: An Encyclopedia of Variety Performers in America.* Vols. 1 & 2. New York, NY: Routledge, 2007.

Curtis, James. *Buster Keaton: A Filmmaker's Life.* New York, NY: Alfred A. Knopf, 2022.

Cutler, Nahum S. *Cutler Memorial and Genealogical History.* Greenwood, MA: Press of E. A. Hall & Co., 1889.

Dennett, Andrea Stulman. *Weird Wonderful: The Dime Museum in America.* New York, NY: New York University Press, 1997.

Foote, Lisle. *Buster Keaton's Crew: The Team Behind His Silent Films.* Jefferson, NC: McFarland & Co., Inc., Publishers, 2014.

Jura, Jean-Jacques and Rodney Norman Bardin II. *Balboa Films: A History and Filmography of the Silent Film Studio.* Jefferson, NC: McFarland & Co., Inc., 1999.

Keaton, Buster and Charles Samuels. *My Wonderful World of Slapstick*. Cambridge, MA: Da Capo Books, 1960.

Kerr, Walter. *The Silent Clowns.* New York, NY: Alfred A. Knopf, 1975.

Kline, Jim. *The Complete Films of Buster Keaton.* New York, NY: Citadel Press, 1993.

Massa, Steve. *Rediscovering Roscoe: The Films of 'Fatty' Arbuckle.* Orlando, FL: BearManor Media, 2020.

Meade, Marion. *Buster Keaton: Cut to the Chase.* London, UK: Bloomsbury, 1995.

McNamara, Brooks. *Step Right Up.* Revised ed. Jackson, MS: University Press of Mississippi, 1995.

Mitchell, Sally. *East Lynne, 1861, Reprint edition,* New Brunswick, New Jersey, Rutgers University Press, 1984.

Muskegon, Michigan Actors' Colony at Bluffton: Buster Keaton & the Muskegon Connection. Muskegon, MI: Dobb Printing, 2016.

Neibaur, James L. *Arbuckle and Keaton: Their 14 Film Collorations.* Jefferson, NC: McFarland & Co., Inc., 2007.

Slide, Anthony, *The Encyclopedia of Vaudeville.* Westport, CT: Greenwood Press, 1994.

Slout, William Lawrence, *Theatre in a Tent: The Development of a Provincial Entertainment*, Bowling Green, OH: Bowling Green University Press, 1972.

Stein, Lisa K. *Syd Chaplin: A Biography.* Jefferson, NC, McFarland and Co., Inc., Publishers, 2010.

Sweeney, Kevin W., ed. *Buster Keaton Interviews.* Conversations with Filmmakers Series. Jackson, MS: University of Mississippi Press, 2007.

Periodicals

Billboard
Camera!
The Cast
Exhibitor's Herald
Jewish Voice, The
Keaton Chronicle, The
Life
Motion Picture
Motion Picture News
Motography
Moving Picture World
National Magazine
New York Clipper
New York Dramatic Mirror
New York Review of Books
Photoplay

Bibliography

The Police Gazette
Variety
Wid's Daily

Newspapers

Akron [Ohio] Beacon Journal
Allentown [Pennsylvania] Leader
Anderson [Indiana] Herald
Arizona Republic [Tucson, Arizona]
The Atlanta [Georgia] Journal
Atlantic City [New Jersey] Gazette Review
Atlantic City [New Jersey] Sunday Express the Sunday Gazette
Aurora [New York] Republican Register
Baltimore [Maryland] American
Baltimore [Maryland] Sun
Bangor [Maine] Daily News
Bayonne [New Jersey] Herald
Bayonne [New Jersey] Herald and Greenville Register
Berkeley [California] Gazette
Birmingham [Alabama] News
Birmingham [Alabama] Post-Herald
Birmingham [UK] Post
Bonner Springs-Edwardsville [Kansas] Chieftain
Boston [Massachusetts] Evening Transcript
Boston [Massachusetts] Globe
Boston [Massachusetts] Post
Bourbon News [Paris, Kentucky]
Bridgeport [Connecticut] Herald
Bridgeport [Connecticut] Times and Evening Farmer
Brooklyn [New York] Citizen
Brooklyn [New York] Daily Eagle
Brooklyn [New York] Life
Buffalo [New York] Commercial
Buffalo [New York] Courier
Buffalo [New York] Courier Express
Buffalo [New York] Inquirer
Burlington [Kansas] News
Burlington [Vermont] Free Press
Carbondale [Pennsylvania] Daily News
Central New Jersey Home News [New Brunswick, New Jersey]
Cherokee [Kansas] Sentinel
Chicago Livestock World

Chicago [Illinois] Tribune
Cincinnati [Ohio] Enquirer
Claflin [Kansas] Clarion
Cleveland [Ohio] Plain Dealer
Columbus [Ohio] Evening Dispatch
Columbus [Kansas] Weekly Advocate
The Commercial Appeal [Memphis, Tennessee]
The Courier [Harrisburg, Pennsylvania]
Courier-Journal [Louisville, Kentucky]
Courier-News [Bridgewater, New Jersey]
Daily Arkansas Gazette [Little Rock, Arkansas]
Daily Enterprise Times [Perry, Oklahoma]
The Daily Item [Lynn, Massachusetts]
Daily North Topeka [Kansas] Newsletter
Daily Press [Newport News, Virginia]
Daily Telegraph [London, United Kingdom]
Daily True American [Trenton, New Jersey]
The Day [New London, Connecticut]
Dayton [Ohio] Daily News
Dayton [Ohio] Herald
Democrat and Chronicle [Rochester, New York]
Denver [Colorado] Post
Deseret News [Salt Lake City, Utah]
Detroit [Michigan] Evening Times
Detroit [Michigan] Free Press
DeWitt [Nebraska] Times
The Dispatch [Moline, Illinois]
Easton [Pennsylvania] Sunday Call
Edmond [Oklahoma] News
Edmond [Oklahoma] Sun-Democrat
Edmonton [Alberta, Canada] Journal
El Paso [Texas] Herald
Ellinwood [Kansas] Leader
Elmira [New York] Star-Gazette
Evansville [Indiana] Courier and Express
Evening Express [Portland, Maine]
Evening Journal [Wilmington, Delaware]
Evening Star [Washington, D. C.]
Evening Telegram [Providence, Rhode Island]
The Excelsior [Omaha, Nebraska]
Fall River [Massachusetts] Daily Herald
Fall River [Massachusetts] Globe
Findlay [Ohio] Republican

Fort Wayne [Indiana] Journal-Gazette
Friend [Nebraska] Telegraph
Galena [Kansas] Evening News
Galena [Kansas] Evening Times
The Gazette [Montreal, Quebec, Canada]
Grand Rapids [Michigan] Herald
Guthrie [Oklahoma] Daily Leader
Harrisburg [Pennsylvania] Daily Independent
Hartford [Connecticut] Courant
Herald Statesman [Yonkers, New York]
Hooper [Nebraska] Sentinel
Houston [Texas] Post
Independence [Kansas] Daily Reporter
Indianapolis [Indiana] Star
Intelligence Journal [Lancaster, Pennsylvania]
The Inter-Ocean [Chicago, Illinois]
Jersey City [New Jersey] News
Jersey Journal [Jersey City, New Jersey]
The Journal [Meriden, Connecticut]
Journal and Tribune [Knoxville, Tennessee]
Junction City [Kansas] Weekly Union
Kansas City [Missouri] Journal
Kansas City [Missouri] Star
Kansas City [Missouri] Times
Kennebec Journal [Augusta, Maine]
Kentucky Irish American [Louisville, Kentucky]
Kinsley [Kansas] Graphic
Ledger-Star [Norfolk, Virginia]
Lewiston [Maine] Daily Sun
Liberal [Missouri] Enterprise
Lima [Ohio] News
Lincoln [Nebraska] Evening Call
Lincoln [Nebraska] State Journal
Lititz [Pennsylvania] Express
Long Beach [California] Telegram and Longbeach Daily News
Los Angeles [California] Evening Express
Los Angeles [California] Evening Post-Record
Los Angeles [California] Herald
Los Angeles [California] Times
Louisville [Kentucky] Courier-Journal
Lowell [Massachusetts] Sun
Lyons [Kansas] Daily News
Massillon [Ohio] Evening Independent

Miami [Paola, Kansas] Republican
Mississippi Blätter [St. Louis, Missouri]
Montreal [Canada] Star
The Morning Call [Allentown, Pennsylvania]
The Morning Call [Paterson, New Jersey]
Morning Journal-Courier [New Haven, Connecticut]
Morning News [Wilmington, Delaware]
The Morning Post [Camden, New Jersey]
Morning Sentinel [Waterville, Maine]
Muscatine [Iowa] Journal
Muskegon [Michigan] Chronicle
Nance County Fullerton [Nebraska] Journal
Nashville [Tennessee] Banner
Nashua [New Hampshire] Daily Telegraph
New Britain [Connecticut] Herald
New Rochelle [New York] Pioneer
New York Morning Telegraph
The New York Press
New York Times
New York [New York] Tribune
Newport [New Hampshire] Herald
Newark [New Jersey] Star-Eagle
Newark [Ohio] Advocate
The News [Paterson, New Jersey]
The News [Providence, Rhode Island]
News Journal [Wilmington, Delaware]
Noble County Sentinel [Perry, Oklahoma]
North Adams [Massachusetts] Transcript
North Bay [Ontario, Canada] Nugget
Oakland [California] Enquirer
Oakland [California] Tribune
Oklahoma Post [Oklahoma City, Oklahoma]
Ottawa [Ontario, Canada] Citizen
Ottawa [Ontario, Canada] Journal
Owensboro [Kentucky] Messenger
Painesville [Ohio] Telegraph
Paola [Kansas] Times
Passaic [New Jersey] Daily Herald
Passaic [New Jersey] Daily News
Paterson [New Jersey] Daily Press
Perry [Oklahoma] Republican
Perth Amboy [New Jersey] Evening News
Philadelphia [Pennsylvania] Inquirer

Philadelphia [Pennsylvania] Record
Pittsburg [Kansas] Daily Headlight
Pittsburg [Kansas] Daily Tribune
Pittsburg Kansan
Pittsburg [Kansas] Leader
Pittsburg [Pennsylvania] Press
Pittsburgh [Pennsylvania] Daily Post
Pittsburgh [Pennsylvania] Post Gazette
Pittsburgh [Pennsylvania] Weekly Gazette
Pleasanton [Kansas] Observer-Enterprise
Portland [Maine] Sunday Telegram
Post Express [Rochester, New York]
Press Telegram [Long Beach, California]
Quad City Times [Davenport, Iowa]
Reading [Pennsylvania] Times
The Record [Hackensack, New Jersey]
The Register [Santa Ana, California]
Richmond [Virginia] Times-Dispatch
Roanoke [Virginia] Times
Sacramento [California] Bee
St. John's [Kansas] Weekly News
St. Joseph [Nebraska] Daily News
St. Louis [Missouri] Globe-Democrat
St. Louis [Missouri] Post-Dispatch
St. Louis [Missouri] Republic
St. Paul [Nebraska] Press
San Francisco [California] Call
San Francisco [California] Chronicle
San Francisco [California] Examiner
Scammon [Kansas] Miner
Sioux City [Iowa] Journal
Spokesman Review [Spokane, Washington]
Springfield [Massachusetts] Republican
Stafford [Kansas] County Leader
Standard Union [Brooklyn, New York]
Star-Gazette [Elmira, New York]
Statesman's Journal [Salem, Oregon]
Sterling [Kansas] Bulletin
The Sun [New York, New York]
The Sun [Wilmington, Delaware]
Syracuse [New York] Evening Telegram
Syrcause [New York] Journal
The Tennessean [Nashville, Tennessee]

Texmo [OK] Times
Times-Union [Brooklyn, New York]
Toledo [Ohio] Sunday Bee
Tribune [Scranton, Pennsylvanie]
Vancouver [British Columbia, Canada] Sun
Virginian [Norfolk, Virginia] Pilot
Waco [Texas] News-Tribune
Warrenton [Missouri] Daily Star
The Washington [D. C.] Times
Waterbury [Connecticut] Democrat
Weir City [Kansas] Daily Sun
Weir [Kansas] Weekly Tribune
Wichita [Kansas] Daily Eagle
Wilkes-Barre [Pennsylvania] Times Leader
The World [New York, New York]
Yonkers [New York] Statesman
Youngstown [Ohio] Vindicator

Films

Back Stage. Directed by Roscoe Arbuckle. Performances by Roscoe Arbuckle, Buster Keaton, Al St. John, Molly Malone, Charles Post, Jack Coogan, Sr., William Collier. Comique Film Company, 1919.

The Bell Boy. Directed by Roscoe Arbuckle. Performances by Roscoe Arbuckle, Buster Keaton, Al St. John, Alice Lake, Joe Keaton, Charles Dudley. Comique Film Company, 1918.

The Butcher Boy. Directed by Roscoe Arbuckle. Performances by Roscoe Arbuckle, Buster Keaton, Al St. John, Josephine Stevens, Arthur Earle, Joe Bordeaux, Alice Lake. Comique Film Company, 1917.

The Cook. Directed by Roscoe Arbuckle. Performances by Roscoe Arbuckle, Buster Keaton, Al St. John, Alice Lake, Glen Cavender, Luke the dog, Bobby Dunn, John Rand. Comique Film Company, 1918.

A Country Hero. Directed by Roscoe Arbuckle. Performances by Roscoe Arbuckle, Buster Keaton, Al St. John, Alice Lake, Joe Keaton, Scott Pembroke. Comique Film Company, 1917.

Fatty at Coney Island. Directed by Roscoe Arbuckle. Performances by Roscoe Arbuckle, Buster Keaton, Al St. John, Alice Lake, Luke the dog, Jimmy Bryant, Joe Bordeaux, Alice Mann, Agnes Neilson. Comique Film Company, 1917.

The Garage. Directed by Roscoe Arbuckle. Performances by Roscoe Arbuckle, Buster Keaton, Harry McCoy, Dan Crimmins, Jack Coogan, Sr., Monty Banks, Alice Lake, Luke the dog, Polly Moran, Molly Malone. Comique Film Company, 1920.

Good Night, Nurse! Directed by Roscoe Arbuckle. Performances by Roscoe Arbuckle, Buster Keaton, Al St. John, Alice Lake, Joe Bordeaux, Kate Price, Dan Albert, Snitz Edwards, Joe Keaton. Comique Film Company, 1918.

The Hayseed. Directed by Roscoe Arbuckle. Performances by Roscoe Arbuckle, Buster Keaton, Dan Crimmons, Luke the dog, Molly Malone. Comique Film Company, 1919.

The High Sign. Directed by Edward F. Cline. Performances by Buster Keaton, Bartine Burkett, Charles Dorety, Joe Roberts, Al St. John, Ingram B. Pickett. Joseph M. Schenck Productions, 1921.

His Wedding Night. Directed by Roscoe Arbuckle. Performances by Roscoe Arbuckle, Buster Keaton, Al St. John, Alice Mann, Arthur Earle, Jimmy Bryant, Josephine Stevens, Alice Lake. Comique Film Company, 1917.

Home Made: A Story of Ready-Made House Building. Ford Motor Company, 1919.

Moonshine. Directed by Roscoe Arbuckle. Performances by Roscoe Arbuckle, Buster Keaton, Al St. John, Alice Lake, Charles Dudley, Joe Bordeaux. Comique Film Company, 1918.

Oh Doctor! Directed by Roscoe Arbuckle. Performances by Roscoe Arbuckle, Buster Keaton, Al St. John, Alice Mann, Alice Lake. Comique Film Company, 1917.

One Week. Directed by Edward F. Cline. Performances by Buster Keaton, Sybil Seeley, Joe Roberts. Joseph M. Schenck Productions, 1920.

Out West. Directed by Roscoe Arbuckle. Performances by Roscoe Arbuckle, Buster Keaton, Al St. John, Alice Lake, Joe Keaton, Ernie Morrison, Sr. Comique Film Company, 1918.

The Rough House. Directed by Roscoe Arbuckle. Performances by Roscoe Arbuckle, Buster Keaton, Al St. John, Alice Lake, Glen Cavender, Josephine Stevens. Comique Film Company, 1917.

The Saphead. Directed by Herbert Blaché and Winchell Smith. Performances by Buster Keaton, Beulah Booker, William H. Crane. Metro Pictures Corporation, 1920.

Frank L. Cutler Plays

—. *Hans, the Dutch J. P.: a Dutch farce in one act.* Clyde, OH: Ames Publishing, 1878.

—. *That boy Sam: an Ethiopian farce in one act.* Clyde, OH: Ames Publishing, 1878.

—. *The sham professor: a farce in one act.* Clyde, OH: Ames Publishing, 1879.

—. *Lodgings for two: a farce in one act.* Clyde, OH: Ames Publishing, 1880.

—. *Lost! or, The fruits of the glass: a temperance drama in three acts.* Clyde, OH: Ames Publishing, 1882.

—. *Cuff's luck: an Ethiopian sketch in one scene.* Clyde, OH: Ames Publishing, 1883.

—. *Old Pompey: an Ethiopian sketch in one scene.* Clyde, OH: Ames Publishing,1883.

—. *Wanted a husband: a Dutch sketch in one scene.* Clyde, OH: Ames Publishing,1883.

—. *Actor and servant: a Dutch farce in one act.* Clyde, OH: Ames Publishing,1884.

—. *The musical darkey: a farce in one act.* Clyde, OH: Ames Publishing,1884.

—. *Pomp's pranks: Ethiopian farce in one act.* Clyde, OH: Ames Publishing,1884.

—. *Seeing Bosting: a farce in one act.* Clyde, OH: Ames Publishing,1884.

—. *The Dutch prize fighter: a Dutch farce in one act.* Clyde, OH: Ames Publishing,1886.

—. *Struck by lightning: a farce in one act.* Clyde, OH: Ames Publishing,1887.

—. *$2000 reward, or, Done on both sides: a change act comedy in one act.* Clyde, OH: Ames Publishing,1887.

—. *A scale with sharps and flats: an operatic and musical comedy in one act.* Clyde, OH: Ames Publishing,1888.

—. *Cousin Josiah: a musical sketch in one scene.* Clyde, OH: Ames Publishing,1891.

—. *The mashers mashed: a farce in two acts.* Clyde, OH: Ames Publishing,1891.

—. *Peleg and Peter, or, Around the Horn: a farce comedy in four acts.* Clyde, OH: Ames Publishing,1892.

—. *Kitty and Patsy, or, The same thing over again: An Irish musical sketch in one scene.* Clyde, OH: Ames Publishing,1897.

—. *Joe, the waif, or, The pet of the camp: a comedy drama in six acts.* Clyde, OH: Ames Publishing,1898.

Abbreviations

MHL-AMPAS Margaret Herrick Library-Academy of Moving Picture Arts and Sciences

LAN Linda Airgood Neil

HRC Harry Ransom Center, University of Texas at Austin

MPCDC-LOC Motion Picture Copyright Descriptions Collection-Library of Congress

NYDM *New York Daily Mirror*

MWWOS *My Wonderful World of Slapstick* by Buster Keaton

Acknowledgements

■■■■■■■■■■■■■■■■■■■■■■■■■■■■■■■

My sincerest thanks go out to Sophia Lorent, Assistant Archivist, Stills, Posters and Paper Collections, Moving Image Department, George Eastman Museum for assisting me with Keaton photos for the project. Ashley Swinnerton, former Collections Specialist, Department of Film, Museum of Modern Art went over and beyond to help me during my visit to her archive, providing much needed scans of Keaton photos for the book as well. Much gratitude and affection go to Rob Arkus for his support with images and overall Keaton information, as always.

This project gave me the opportunity to reconnect with Dr. Vergil Noble, who so graciously provided copies of his work on the Cutler family, the family of Buster's mother Myra, that served as the basis for Chapter 1. He suggested to me that Linda Neil had also worked out much of the genealogical information. Making her acquaintance led to copious amounts of family information that I have used gratuitously in the book. I only wish I could have included it all. I can't begin to thank Linda enough for sharing her information so graciously.

I am also indebted to Allison Weber, Administrative Specialist at Ohio University Alden Library for her help retrieving sources and Miriam Intrator of OU Special Collections for assistance during my visit. The librarians at Nashua Public Library in Nashua, New Hampshire must also be thanked due to digging out a source totally unavailable to me elsewhere. I thank Rory Morgan of the Easton Pennsylvania Public Library and local Easton historian Kenneth Klabunde for assistance uncovering pertinent Keaton vaudeville information. I also thank Heidi from the Western History and Genealogy department of the Denver Public Library for some much needed Keaton venue items.

Thanks also to my supporters at Ohio University Zanesville: Dean Hannah Nissen, Angela Richcreek, and Cindy Oliver. Thanks also to Dr. Pamela June, John Prather, and the members of the RHE Faculty Development committee for awarding me an RHE summer stipend, that allowed me to work in the archives during the summer of 2022.

Index